Mao Tse-tung

Mao Tse-tung

THE MAN IN THE LEADER

Lucian W. Pye

Basic Books, Inc., Publishers

NEW YORK

Excerpts from Edgar Snow's *Red Star over China*, copyright © 1968 by Edgar Snow are reprinted by permission of Grove Press, Inc., and Victor Gollancz Ltd.

Union Press photographs are reprinted by permission of Union Press, Ltd., Hong Kong.

Library of Congress Cataloging in Publication Data

Pye, Lucian W. 1921–
  Mao Tse-tung: The Man in the Leader

  Includes bibliographical references and index.
  1.   Mao, Tse-tung, 1893–
DS778.M3P93   951.05'092'4 [B]   75–31832
ISBN–0–465–04396–8

CONTENTS

Contents

PART THREE
The Public Man

PREFACE

AT THE OUTSET a word of warning. Some people are allergic to psychological interpretation. It is a scientific fact, as solid as that behind the Surgeon General's Warning, that some people become agitated, indeed inflamed, at the suggestion that childhood experiences can color adult behavior, and, more particularly, their blood will boil at the idea that such might be the case with great men of history. Anyone who suspects that he is so inclined should not read on.

Those who are prepared to go on have every right to ask what my biases are in the application of psychological insights to the study of great political leaders. In recent years there has been some interest in a new field of study called psychohistory. I have been greatly influenced by Erik H. Erikson, but I have also learned much, and at an earlier stage in my intellectual development, from other pioneers in the effort to apply an understanding of the unconscious to public affairs. As a political scientist I am deeply indebted to the work of Harold D. Lasswell, Gabriel A. Almond, and Nathan Leites, and I have been inspired by the studies of Alexander George, Arnold Rogow, Robert Lane, and James David Barber; as a social scientist I am indebted to a pantheon of scholars: Abram Kardiner, Ralph Linton, Clyde Kluckhohn, Alexander Inkeles, Ruth Benedict, Geoffrey Gorer, and many others. My inclination, therefore, is to accept my identity as a political scientist and not profess adherence to a new discipline, for to do so would be unjust to the variety of social scientists who have worked in the various parts of the vineyard that Freud first staked out.

Unquestionably, there are many situations in which it would be most prudent for a political scientist to skirt the morass of psychology. But for the student of contemporary China, this seems impossible because there is widespread agreement that the personality of one man, Mao Tse-tung, has completely dominated the politics of the People's Republic. Yet, curiously, there have been almost no attempts to analyze systematically this most remarkable personality. Much, of course, has been done to study the writings of Mao and to place his works in the context of Chinese intellectual history. As for his personality, however, there has been little more than two embryonic theories: one which describes him as a revolutionary romantic, a dramatizing character, and the other depicting him as sensitive to death and immortality. But neither theory seeks to relate these traits to the emotional development of the man.

This hesitation of Mao's biographers to deal with the private man means that we may have been deprived of knowing him as a complete human being as we know, for example, Roosevelt, Churchill, Wilson, Luther, Gandhi, and other great men. It is true, of course, that great men, like all individuals, should have rights of privacy. There are several reasons, however, why scholars also have a responsibility to try to understand the human and even intimate side of public figures. There is, for instance, the importance of motivations: We know that private motives are always an element in influencing public behavior. Also, with a leader whose greatness has involved the creation of strong collective emotions, as Mao has done in appealing to Chinese nationalism and in calling for commitment to social change, it is legitimate, and indeed essential, to ask how he came to understand human feelings and how he managed his own passions so as to be so skillful in influencing the affects of others.

Anxieties about psychological interpretation generally take two contradictory forms: "too much is being explained"—the analysis is too deterministic because it suggests that so much in later life could follow from such small beginnings; or "too little is being explained"—many people have had comparable private experiences without the same public consequences. When these two objections are combined they produce a third which says "too much is being made of too little evidence." Yet, the canons of psychological interpretation should be no different from the general requirements in analyzing behavior. The real problem is that in the social sciences we are generally able to deal with the "necessary" conditions, but at our stage of knowledge we can rarely deal with the "sufficient" conditions for explaining why something happened. Therefore, the problem of psychological interpretation is essentially the same as that of, say, the intellectual historian who, in dealing with Mao's cognitive development, can identify particular writings and books that Mao read and that presumably influenced his thinking in certain discernible directions, but who cannot explain why countless other people who have read the same works were not similarly influenced. So it is with psychological interpretation: The only difference is that some people seem to expect more, or hope that less can be said.

As with so many aspects of understanding China, a major problem in studying Mao's personality is a shortage of information. Aside from the remarkable autobiographical account Mao gave to Edgar Snow in a cave in Shensi 40 years ago, factual information about the private Mao is as scarce as that about the workings of the Chinese political process. All we can do is to try to piece together all the scraps of information that are available and then to seek an interpretation that seems most consistent with most of the information. The structure of this book has emerged out of a process of going back and forth over the data of Mao as a public man and Mao as a private man.

More specifically what I did was, first, to juxtapose all available information about various psychologically critical relations: I thus put together all that he and others had to say about his relations with his mother, and then I examined how he later related to women and how he treated his wives; I looked at what we have been told about how Mao acted as a "son" to his father, and then how he performed as "father" to his sons and daughters; his relationships with his brothers and sister were put in the context of his later collegial relations. Concrete understanding about one relationship could be used to help fill out our understanding of another. Our purpose was to arrive at an interpretation of personality which was most consistent in terms of these critical relationships. The second step was to juxtapose this picture of Mao the private man and the record of Mao the public figure and then to make further adjustments in our search for the man in the leader.

Our method of analysis has meant quite frankly that from time to time we have speculated that certain events must have taken place even though we lack objective proof. We are led to these educated speculations because our theory of personality holds that in all lives there is coherence and that the traits which appear at different stages of life are related to what precedes and what follows.

This approach has led us to a new emphasis and a new set of concerns in explaining the psychology of a great political figure. Conventional theories in psychology have dealt with the issues of authority and rebellion primarily in terms of the tensions and repressions associated with the father-son relationship. We have found, however, that in the case of Mao Tse-tung the critical developments were related to pre-Oedipal experiences and involved primarily Mao's relationship with his mother, a relationship which gave him strong feelings of narcissism but which also gave him a sense of being unjustly treated when he could no longer command her undivided attention. Our hypothesis is that this range of primary experiences best explains Mao both as rebel and as charismatic leader. It also illuminates his extraordinary appeal to radical youth in Western societies who likewise need to rebel because of their frustrations and rage that the world has not fulfilled the expectations of life that they had first glimpsed during the exceptional security and indulgence of their phase of infant omnipotence and bliss.

At the outset we must stress the tentative nature of our analysis. Hopefully, in time, if more information becomes available, it will be possible to modify or further confirm our interpretation of Mao Tse-tung. In the meantime, this is a particularly appropriate moment to examine the psychological dimensions of Mao's greatness when the Chinese political system is absorbed with the question of succession. Any attempt to understand how Mao conducts himself with respect to this last great issue in his public career requires a developmental perspective toward his entire life. Furthermore, while one cannot foresee what will happen after his passing, it is highly likely that his life will soon become enveloped in an ever thicker cloak of myth. Therefore, it seems especially desirable to make this initial analysis at a time when much of his life is already a part of history, but while he still has a last act to play before becoming a part of static mythology.

In carrying out this research I incurred a debt to Alan P. L. Liu for his extensive contributions in mining hidden facts

Preface

on Mao's life. Originally, we planned to co-author this study, but the distance between Massachusetts and California proved to be insurmountable and, without constant contact, I drifted off into my own interpretation of Mao's personality. Liu's work, particularly on how others perceived Mao and on Mao's relations with his colleagues, which was relied upon for Chapters II and X, stands on its own as an important study of Mao.

My psychological interpretation of Mao was decisively shaped out of long and stimulating discussions with Steve Pieczenik, M.D., who constantly pushed me to seek ever deeper explanations of behavior. He guided me to certain useful works of Helene Deutsch and Otto Kernberg. Dorothy Grosse Fontana helped gather data on Mao's relations with his associates.

I have benefited from careful and critical readers who have examined this manuscript from the perspectives of psychology, Chinese history, Mao's political career, and prose style. Jean MacKenzie Pool grasped the full dimensions of my interpretation and with great sensitivity challenged me with further subtle hypotheses. Harold R. Isaacs, whose understanding of the early years of Chinese Communism is second to none, reaffirmed the ideal of the academic colleague by critically reviewing my words one by one. Michel Oksenberg generously gave of his time and shared his wealth of knowledge about Mao's style of rule. Richard H. Solomon gave invaluable help from the perspectives of both Chinese psychology and Communist history. Roy Hofheinz tested my words against his extensive knowledge of the Chinese Communist movement, and Edward Rice helped me on several details of fact about Mao's children. Other readers to whom I am indebted are Gabriel A. Almond, Suzanne Berger, David Denoon, Harold D. Lasswell, Ithiel de Sola Pool, and Myron Weiner.

For unearthing certain critical items and for being most generous I am indebted to Sidney Liu.

I truly appreciate Virginia Peltier's understanding patience in deciphering my illegible handwriting and typing my seemingly endless revisions.

Once again, Mary W. Pye has played a major role in polishing my prose, challenging my reasoning, and working at every stage of editing and proofreading.

Although I would feel much more comfortable if I could share responsibility for this work with all who have helped me, I must, of course, personally accept full accountability for its limitations.

LUCIAN W. PYE

ILLUSTRATIONS

Following page 130

Listed in the order in which they appear in the book

Mao's birthplace in Shao-Shan: The secure world of his childhood. (*Marc Riboud/Magnum*)

The room Mao was born in: Note the photographs of his mother and father on the wall. (*Rene Burri/Magnum*)

Mao (far right), his two brothers Mao Tse't'an (left), Mao Tse-Min (center), and his mother. (*Union Press Ltd.*)

At his mother's funeral: From left to right: Younger brother Mao Tse't'an, father, uncle, and Mao, wearing black mourning band. (*Rene Burri/Magnum*)

Mao Tse-tung (fourth from left) with classmates at the Hunan First Normal School, about 1917. (*Rene Burri/Magnum*)

The young radical Mao at the beginning of his career (1919). (*Union Press Ltd.*)

Mao's first wife, Yang Kai-hui, and their two sons Mao An-ying and Mao An-ch'ing (standing). (*Union Press Ltd.*)

Mao and his third wife, Chiang Ch'ing, at the time of their marriage. (*Eastphoto*)

As party intellectual (1923). (*Union Press Ltd.*)

As soldier (1937). (*Union Press Ltd.*)

As young orator (1938). (*Union Press Ltd.*)

As old orator (1945). (*Union Press Ltd.*)

As writer. (*Eastphoto*)

Reading. (*Eastphoto*)

Mao in military action. (*Union Press Ltd.*)

Comrade Mao Tse-tung and his close comrades-in-arms. All, in varying degrees, were at one time abandoned by Mao. From left to right: Chu Teh, Chou En-lai, Ch'en Yun, Liu Shao-ch'i, Chairman Mao, Teng Hsiao-p'ing, Lin Piao.

PART ONE

Introduction: The Monkey and the Tiger

". . . in truth I have a tigerish nature as my main characteristic and a monkey nature as my subordinate characteristic."

Mao Tse-tung

CHAPTER

1

The Problem

BY ALL STANDARDS, Mao Tse-tung belongs in the company of the few great political men of our century. Born and raised in the obscurity and restrictions of nineteenth-century rural China, he rose to assume the leadership of the Chinese Revolution, rule the largest population in the world with the most pervasive and intense government known in history, and finally has clung to life long enough to become the last of the political heroes of the great generation of World War II. His life spans the emergence of modern China and his character has shaped the manner and style of the Chinese Revolution.

To say that Mao Tse-tung has been the most revered and the most ecstatically worshipped man of the century may seem like paying him a slight compliment in the light of the awesome statistics of China. With some 800,000,000 Chinese presumably holding Mao Tse-tung in absolute reverence as a demigod, what other mortal of our times can claim to be his competitor in popular appeal? Yet, Mao Tse-tung's appeal has reached far beyond the citizenry of his native land, however large. Few have not been touched by his existence, whether in admiration or hatred, in respect or scorn. His name has become the label for revolutionary extremists throughout the world, "the Maoists," yet it is Mao Tse-tung with whom leaders throughout the world seek audiences. The Pope in one day admits to his presence more people than Mao Tse-tung grants audiences in a year. When Mao last appeared publicly, more than a million people expressed tumultuous joy, and since then the occasions for allowing a select few into his presence have been newsworthy throughout the world. The announcement that the American Secretary of State has had a couple of hours of discussion with the Chairman is a signal to all that the Secretary has been favored, indeed, honored; and, of course, when a trip to China does not include a visit with the Chairman, the universal interpretation is that favor is being withheld.

The extraordinary appeal of Mao Tse-tung is hard to identify. Some may suggest that it lies less in the man and more in the nature of Chinese society, for the Chinese do seem compelled to make all of their leaders into imperial figures. Yet, the fact remains that many non-Chinese, who have no affinity for his rural origins but represent a host of varied social and personal backgrounds, seem to find inspiration for their political lives in his words and his example. Restless youth scattered throughout the world who have more formal education than he had feel that in his revolutionary ardor and purity he speaks for them.

Indeed, Mao casts a powerful appeal even to those who have no sympathy whatsoever for his ideals, yet respect him as a statesman and strategist of a new world balance of power.

Politicians of old and new states make visits of deference to this man of seclusion and mysterious power. And besides them, the personal fascination of Mao Tse-tung has also excited the imagination of intellectuals such as André Malraux who seek audiences in their turn.

What is the character of the man that lies behind all this greatness? Merely to raise the question is an act of sacrilege for many. For the Chinese and other worshippers of Mao and his thoughts, it is enough to dwell on his public virtues, read only hagiographies, and reject all else as being in bad taste. For his detractors, the whole spectacle is revolting, and Mao the man must be the devil behind the Chinese version of socialist totalitarianism. Yet between these extremes there are those who are honestly curious. It is to such readers that this book is addressed.

The public record reveals a man at home in rural China, a man of the peasantry, who knows the myths and folklore of traditional China. Yet, although he received a Confucian education, Mao was also part of the first full generation of Chinese to explore Western knowledge. From his rural isolation, he moved effectively into the chaotic, competitive world of Chinese student politics and revolutionary scheming. As soldier, ideologist, and planner, he became the symbolic leader of the Chinese Communist guerrilla struggle. As victorious ruler he was a visionary who looked beyond immediate problems of administration to the goals of a new society and to the molding of a new form of man. Chinese to the core, he also has been a principal shaper of our two contemporary international systems: His judgment helped to create the postwar world of two sharply divided blocs, and his decisions contributed to the 1970s concept of a more fluid and complex balance of states. His genius has thus extended from the era of China's first awakening, through the drama of World War II, the intense bitter struggles of the Cold War, to a new era of the future, whose outlines we can barely perceive today.

In recent years, numerous attempts have been made to understand what lies behind the renown of Mao Tse-tung. Students of intellectual history, for example, have tried to suggest ways in which he has enriched Marxism; but while they have shown Mao to have been an astute, indeed shrewd, thinker, they have all had to concede that his ultimate claim to greatness does not lie in his work as a philosopher. Others have suspected that his reputation springs from his successes as a military strategist; but in spite of all their sympathetic effort, it is clear that Mao's genius lies elsewhere. Still other champions of Mao's fame have argued that he envisaged entirely novel goals for the economic order which would render obsolete all conventional ambitions for greater industrial and material well-being; but a careful review of Mao's policies makes it clear that he appreciates the near universal craving for higher standards of living and greater personal security.

The paradox of Mao Tse-tung is that while his claim to greatness is unassailable, in every specific sphere whether as philosopher, strategist, economic planner, ideologue or even world statesman, his qualities are not the match of his right to greatness.

The secret of his greatness lies elsewhere—in his extraordinary ability to understand, evoke, and direct human emotions and the innumerable ways in which he has used his own persona to command the sentiments and passions of others. In modern China the realm of emotions has been peculiarly problematical: In traditional Confucian China the essence of correct behavior was the complete mastery and indeed repression of passion, and especially aggression; but out of the frustrations of impotence in the modern world the Chinese have been responsive to the appeal for acts of public passion. The need to ritualize emotions as a means of controlling feelings contributed to the traditional Chinese appreciation of drama and theater; and the modern need to find expression for feelings has multiplied the numbers of those who want to be heroic and to find drama in their own lives.[1] Mao Tse-tung as a person has been uniquely capable of responding to this need of the times in China, for he is possessed of a personality that fits the definition of a "dramatizing" character whose skill lies in commanding the "immediate affective response in others." [2]

Since Mao's greatness lies so clearly in the realm of emotions, the problem of Mao Tse-tung is a problem in political psychology. To treat Mao merely as an intellectual or as a calculating strategist is to miss the essential dimensions of his historic role. Furthermore, if we are to understand how Mao came to be so successful in mobilizing the feelings of the Chinese, and of others, we must explore his own emotional world and discover the dynamics of his psychic relations with others.

As an individual, Mao is intrinsically fascinating. His acts and his words are startling and unexpected. In his conversations he will bring up the most unlikely subjects: Why are some Africans more dark-skinned than others? Have not all the advances in medical science only increased the number of diseases? The Chinese people have always known Marxism because they have always appreciated contradictions. A dedicated materialist, Mao can suddenly speak as a conventional believer in the hereafter: "I shall soon be seeing God." "When we see God, or rather Karl Marx, we will have to explain much." At times he has depicted himself as an outstanding hero of Chinese history: "Yes, we are greater than Ch'in Shih Huang-ti." "We must look to the present to find our heroes." At other moments Mao has modestly belittled himself and indulged in self-pity as when he pictured himself wandering through life as "a lonely monk with a leaky umbrella." At times his speeches have been witty and caustic; at other times he has allowed his words to ramble. His style is generally vivid, sensitive to nuance, reflective of emotions, and often playful and teasing.

Intrinsic fascination aside, Mao's character demands serious analysis because there is much in the history of modern China that cannot be explained except in terms of Mao Tse-tung's personality. In the fluid circumstances of the Chinese Revolution, time and again events and processes took on decisive form in direct response to the personality of Mao Tse-tung. In stable societies with solid institutions the scope for the influence of personality considerations is constrained to the narrow limits of how different individuals may perform established roles. In the case of Mao Tse-tung there was no defined role for him to fill; rather his own personality created his own roles and thereby shaped Chinese history.

Thus, the modern history of China is a complex blending of objective developments, individual style, and a considerable element of chance and accident.

According to most conventional accounts, the dynamics of modern Chinese history were the interplay of massive social and economic forces: the rise of nationalism, the distintegration of the rural economy, the impact of the West, the collapse of Confucian ideals, and the like. In such a view of history there is little room for the force of personality, but rather, events are visualized as the products of huge waves which may carry along on their crests, almost like whitecaps and flotsam, a few people who may seek to convey the illusion of being in command of the forces they are riding, while others, less lucky in catching the crests, are violently thrown into the troughs and destroyed.[3]

Such a vision of the impersonal workings of Chinese his-

The Problem

tory is often juxtaposed with analyses that treat in great detail the convoluted relationships of the host of men whose names appear in all the conventional accounts of modern China. Thus, one chapter will elaborate the forces of social change and the next will pick up the story of a multitude of friends and foes trying to manage China's modernization. What is missing is a coherent linkage between the flow of history and motivations. The same analysis will attribute the Chinese Revolution to impersonal factors and then declare that the culmination of that revolution, Chinese Communism, has been shaped by the idiosyncratic character of Chairman Mao. Like scientists accepting both wave theory and quantum theory in explaining light, so historians of modern China tolerate their two approaches and feel little need to explain any causal relationship between them.

When the story of modern China is systematically related to the activities of Mao, a key element of Mao's genius is immediately highlighted: his remarkable capacity to perform different, and even quite contradictory, roles at different times. As Mao took on the roles of peasant organizer, military commander, ideological spokesman, political strategist, and ruling statesman, he also vacillated between such contradictory public persona as fiery revolutionary and wise philosopher; dynamic activist and isolated recluse; preacher of the sovereign powers of the human will and patient planner who knows that history cannot be rushed.

In a very strange manner Mao Tse-tung has been able to communicate a sense of the integrity of the human spirit precisely because he has defied logic and spoken for exactly opposite points of view. He has praised books (indeed sanctified the presumed magic of his own "Little Red Book") and he has denounced bookish knowledge—"Reading books only makes myopic children." He has equally extolled and denounced vio-

9

lence. He has championed reason and also scorned the paralyzing impulses of reasonableness. His intellectual integrity is as unassailable as folk wisdom, with its appropriate sayings for every option.

For the politician, especially for the man who deals in the hard currency of truth and falseness in the subtle universe of human affect, the question of integrity of role is complicated. For he must deal with both desires and reality, the elements which must be mixed in the daily marketplace of political exchange, and thus he can obscure the differences between objective fact and subjective reality, for they are to him matters of interchangeable importance.

Mao Tse-tung supports the critical insight of the founder of political psychology, Harold Lasswell, that basic to all public figures is an element of "playing a role, of being an imposter," and of indulging in the necessary degree of "self-deception" to make it possible to engage enthusiastically in the make-believe of the political "game." [4]

With Mao Tse-tung, as with most political leaders, the problem of explaining public successes involves an understanding of certain private needs which can only be satisfied by public acts. The purpose of such explanation, however, is not to trivialize the great man by making his historic acts only grotesque amplifications of slight distortions in the experiences that all people must pass through. On the contrary, great men are not belittled by discussions of their period of dependency, for the very essence of humanity in all people is the common drama of personal development from utter helplessness to self-realization.

Indeed, the bond between the great man of history and his acclaiming public has to be forged in the life experiences of Everyman. Therefore, there is a need to look into the story of the private Mao Tse-tung, in order to uncover the secrets of both his maturation and his public appeal. Although in theory there may be no reason to suppose that whatever may have driven a man to public life would also have to be the source of his public appeal, in the case of Mao Tse-tung there are reasons to believe that the two are associated because his successes and his failures lie so completely in the domain of the management of affect.

In examining the details of the private man, we must look for clues that will illuminate how Mao was able to adapt to so many roles and situations, and why he was able to touch the emotions of so many people with such different backgrounds. Mao Tse-tung's appeal as a rebel does not seem, for example, to spring from any need on his own part to play out on a grander stage any deep feelings of hostility toward an autocratic and repressive father, for too many people who have not had such difficulties with their fathers have resonated to his call for rebellion. (We shall see that Mao's relationship with his father was neither so simple nor so oppressive.) Instead, we shall discover that Mao's style as a rebel taps a different set of memories, locked in the unconscious of a wider range of people: He speaks to the anguish and the anger of all who feel the frustrations of being "ignored," of not being "respected as an individual," of not being able to "participate in the decisions which affect one's life"—that is to say, all who feel that life has let them down because reality will not allow them to recapture the sense of infantile omnipotence that they once knew when they were the center of a universe in which their every wish could command as magic the attention of others. As we shall see, there is a clear psychological basis for Mao's appeal as a rebel—his ability to touch responsive chords in middle-class youth throughout the world who have known indulgence and whose parents once gave them levels of attention that could not be sustained.

Introduction: The Monkey and the Tiger

The idea that Mao's greatness lies in the relationship between his own psychological needs and the psychological needs of masses of people is a part of Mao Tse-tung's political consciousness. When Mao saw Edgar Snow after the Cultural Revolution he confessed that the Chinese people had probably gone too far in attributing magical power to his Thoughts, but then he added that there are times when there is a need for a personality cult, and that in human affairs one thing that will always exist is "the desire to be worshipped and the desire to worship."

With these words Mao identified the essential relationship between leader and follower: The politician serves a psychic function for the crowd just as the crowd performs a function for the politician. Leaders and followers are each dependent upon the other and they need to extract from the other something which fulfills their needs, and yet there is a peculiar singularity but vital difference in what each seeks. The desire "to worship" and the "desire to be worshipped" are symmetrical, but not similar sentiments.

Mao's insight into the needs of leaders and followers takes us directly to the essence of charismatic leadership. The need to worship taps the basic human need for dependency; the need to be worshipped goes to the core sentiment of narcissism; and, of course, dependency and narcissism have their common roots in infancy. The comforts of dependency and the exhilarations of narcissism are linked in the earliest of human experiences when the self has not been differentiated from others or from the environment, and when there is a confusion of omnipotence and helplessness. At that stage the distance is infinitesimal between the cries of weakness and vulnerability, and the joys of every wish becoming an instant command for attention. Out of this universal experience most people, in varying degrees, can sense that their hero's joy in being worshipped barely masks his anxieties over being ignored; and most leaders, in even more subtle degrees, can sense that lurking in the dependency of their followers is a mighty craving for potency, and that a people's sense of justice rests upon the infantile longing that their own inherent goodness will be rewarded by the blessing of their own total command of their situation. The followers can see their leader's psychic vulnerability, but they do not want to see through him for fear of destroying the memories of the only magic that ever worked in their lives. The capacity for the leader to tap his own narcissism reminds his followers that they too have their potential for greater goodness and strength.[5]

The strange dynamics of narcissism also feed the universal myth, inherent in political systems, that goodness should be rewarded by becoming powerful, and that power should always have the goodness of authority. This goodness insures that those who need dependency will be safely nurtured. Therefore, to understand the linkage between the dramatic and self-asserting Mao Tse-tung and a Chinese people who want both security and effectiveness, we must carefully identify both the private experiences of the leader and the cultural patterns of the masses that have made it possible for such a great charismatic leader to emerge in the revolutionary context of China.

Out of the interplay of narcissism and dependency those who need to be worshiped and those who need to worship are linked together as each depends upon the other's vulnerabilities.[6] The charm of the great man is that we can see his capacity for both self-deception and for having fun with the public; the great man in turn is charmed and exhilarated that his actions can bring such exaggerated responses from the public. A Franklin D. Roosevelt could never completely hide his pleasure at being able to manipulate public passions, and the American public never completely hid their pleasure at being able to see through the self-satisfaction of their popular president. The great appeal of John F. Kennedy was based on a very human relationship in which his admirers appreciated his refusal to take himself too seriously, and he understood their readiness to be teased and humored. The key to why the sly element of the imposture inspires heroism in the viewer rather than disenchantment seems to be the universal human appreciation of narcissism. People can instinctively understand that the great man enjoys his sense of greatness, and they may respond in kind by relaxing their inhibitions about their own narcissistic urges and in their turn aspire to act in ways which rise above their humdrum roles.

Mao Tse-tung in a moment of self-revelation once wrote his wife a letter, which we shall analyze later, in which he tellingly described his own personality as being part "monkey"—impish, quixotic, mercurial, unpredictable, and always quick to provoke, tease, and change—and part "tiger"—the lord and ruler who is fierce and dangerous, respected and feared by all.

This mixture of the monkey and the tiger, which gives an intriguing quality to Mao's behavior, leaves him free to maneuver. As the ideologue of willpower he suggests that his commitments are absolute; yet, his basic ambivalences make it possible for him to alter policies and dramatically change his positions.

As the master of mass emotions it would seem that his own feelings must be more intense and unruly than most people's. Yet, in fact, over the years his capacity to act out many roles and to champion a variety of contradictory positions points to his ability to control completely his own feelings. He himself once wrote that a cardinal principle of life is that: "It is permissible to arouse emotions [in others] but not ever to give vent to them." [7]

The ability to move other people's feelings while always guarding his own explains much of Mao's political genius. But there is much more to the mystery of Mao Tse-tung that can only be explained in psychological terms. As we shall see, all manner of contradictions seem to abound in Mao's political style. He has idealized conflict and struggle; yet he has been hypersensitive to criticism and competition. He has throughout his life attacked authority for being irresponsible; yet he has been reluctant himself to assume the full responsibilities that go with power. He has upheld as ultimate values dedication, loyalty, and absolute commitment; yet he has practiced flexibility and even moderation. He has upheld the idea of pure fraternal relations; yet over the years he has abandoned his closest comrades one after the other.

Indeed, before we can explore the psychic dynamics of this most remarkable leader, we need further introductions to his manifest characteristics. First, we must take into account the descriptions and general impressions of those who have met him. Then, we need to identify the principal traits of Mao as a public figure. Only after we have been introduced to the mature man and have arrived at a greater appreciation of the complexities of the emotional basis of his behavior, will we be ready to examine the private man and learn about his emotional development, his defense mechanisms, and his manner of dealing with others. The private Mao begins with his childhood, and therefore we must examine with care the nature of his relations with his mother, his brothers and sister, his father, his schoolmates and teachers, and finally his wives and children. These are the basic relationships that great men and common men alike experience, and that provide the emotional drama which shapes personal traits and styles. We will deal with matters central to all men: growing up in a family, learning to deal with peers, establishing one's own family, and having one's own children. Rather than stopping with childhood and then seeking to relate the boy to the man, our view of the private man will include the full cycle of Mao as both son and father. We will do this for both practical and theoretical reasons. In interpreting a man's account of his childhood, it is useful to juxtapose his descriptions of how his father treated him with the record of how he in turn as a father treated his own offspring. Indeed, much is revealed by the similarities and differences between the family of one's dependent years, which is largely beyond one's shaping, and the family of one's adult creation.

After we have completed our exploration of the private Mao, we shall then return to Mao as a public figure. Our purpose will not be to review his entire public record, which is already available in numerous biographies and histories, but rather to concentrate on how his personality contributed to his remarkable political successes. As a political creator, Mao's great ability has been in his mastery of words and ideas and his management of power. He has been one of the rare public figures in history who has been both an ideologue and a strategist. His skills in these areas seem to be directly related to his emotional character.

Finally, there is the problem of Mao's capacity to leave enduring institutions. The very developments that generated his creative powers as ideologue and strategist have apparently compelled him persistently to abandon his personal associates, and thus as a great charismatic leader he has floundered in passing his power to his lieutenants. Precisely because of certain qualities in his personality, which we shall identify and which account for his greatness, he has been unable to institutionalize his great creative act of carrying out the Chinese Revolution.

2

Impressions of the Private Man

THE MAGIC of greatness has so obscured the image of Mao Tse-tung that the man himself has rarely been described in straightforward terms. Even his public life has been a secret life. The most meticulous analysts of China have been prepared to discern Mao's hand behind all manner of policy turns, while quite shamelessly admitting that they know next to nothing of the private activities of the man.

This combination of public myth and private secrecy means that before we begin to speculate about the inner qualities of this great man, we need to describe him through the words of eyewitnesses. Yet, for a man who has lived at the vortex of the Chinese Revolution, and risen to be the revered leader of the most populous country in the world Mao Tse-tung has remarkably few witnesses. From his days as a guerrilla fighter hiding in mountains, evasively marching through the backlands, and lurking in secluded caves, to the period of authoritarian isolation in grounds where emperors once indulged their private pleasures, Mao Tse-tung has been niggardly in sharing his presence. Instead, there have been numerous theatrical occasions where the drama obscures the nature of the man.

Objective reporting about such simple matters as the physical qualities and manner of the man has been almost impossible because nearly every witness has been so overwhelmed by the event of meeting such a great figure that he has generally been able to describe only his own subjective reactions to the experience. A Henry Kissinger speaks of how Mao exudes power and a grasp of history. An André Malraux tells of seeing an oracle, given to word play and intellectualization. A delegation of Japanese socialists reports that they met a man of compassion and empathy. From the time that Edgar Snow contrived to slip into Yenan and bring back the first Western journalistic reports on the Red Army and his meetings with Mao Tse-tung, the tradition was established that a meeting with Mao was an exceptional event that would add to the luster of anyone who was fortunate enough to be granted an audience.

When we assemble all the words of those who have met Mao, even after making appropriate allowance for those who were either awestruck or politically prejudiced, one must conclude that they could not be speaking of the same man, but rather of several different men. To some he has appeared tall, vigorous, animated; others have seen him as stooped, soft, retiring. Some have seen him as open and friendly; others as aloof and even lonely. He has been described as verbally sharp, intense and argumentative, and also as reflective, relaxed and philosophically inclined.

The first conclusion, therefore, might be that Mao is a man of moods. Mao's orderly during the Long March, who saw no faults in him, has suggested that Mao's spirit changed frequently according to circumstance.[1]

Others who have seen Mao over time have commented about the paradoxes and contradictions in his behavior. In a serious meeting with high officials Mao will suddenly use earthy, salty language. When others are grim, he appears relaxed. When others are satisfied, he will express dissatisfaction and call for struggle and greater efforts.

Before looking more carefully into the character of Mao's moods and ambivalences, we should note that these differences in eyewitness descriptions reflect with remarkable precision the various roles which Mao has assumed at different times in his life. He seems to have been a man who has always readily portrayed what others perceived as appropriate, and indeed ideal, qualities of whatever role he was cast in at the time. As Mao Tse-tung progressed from country boy to adolescent school boy, to radical intellectual, then party organizer, guerrilla leader, party spokesman and ideologist, to national leader and revolutionary symbol, people tended to describe him in quite different ways.

One of Mao's earliest schoolmates, Siao Yu, who knew him when he was an obscure country boy seeking the acceptance of younger classmates, recalled: "Mao was not unusual in appearance, as some people have maintained, with his hair growing low on his forehead, like the devils pictured by old-time artists, nor did he have any especially striking features. In fact I never observed anything unusual in his physical appearance. To me he always seemed quite an ordinary, normal-looking person. His face was rather large, but his eyes were neither large nor penetrating, nor had they the sly, cunning look sometimes attributed to them. His nose was flattish and of a typical Chinese shape. His ears were well proportioned; his mouth, quite small; his teeth very white and even. These good white teeth helped to make his smile quite charming, so that no one would imagine that he was not genuinely sincere." [2]

Then a few years later, when Mao was in normal school and passing through his adolescent crisis, he became known as an "unkempt person" (*pu hsiu pien fu*). At that time he started to allow his hair to grow longer than Chinese youth fashions of the day. He conveyed the impression of one who was unconcerned with clothing and physical possessions. Whereas when he first entered primary school he was hypersensitive about the quality of his clothing, he now took the lead in affecting the casual, and indeed sloppy, appearance of the free-spirited student and aspiring scholar. A classmate of that period, Li Jui, writes:

> When comrade Mao Tse-tung first enrolled in the Fourth Provincial School, he was issued a blue-greenish uniform which he wore for several years even after it became torn and discolored. Aside from wearing this uniform, he often had a gray gown on. During winter, he wore a padded cotton shirt inside. He seemed to have never changed the white-cloth pants throughout the year. In summer he often did not have socks on and his cloth shoes were torn. His quilt was old and hard as those used by the peasants in Hunan. . . . His classmates regarded him as an especially "unkempt" person. [3]

From the time he was a schoolboy until he reached the pinnacle of power in 1949, he wore baggy cotton uniforms; when he became leader of the Party he only changed the color from black to gray. [4] On the other hand, before Mao entered his phase of adolescent slovenliness he had been meticulous in his dress, and interestingly, once he achieved national authority he reverted to earlier character and again dressed to fit a role of respectability.

In fact, adolescence brought out traits that were to characterize Mao's entire life. For example, Li Jui's descriptions of Mao's schoolboy days in Changsha in 1913–18 suggest that even then the aloofness and solitariness, which characterized so much of Mao's later life, were already evident. On Sundays other students would gather in groups of three or five, cooking their own meals and eating together. "Only comrade Mao Tse-tung alone gathered some cold rice and dishes, sat by himself, finished his meal and left quietly." [5] Similarly, Chou Shih-chao, another of Mao's classmates, recalled that Mao, "in class, was a well-behaved and gentle person; he never skipped while walking. His speech was never crude. Often he sat solemnly and erect, saying few words." [6]

Yet, those who were to describe Mao only a few years later when he was a guerrilla leader have spoken of his rude habits: As a chain-smoker he sucked his breath "with a strange noise quite unpleasant to those who heard it." [7] And Edgar Snow tells of how in his Yenan cave Mao would absentmindedly turn down the belt of his trousers and "search for some guests" and of how once in a briefing session he stripped off his pants because of the heat. [8] Visitors who have met Mao after he became the ruler of China have been impressed with his quiet dignity and his gracious manner.

Those who knew Mao during the years after he graduated from normal school, but before he became a full-time Party organizer, that is when he was entering the world of intellectual Marxism, have commented about his scholarly mien. At that time Mao had moved to Peking to become assistant librarian of Peking National University and was surrounded by scholars and students with whom he wanted to mingle. From the observations of others there was little on the surface that revealed that at that time Mao was personally distressed over his poverty and felt inferior. The philosopher Hu Shih tells of how he met Mao in Peking and assumed that he was a regular student.

In the next phase of Mao's life as he started his career as a professional revolutionary he maintained some elements of the radical intellectual role; and he did not entirely shed his rural and unkempt schoolboy qualities. Li Ang, one of the early members of the Chinese Communist Party, in describing Mao's appearance in 1921 when the Party was just established, said: "He [Mao] left me with a strange impression. I saw in him the plain and sincere quality of a rural youth—he wore torn cloth shoes and a gown of coarse fabric. It was rare to encounter such a person in a place like Shanghai. But I also saw in him the decadent manner of those scholar-celebrity types. . . ."[9] A participant at that First Congress, Chang Kuo-t'ao, has recalled that Mao appeared to him to be a ". . . palefaced scholar, wearing a gown."[10] Another acquaintance reports that, "At that time Mao wore a long gown and a pair of cloth shoes. . . . When I attended meetings with Mao I discovered that he would not talk at first. He would rise toward the end of the meeting to sum up and suggest solutions."[10a]

In the next phase of his career when he was busy as an agitator and organizer among workers and peasants, reports of Mao's appearance changed again. Two former workers at Anyuan Mine in Hunan where Mao and his comrades started the labor movement after 1921 recalled that Mao dressed like a common laborer, wearing a straw hat and tying up his trousers around his knees "as if he had just returned from labor work."[11] "Often Mao was seen wearing a ragged uniform with a large T-shaped patch on his back and, like other workers, ate his meals squatting, dabbing his chopsticks into the vegetable dishes on the ground." [12] We have the report of Li Jui that Mao consciously studied the style of workers' behavior, observing carefully their mannerisms, playing the role of worker rather than becoming a laborer himself, for that would have inhibited his freedom for agitational work. According to Li Jui, "Comrade Mao Tse-tung had done some hard and serious work prior to his approaching the laborers. He often put on a straw hat, straw sandals, a coarse jacket, and short pants so as to be closer to the workers. For example, to understand the conditions among rail workers on the Yueh-Han line, he spent several days in a teahouse in the northern station of Changsha, drinking tea with the workers. Finally he made friends with workers." [13]

In Mao's next phase as guerrilla leader, he lost the quality of being indistinguishable from the masses and assumed a command presence. Initially, Mao continued to act the part of the peasant-worker-soldier, but even as early as 1930, he was seen as a definite personality, with elite status and no longer one among many. A Party newsletter, in describing a mass meeting in western Fukien, organized to bid farewell to the Red Army, said that, of the more than twenty people who addressed the audience, "all were workers or peasants except Chu Teh, Mao Tse-tung, and a delegate from Taiwan." [14] As Mao rose in power during the Long March, descriptions of him changed. Both critics and supporters suddenly found him to be a man of decisive action, great energy, and increasing aloofness.

After the Long March, Mao became the dominant figure in the Chinese Communist Party. Reports of his appearance suddenly changed as people again began to see in him a scholarly figure, exuding wisdom, and suggesting great decision-making skills. At this stage, witnesses began to sense in Mao Tse-tung mystical powers and magic in his remoteness. Edgar Snow, recalling his first impression of Mao in Yenan in 1936, wrote:

> I met Mao soon after my arrival: a gaunt, rather Lincolnesque figure, above average height for a Chinese, somewhat stooped, with a head of thick black hair grown very long, and with large searching eyes, a high-bridged nose and prominent cheekbones. My fleeting impression was of an intellectual face of great shrewdness, but I had no opportunity to verify this for several days. . . .[15]

As Mao became widely known as the leader of the Chinese Communists, he received increasing numbers of Chinese and Western correspondents in his cave in remote Yenan. One of the Chinese reporters wrote later of his first impression of Mao:

> Elegantly tall but not striking in appearance. A woolen uniform that was apparently old and worn. The collar was typically unbuttoned and, like in his photograph, the white shirt inside was exposed. His eyes stared at the person introduced to him as if he was making an effort to learn the name of the visitor.
>
> His speech had a heavy Hunanese accent. He had a tired look, maybe due to work and tension, and he was unsmiling throughout the conversation. And yet his manner was gentle and scholarly. He uttered each syllable clearly and his wording was proper and well ordered. He followed his talk accordingly which was a theoretical exposition, not a hortatory lecture.
>
> This is Mr. Mao Tse-tung, leader of the Chinese Communist Party.
>
> While listening to his talk, I had more time to watch him. With thick hair and a somewhat plump face, he does not look like an action-man. His broad forehead and his straight, high-

bridged nose show an aristocratic air about him. His eyes were always staring forward, signifying a profound thinking man.[16]

In 1946 the British writer Robert Payne interviewed Mao in Yenan, and was again struck mainly with his scholarly academic appearance. Payne wrote:

> . . . He is fifty-three and looks thirty. You will see him any day on any campus in England or America.
> . . . Ultimately, a man is what he is without his cap. Remove the cap, and Mao Tse-tung gives all the appearance of a scholar, with all the odd chameleon strengths and weaknesses which come from an intense absorption in scholarship. The course of study he has set himself is the revolution of China.[17]

Descriptions of Mao's health and physical vitality have also varied according to periods of his life. In his youth he was weak and prone to illness; in adolescence he went to great lengths to build up his body. His health deteriorated on numerous occasions, at times because he could not afford an adequate diet, more often because he had no time for food or exercise, and in several notable cases, because of tensions from being "ignored" and distress over failure.

While Mao was still under the influence of his father he was, as we shall see, vulnerable to the charge of being lazy, but once he began to find himself, he frequently demonstrated tremendous outpourings of concentrated energy. When Edgar Snow was interviewing him in Yenan, Mao showed no sign of fatigue as they talked late into the night. Snow learned that Mao customarily worked a thirteen- to fourteen-hour day and usually did not retire until two or three o'clock in the morning.[18] And when in 1944 Gunther Stein interviewed Mao from three in the afternoon to three in the morning, Mao still seemed "fresh and animated."[19] The most dramatic account of Mao's animal energy is his bodyguard's account of how Mao wrote the famous essay *On Protracted War*. For two days he did not sleep at all, on the fifth day he was visibly thinner, on the seventh day he was still so absorbed in his work that he burned his toe because he did not notice that his foot was stuck in the charcoal fire, then finally on the ninth day he finished the essay.[20]

When Mao first came out of the obscurity of Yenan to assume a national role he was perceived as an articulate spokesman who could speak spontaneously with and for all elements of Chinese society. In 1945, when Mao went to Chungking to negotiate with Chiang K'ai-shek on the eve of the civil war, he was seen as being less polished and refined than the Generalissimo but also as a readily accessible and friendly personality.[21] At that time the Party was courting all "independent" and non-Kuomintang elements, and speaking in terms of a new version of democracy for China. Yet almost as soon as the Communists came to power the public personality of Mao changed to that of the remote and isolated decision maker.

The aura of mystery in Mao's style of authority was finally established when, less than three months after coming to power in Peking and establishing his residence in one of the palaces of the emperors, he left his country for a visit of nearly four months to Moscow. Khrushchev reports that the Soviet elite found him an uncertain leader who had to be entertained but who could not effectively communicate his purposes.[22] Yet a few years later Khrushchev was impressed by the decisiveness of Mao and how he "sounded like Stalin" because he "had nothing good to say about anyone." [23]

Once Mao Tse-tung felt secure in his role as China's national leader his image was soon caught up in myth-making campaigns. In this process Mao was steadily stripped of a normal personality and made into an abstract symbol, which had different facets at different times depending upon the themes being stressed by the Chinese media and the Party activists. Describing Mao after his first decade in power, Howard Boorman found it appropriate to speak of him as a "lacquered hero." [24]

As the stereotypes became stronger, those who met Mao were often startled to find that in the flesh he was a man of strong words and emotions. By the late 1960s when Mao's health became more and more a matter of worldwide speculation, reports of visitors often dwelled mainly on impressions of his well-being, which seemed to be rather unstable.

Among all the eyewitness accounts of Mao's appearance during this late phase of his life, possibly the most significant is that of Secretary of State Kissinger as told to C. L. Sulzberger:

> He [Mao] was grossly overweight but he had a remarkable capacity to dominate things around him. Physically he exuded willpower. De Gaulle dominated any room in which he stood because of his serenity. Mao dominates equally—by his feeling of will.
>
> We only talked for a little over an hour and I have no way of knowing if Mao has more than an hour or two of effective mental force during a day. But he did convey this impressive atmosphere of tremendous power. Very recently I reviewed the transcript of our conversation and I found it like the overture of a Wagnerian opera. Every single thing we discussed in the subsequent conversation with Chou En-lai was previously mentioned in that single talk with Mao." [25]

Other eyewitnesses have mentioned this sense of willpower, as well as his quality of aloof serenity. Indeed, next to Mao's remarkable capacity to adapt himself to his different roles a second striking observation of eyewitnesses is his abil-

ity to command his emotions and to suggest that he is emotionally detached from immediate matters.

Even as a child his classmates noted his "grave manner,"
and as he grew older people were increasingly struck with his
calm exterior. This quality of aloofness was combined with
very rare demonstrations of any form of affect and emotion.
Even when he conveyed a sense of action and was evoking
feelings in others, he seemed personally to be withdrawn and
in closer touch with his inner world. Thus, a former worker of
the Anyuan Mine recalled his first impression of Mao in 1920:

> At that time the labor movement was at a low ebb but he had
> the attitude of "sitting solidly on a fishing boat regardless of the
> rise of winds and waves." He was completely at ease as if he al-
> ready had everything planned within himself.[26]

After achieving his position of leadership Mao's reserve in
expressing affect strengthened his appearance of having great
wisdom. He was seen as a man who was completely in command not only of his own emotions but also of the entire situation. The first Westerners who ever met Mao were uniformly
impressed by his calm exterior and his apparent perfect control of his emotions. In August 1937, when the war with Japan
had just begun and excitement was everywhere in China,
Nym Wales, the wife of Edgar Snow, observed: "Mao speaks
in quiet decisive syllables like someone reading from a familiar
book. He never shakes the shaggy black mane away from his
eyes. He never plays with a pen or pencil. His large shapely
hands are as quiet as his voice.[27]

In 1938, British explorer Violet Cressy-Marcks interviewed Mao in Yenan and later wrote about her first impression of him: "His ears were different from any man's I have
ever seen—quite flat on top—and his thick black hair was

parted in the middle. His fingers were thin and his hand nicely shaped. He had a quiet manner and voice: I had expected to see a man who would have given outwardly the appearance of fire and strength. . . ." [28]

When Edgar Snow saw Mao a second time in 1939 he was struck more than ever with Mao's control of his emotions. "I found Mao living in a 'modern' three-room cave 'apartment' in the loess hills a few *li* outside Yenan. I noticed again the unusual repose of the man; nothing seems to ruffle him. He is gradually acquiring a kind of benignity. He is pronouncedly less 'tense' than Chiang Kai-shek. . . ." [29]

It is significant that the more dramatic and theatrical the setting, the greater Mao's control of affect. In the Yenan years Mao developed his public speaking style which maximized the contrast between passionate words and the disciplined, unimpassioned speaker. A female journalist who stayed in Yenan for several years during the war against Japan recalled her first impression of Mao's public style: "His voice was not high, but his quietness, *the kind of quietness as if there was no connection between him and the audience,* captured the attention of everyone. He did not speak long but people clapped wildly" (italics added). [30]

At about the same time, Violet Cressy-Marcks witnessed a similar performance by Mao in a mass meeting in Yenan:

Mao Tse-tung, I think, is the only orator I have ever seen *who made no gesture whatsoever. He kept his hands clasped behind him and he spoke for three hours.* [italics added] He had no notes and just looked at the audience. Outside it was very dark and inside the hall there was only a lantern or two swung over a line in front of the stage. The rest of the hall was in darkness. All around me the tense faces with solemn eyes never left Mao Tse-tung's face. The silence was such that a pin could have been heard if it dropped. [31]

Introduction: The Monkey and the Tiger

The capacity to stare down others, to hold the eyes of individuals or groups, requires enormous psychic energy, complete determination to shield the self while penetrating the other, and is a masterful technique for controlling others.

After gaining national power and becoming a semidivine hero, Mao's style of public speaking remained the same. Whenever he faced large crowds he became distant, reticent, and a solitary figure. In secret Party congresses and when addressing leading cadres, Mao could be biting, sarcastic, humorous, and rambling. Over the years, however, he has tended less and less to make the effort of public addresses. We know that, from time to time, Mao has moved around the country, inspecting projects, testing opinions, and talking with supervisors. Frequently, on these occasions, large masses of people are mobilized to hear him, but almost invariably he has chosen not to speak but only wave to them; typical was his visit to Wuhan University in 1958:

> After inspecting the factories built by university students, Chairman Mao appeared in the track field of Wuhan University. There waited some 13,000 students and staff. . . . From these came thunder-like applauses and greeting. "Long Live Chairman Mao." The responsible persons of these schools shook hands with Chairman Mao. . . .
>
> Mao walked up the steps of the Administration Building and raised his arm, waving at the crowd to show his appreciation. Then he departed.[32]

It is in the small group setting that Mao is most responsive. He is particularly skillful in making a few joking remarks to disarm his visitors. In 1945 while in Chungking negotiating with Chiang K'ai-shek, Mao received two young couples, one being factory workers and the other college students majoring in agronomy. When the two couples were introduced to Mao, he responded smilingly: "Ah, two pairs of husband and wife, four youths; two study agriculture and two are workers. Then you are 'worker-peasant alliance.' Very good. Very good!" As these youths recalled: "Chairman Mao's words were spoken slowly, sentence by sentence. They made the whole room fill with laughter. A mood of relaxation now prevailed." [33]

Several people who have had private meetings or dinners with Mao report that while he has great ability to express a wide range of apparent emotions, he often does so with such rapidity that some suspect that he is prone to dramatize and to pretend to feelings.

Kung Chu who met Mao in Kiangsi in 1928, recalled Mao's dramatic behavior:

> During dinner, Mao smiled often. When he talked about the good prospects of the future, he laughed heartily. But his expression changed to a worried and sad look when he talked about current economic and food problems. He became extremely angry when he mentioned how he was given several warnings by the Party Center who criticized his attack on Ping Chiang and Liu Yang as "military adventurism" and "an opportunist unwilling to mobilize the masses." He was called a "deserter abandoning the masses" when he retreated to Chingkangshan. Mao clenched his fist and railed at the responsible Central leaders for their knowing only empty talk without heeding real situations. His manner suggested that he would not be satisfied until he had his vengeance. I feel that Mao had a talent for acting. In a short time he displayed all the sentiments of joy, anger, sadness and happiness. [34]

Mao has always had a fondness for the theater, and apparently greatly enjoys the freedom of playing with his own emotions in the safety of a make-believe setting. Chao Ch'ao-kuo reports how at theatrical performances Mao became lively and engaged in "hearty laughter." [35] Robert Payne also saw

Mao at theatrical performances, alternately "giggling almost to sickness" or assuming a reverential posture:

> In those rare moments when Mao Tse-tung was not about to fall from his seat, you noticed that he put his palms together in the attitude of someone praying and his face was grave. You wondered where you had seen it all before. Then you remembered that the boy at his first party had changed instantly to the vicar in the parish hall who would make a speech in a moment and call on everyone present not to forget their subscriptions for the harvest offerings.[36]

The theater is one of the most popular forms of entertainment for most Chinese—indeed one of the few remaining forms of public entertainment permitted under the generally austere Communist regime—and Mao's enjoyment of stage performances may merely seem to make him typical of his culture. Yet the fact that the theater has been given such legitimacy under his rule, and that he married an actress at just the time when he himself was ready to mount the national political stage does suggest a special feeling for the theater.

Although in the folklore of Chinese Communism it is widely presumed that Mao is capable of outbursts of anger, it is significant that we have no witnesses to any scene of uncontrolled rage. But we do have several reports suggesting that Mao at times bluffs his emotions. Thus, Edgar Snow reports: "I never saw him angry, but I heard from others that on occasion he had been roused to an intense and withering fury. At such times, his command of irony and invective was said to be classic and lethal." [37] And Robert Payne tells of seeing Mao make a "violent gesture, throwing out his clenched fist" as he sought to emphasize his anger at those abroad who supported the Kuomintang.[38] This quality of petulance and of shifting moods has made Mao seem slightly feminine to some.

Indeed, numerous Western and Chinese observers of Mao have commented that not only his manner in changing emotions but even some of his physical characteristics suggest a feminine quality. Agnes Smedley, for example, described her first meeting with Mao in Yenan. "The tall forbidding figure lumbered toward us, and in a high-pitched voice greeted us. The two hands grasped mine; they were long and sensitive as a woman's. . . . His dark inscrutable face was long, the forehead high, the mouth feminine. . . . I was in fact repelled by the feminine in him. . . ." [39] Later Smedley contrasted the athletic, outgoing, physically active Chu Teh with Mao and his ". . . strange, brooding mind . . . sensitive and intuitive almost to the point of femininity . . ." [40] Adrdré Malraux tells of his meeting with Mao, "I go to take leave of him, and he holds out an almost feminine hand, with palms as pink as if they had been boiled." [41]

Others have also noted that Mao's handshaking became increasingly flaccid as he aged. A diplomat stationed in Peking in the late 1950s was surprised by the lack of vitality in his grip and the sensation that "he had no bones in his hand." [42] In Chinese culture a soft rather than a firm handshake is, of course, the norm; but Mao seems to exaggerate the limp quality.

Mao's manner of walking also seems to be strikingly non-masculine. A former Shanghai businessman recalls meeting Mao in December 1955: "The Communist Chairman is tall for a Chinese; he is a heavy, soft-looking man who appears younger than his pictures usually suggest. He is very slow. He walks with his toes pointed out; he takes short steps and swings his arms more than seems necessary for his ponderous gait." [43] This is not just the consequence of aging for even when Mao was in high school, his gait reminded people of the slow but jerky movements of Chinese women with bound feet. Siao Yu tells that "he walked rather slowly, with his legs somewhat separated, in a way that reminded one of a duck waddling. His movements in sitting or standing were very slow." [44]

Later we shall find more significance in these observations. Here we should merely like to note that there is something very mysterious in the greatest revolutionary of our times, a warrior, and an ideologist of passionate actions seeming to be a gentle, passive, and physically undynamic person. This quality of mystery, of contradictions and polarities, is possibly the most striking feature that acquaintances have noted in Mao. Another of Mao's early classmates, Hsiao San, brother of Siao Yu, confessed to Robert Payne, "Mao is the most complex person we have. . . . None of us have really understood him. I have known him longer than anyone else, but I have never got to the root of him." [45] Mao himself seems to appreciate his capacity to convey mystery and ambiguity. Nym Wales tells that, "In the gregarious elbow-to-elbow world of Yenan, he was an Olympian figure indeed. When you went to call on him at night, the affair seemed as ceremonial as keeping a tryst with an oracle." [46] Agnes Smedley, the other Western woman who knew Mao before he had become almost completely unapproachable, noted that in spite of being personally repelled by the "feminine in him," "the few who came to know him best had affection for him, but his spirit dwelt within itself, isolating him." [47] Also echoing Hsiao San, who told Robert Payne that "there were secret springs in Mao which he never disclosed," [48] Smedley further noted: "I had the impression that there was a door to his being that had never been opened to anyone." [49]

Robert Payne described Mao in Yenan, when he was the most accessible at any time in his career, as being "remote," "intangible," and "aloof." [50] This quality of lonely isolation and mystery existed even in Mao's relations with his wives. Although we do not have any direct testimony from his second wife, Ho Tzu-chen, Edgar Snow, when he was recording Mao's autobiographical recollections, observed: "During Mao's recollections of his past I noticed that an auditor at least as interested as I, was Ho Tzu-chen, his wife. Many of the facts he told about himself and the Communist movement she had evidently never heard before, and this was true of most of Mao's comrades in Pao An." [51] This was true in 1936 when Snow first met Mao who, by that time, had been living with Ho for eight years.

Some three decades later, in 1967, during the height of the Cultural Revolution, Chiang Ch'ing spoke to the enlarged meeting of the Military Affairs Committee:

> The Chairman has always been strict with me. He treats me first and foremost as my strict teacher. To be sure, he does not coach me literally by holding my arms, like some others do. But he is very strict with me. Many things are unknown to me. *The Chairman as a person, I think, you comrades know more than I do. We live together but he is a man with few words . . .* [52] (italics added).

Most significant of all, Mao Tse-tung, when he has had the occasion to speak of his own personality, has in various ways identified his own underlying ambivalences. For example, in a candid talk at Hangchow on December 21, 1965, Mao observed: "Marx's *Das Kapital* began with an analysis of the dual nature of commodities. Even things which are not commodities also have a dual nature. Our comrades have dual nature, too; namely, right and wrong. Don't you have a dual nature? I myself have duality. . . ." [53]

Mao has himself identified the character of his inner ambivalences as a clash between self-confidence and self-doubt, between solid strength and impish trickiness. Late in Mao's life in a letter to his wife, Chiang Ch'ing, he expressed in remarkably objective fashion the strong sense of confidence in his own personality that was usually adequate to conquer his residual elements of self-doubt, largely because on both the scales of confidence and doubt he had grander proportions than others.

> Although I have confidence, yet at times I am doubtful. I once said when I was in my teens: I believe I should live two hundred years and sweep three thousand *li* [Chinese miles]. I was haughty in appearance and attitude, but somehow I also always doubted myself. I always felt that when the tigers are absent from the mountains, then the monkey will call himself king. I have therefore become the king of the jungle, although I am just a monkey. This is not vague compromising, for in truth I have a tigerish nature as my main characteristic and a monkey nature as my subordinate characteristic.[54]

Ambivalences between the "tiger"—the symbol of the powerful, self-assured, all conquering personality—and the "monkey"—the impish, erratic, unfettered, and changeable spirit: Once again Mao's own words seem to capture perfectly the structure of emotions. The Westerner, although accustomed to thinking of the lion as the king of beasts, has no problem appreciating that in Chinese culture that role is ascribed to the tiger; but what may need explanation is the place that the monkey occupies in the Chinese imagination. A hero of one of the greatest stories in Chinese folklore is a great monkey who had magical powers to change himself, and was thus the quick imposter, the impish spirit who could dart about, appearing and disappearing without enduring commitments, but with maximum dramatic effect. Mao in his poetry has spoken of his empathy for the Golden Monkey.*

Using the work of the anthropologist Ruth Bunzel, Margaret Mead and Martha Wolfenstein have summarized all that the monkey image holds for Chinese such as Mao Tsetung who were brought up on the legend.

> Monkey is of supernatural origin, yet his character is quite humanly aggressive and assertive. He is extremely self-confident, fearless, and reckless, with a strong urge for activity. He is also very frank in stating his opinions and uninhibited when speaking to his superiors, since he has no sense of status difference or of behavior adjusted to status difference, and, least of all, "face" (*mien-tzu*). Being highly intelligent, he manages very early in his existence to equip himself with all the powers necessary to assure him victory in any kind of struggle. He is very proud of his superior physical and mental abilities, which he believes entitle him to a dominant position in the universe. His sense of justice and fairness is based upon this belief. Monkey has an insatiable desire for prestige and power.[55]

Mao, in writing to his wife about the contradiction in his nature between his self-assured "tiger," and his spontaneous and affect-free "monkey," indicated that there is a burden in self-confidence as he explains that people do not appropriately appreciate the pain that a morally superior person experiences when others fail to recognize his virtues. Mao wrote to his wife,

> I must quote several sentences of a letter by Li Ku of the Han dynasty to Huang Ch'iung as an explanation of my situation,

* In the summer of 1974 during the wall poster campaign associated with the "anti-Confucius, Anti-Lin Piao" campaign, a series of large character posters appeared on the walls of the Peking Revolutionary Committee headquarters, criticizing local leaders for not being adequately committed to Mao Tse-tung's revolutionary spirit, and significantly signed "The Golden Monkey."

Introduction: The Monkey and the Tiger

"Hard objects break easily; white substances become easily soiled. Sophisticated music like the song White Snow in Early Spring has few who can appreciate it; it is difficult for a person of great renown to match his deeds with his reputation." These sentences are an apt description of myself. Once I read the above sentences at a meeting of the Standing Committee of the Politburo.[56]

Mao Tse-tung's judgments about himself thus give further substance to the views of others that he is a man of ambivalences, in some ways scornful of his environment and in other ways hypersensitive to others' views of him, and quite able to "play up to" the expectations of any audience. Behind these hints of Mao's appearance of self-confidence lurk uncertainties as to whether others in fact appreciate what he wants to believe to be his own innate goodness, we have moved beyond the level of impressions toward the search for deeper explanations. But before we take up this investigation of the private man, it is necessary to gain some first impressions of Mao as a public man.

CHAPTER

3

Impressions of the Public Man

ON THE FACE OF IT, it would seem much easier to characterize Mao the public man than Mao the private man. Understandably, his private life has been obscured while the attention of one of the most powerful public information organs in the world has focused on his public role. Yet, paradoxically, the legend of Mao Tse-tung has in a strange way more effectively obscured the realities of Mao Tse-tung as a decision maker than of Mao as a private person. The building of the myths of Mao Tse-tung the Helmsman has provided a cloak of near total secrecy around the actual operation of the Chinese political system.

Furthermore, while for the early private man there exists Mao's own autobiographical account to Edgar Snow and eyewitness reports of him in various informal contexts, there are no complete memoirs by either Mao or his colleagues that would reveal Mao's actual political role. According to legend, everything positive in the New China stems from the personality and the thoughts of the Chairman. Mao Tse-tung himself has suggested that the cult of his personality may have been exaggerated because of the "habits of 3,000 years of emperor-worshiping traditions," [1] but then he has also defended such legend-building and observed that, "Probably Mr. Khrushchev fell because he had no cult of personality at all." [2]

The myth of Mao Tse-tung is not just the product of sycophantic followers and propagandists of the New China. Scholars and commentators throughout the world have advanced the view that Mao has placed his personal stamp on the Chinese Revolution and that the distinctiveness of Chinese Communism stems from his personal genius. Yet, on reflection it should be self-evident that it is unrealistic to believe that the mind and spirit of one man could shape all of modern Chinese history.

Other more cautious scholars have limited Mao's role by depicting much of the history of Chinese Communism as a struggle between Mao and those who do not share his political visions. Yet even this view of Mao, which came out of the surprising turmoil of the Cultural Revolution, is tainted with the stuff of legend for it emphasizes the coherence of Maoism as an ideology rather than the complexities of Mao's full career as a public man. From non-Chinese versions of the ideology of Maoism it would appear that Mao as a political figure is an incurable romantic, a believer in revolution for its own sake, and an utopian completely incapable of appreciating practical considerations.

Stanley Karnow, for example, in his detailed account of the Cultural Revolution sums up Mao's style by pointing to the fact that "Not once during the Cultural Revolution . . . did Mao outline a clear-cut, practical program aimed at precise objectives. Instead, he exhorted his followers to destroy his opponents so that an undefined utopia might emerge at some unspecified point in a faraway future." [3] Robert S. Elegant theorizes that "Mao was obsessed with grandiose theories and transcendent policies." [4] And Robert J. Lifton has interpreted the entire Cultural Revolution in terms of an aging Mao's response to death. More specifically, "Mao's ultimate dread—the image of extinction that stalks him—is the death of the revolution," for to him the "Revolution" had become a "sacred thing itself." [5]

Most of these writers would agree with A. Doak Barnett that there is a difference between the political ideology of Maoism and Mao's personality.

> Many labels have been used to characterize Mao's strategy of revolutionary development and the basic assumptions, predispositions, values, and goals that presumably have motivated his actions. All involve great oversimplification, and none is therefore wholly satisfactory. Yet most of them have a certain validity. Terms such as revolutionary nationalism, idealism, radicalism, romanticism, populism, and egalitarianism highlight distinctive characteristics of his thought, but each of these labels is also misleading in some respects when applied to Mao. [6]

Partly the labels are misleading because, as Michel Oksenberg has observed, Mao Tse-tung has been "trying to reconcile conflicts of the modern age—between egalitarianism and industrialism, freedom and bureaucracy, participation and order." [7] The tendency to exaggerate Mao's preferences in these contradictions becomes pronounced in many attempts to explain the Cultural Revolution as a struggle between the "two lines" of "Maoists" and "Liuists." [8]

Introduction: The Monkey and the Tiger

Yet all of these attempts to see the "real" Mao in the phenomenon of the Cultural Revolution had to depend upon indirect evidence for Mao did not make "a single public statement during the entire Revolution." [9] Indeed, if we were able to blank out the period of the Cultural Revolution from our minds we would have quite a different picture of Mao as a political man. Thus, far from distrusting organizations, it was after all, Mao Tse-tung who in the 1920s had opposed the undisciplined and unrealistic leadership of the first Chinese Communist leaders and especially of Li Li-san who, in Mao's words, "failed to recognize that the revolution required adequate preparation by the building up of its own organizational strength." [10] And later it was Mao Tse-tung who successfully Bolshevized the Chinese Communist Party through the *chengfeng* campaign of 1942–44. [11]

Again, the ideology of Maoism stresses not only revolutionary fervor but also self-reliance and autonomy. Yet it was Mao himself, who after struggling for years alone to gain national power, took off for Moscow shortly after victory for a prolonged visit in search of alliance and aid. No other leader of a newly independent African or Asian country could have conceivably abandoned his country for so long as soon after coming to power in order to negotiate with a potential patron. Yet Mao, according to Khrushchev, openly manifested ambivalences of dependency and autonomy toward Stalin and the Russian leadership. [12] Even at the cost of his self-esteem, Mao personally insisted in the councils of the Chinese leaders that they commit China to the policy of "leaning to one side" and accepting the guidance of "the elder brother," the Soviet Union.

The ideology of Maoism cannot be taken as a guide to Mao's political thoughts above all because it was he himself who terminated the activities of the radical "Maoists" and the Red Guards at the end of the Cultural Revolution. Finally, Mao was as much behind the decision to invite President Nixon to visit China and to sanction a new relationship with the United States as the decision to have a Cultural Revolution.

In sum, Mao the public man has been as active in China's consolidating, "pragmatic" policies as in her radical and utopian efforts. Therefore, in seeking even initial impressions of Mao the public man, we should avoid the error of seeing him only in terms of the popular conception of Maoism. There is more to Mao's political style than just the glorification of revolution and the radical spirit or belief in egalitarianism, spontaneity, and populism, or faith in peasants, the untutored, and distrust of city ways, formal education, and bureaucratic processes. Yet these are all elements of what he has brought to Chinese politics.

In seeking a first impression of Mao the public man to guide us in our psychological study, we are, therefore, interested in more than just the spirit of Mao implicit in Maoism, and yet we need a picture that is more precise and sharply focused than that of the legend of Mao the Helmsman.

We need to grasp the ways in which his personality shapes his choices even when he is being a "pragmatic" and calculating decision maker. Therefore, we are concerned with his style in dealing with power, his manner in strategy, and his use of action; in a phrase we are interested in what some have called his "operational code." Before we can appreciate the relationship of the private man and the public figure, we need to describe Mao's idiosyncratic traits as a decision maker according to a series of generalized themes appropriate for characterizing any great political figure.

Introduction: The Monkey and the Tiger

Consistency vs. Contradiction

A key question that needs to be asked about the world view of any political leader is whether he tries to be consistent in his statements and policies, and precise and logical in his basic mode of reasoning, or whether he tends to shift his position easily, accept the need to respect the realities of changing circumstances, and in his thinking is he highly tolerant of ambiguities and contradictions?

Mao clearly belongs to the school that believes that consistency is the hobgoblin of the small mind. Throughout his career he has found it easy, and often enjoyable, to change his position and to give expression to various ambivalences. Indeed, the zigzags of Chinese policies over two decades seem to reflect in large measure Mao's bemusement with the very concept of contradictions. Some scholars have argued quite convincingly that the most striking characteristic of Mao's political thought is his fascination with the notion of contradictions.[13]

Of course, as both a Leninist and Marxist, Mao is expected to be flexible in tactics and committed to a dialectical view of history. And in his own philosophical writings Mao has concentrated to a large degree on the question of contradictions. Yet when reviewing Mao's use of the concept of contradictions it does not require any special perceptiveness about personal styles to recognize that Mao's fascination with contradictions has gone beyond that of most Marxists, and that his concept of the dialectic has at times been extraordinarily idiosyncratic, indeed to a point which would make it seem to be non-Marxian. There is nothing, for example, in the history of Marxism that would prepare one for the idea which Mao expounded to Party cadres when he said: "Fearing and not fearing, being happy and being unhappy, solving problems and not solving them: this is dialectics. For instance, in waging war, at the beginning one is quite afraid, but the more he fights, the more courageous he becomes. Without having had several errors in line, we could not be so good today." [14]

In other statements Mao has revealed this same propensity to treat any pair of opposites—"good and bad," "hot and cold," "young and old"—as being in the same class as Marx's concept of dialectical materialism. The awkward fact is that Mao persistently associates the contradictions of dialectical materialism with the pairs of opposites basic to traditional Chinese thought. Indeed, he has seemingly recognized that he is addicted to classical Chinese modes of thinking by shifting in the same paragraph from elucidating his notion of Marxian opposites to cite the work of traditional Chinese philosophers. "The sky and the earth are the unity of opposites. Voluminous words are not required when it comes to good things. Lao-tzu wrote only a little over 5,000 words in his lifetime." [15] Furthermore, the enthusiasms with which Mao greets any example of the "unity of opposites" suggests that he has a benign view of pairs, more consistent with the traditional Chinese view of the "harmony" of the *yin* and the *yang* than with the conflict implicit in the notion of contradictions in Western Marxism.

On occasion, Mao has said explicitly that traditional Chinese thought is consistent with Marxism because it contained the notions of both the harmony of opposites and the dynamics of imbalance that are to him the essence of Marx's theory of contradictions and dialectics. "It is always so that people do not think alike. Imbalance is the law of universal progress. Mencius said: 'All things are not alike, and all things complement each other.' People do not think alike and yet it is possible to reach accord. Progress is made in a zig-zag spiral pattern." [16]

It would be wrong, however, to believe that Mao's concept of contradictions is merely a revival of traditional Chinese concepts. Mao has made his own modifications. For example, the classical Chinese pairs of opposites were vivid and immutable, poles of enduring differences. Mao, on the other hand, holds that little endures for anything can change into its opposite.

> Hard battle and rest and consolidation are the unity of opposites. This is the law. They also are mutually transformable. There isn't anything that is not mutually transformable. High speed turns into low speed, and low speed turns into high speed. Labor turns into rest, and rest turns into labor. Rest and consolidation, and hard battle are also like this. Labor and rest, and high speed and low speed also have identity. Getting out of bed and going to bed are also the unity of opposites. An old saying goes: "He who has slept for a long time thinks of getting up." . . . Sleeping transforms into getting up, and getting up transforms into sleeping. Opening a meeting transforms into closing a meeting. Once a meeting is opened, it immediately embraces the factor of closing the meeting. [17]

But Mao's attachment to the concept of contradictions becomes psychologically interesting when he uses it as a way of neutralizing subjects that we know are highly emotional to him, such as the relationship of sons and fathers, and husbands and wives. In one rambling recounting of the concept of dialectical contradictions, Mao revealingly suggested that it was possible to dismiss the inherent tensions of both generations and sexes by simply holding that the differences do not really exist: "Sons transform into fathers, and fathers transform into sons. Females transform into males and males transform into females. Direct transformation is not possible. But after marriage when sons and daughters are begotten, is that not transformation?" [18] By thus blurring distinctions, Mao wards off problems of a deeply personal nature. He has gone even further than just the matters of generations and sex, and has used the concept of contradictions as a comforting shield against the disturbing fact of the inevitability of death. At a Party Congress Mao once spoke of how the Chinese people had a national affinity for Communism because of their instinctive appreciation of the "unity" of weddings and funerals, and by jesting about both, he stripped them of their customary emotional dimensions:

> There are red and white happy events. . . . The Chinese people consider weddings as red happy events and funerals white happy events. . . . The Chinese know dialectics. Weddings will produce children. A child is split out of the body of the mother. It is a sudden change, a happy event. One individual is split into two or three, or even 10, like planes off an aircraft carrier.* The common people find the occurrences, changes, and deaths of new matters happy events. When a person dies, a memorial meeting is held. While the bereaved weep in mourning, they feel it is also a happy event. Actually, it is. Just imagine if Confucius were still living and here at this meeting in Huai-jen Hall. He would be over 2,000 years old, and it wouldn't be so good. [19]

Beyond jesting, however, we have examples of Mao essentially denying the reality of death by his use of his version of the dialectic, which he seems to know to be different from the Soviet version of the dialectics. For example, he has written: "Life and death are mutually transformable. Life transforms into death, and lifeless things transform into living things. . . . It is a natural law. . . . The Soviet Union's

---

* The Chinese word for aircraft carrier is "aviation mother-ship."

'Concise Dictionary of Philosophy' takes upon itself to differ with me. It says that the transformation of life and death is metaphysical and that the transformation of war and peace is erroneous. Who is right after all?" [20]

Mao thus makes use of the concept of contradiction in numerous ways: At one moment he can be impish and cute as he plays with differences that are sobering to most people; at the next moment he can startle by suggesting that what others accept as normal differences are profound matters. By playing with contradictions he shocks others and, as the clever "monkey," he tears down distinctions and suggests that what is good is bad, and what is bad can be good.

One can see this spirit as he tells how,

> I once asked some comrades around me whether we lived in heaven or on earth. They all shook their heads and said that we lived on earth. I said no, we live in heaven. When we look at the stars from the earth, they are in heaven. But if there are people in the stars, when they look at us, wouldn't they think that we are in heaven? Therefore, I say that we live in heaven while also on earth at the same time. The Chinese like the gods. I asked them whether we were gods. They answered no. I said wrong. The gods live in heaven. We live on earth, but also in heaven; so, why shouldn't we be considered gods also? If there were people in the stars, wouldn't they also consider us as gods? My third question was whether the Chinese were also foreigners? They said no, only the foreigners were foreigners. I said wrong, the Chinese were also foreigners, because when we consider the people of foreign countries as foreigners, wouldn't they also consider us as foreigners? It explains the superstitious ideas on this point. [21]

Yet at other times Mao has become sober and even threatening as he has talked about contradictions. That was clearly his mood when he mentioned that he himself has contradictions and that, "the world is full of contradictions. There is no place without contradictions." [22] Nor did he believe that contradictions were a laughing matter when he warned a conference of cadres that "Exposing contradictions may lead to settlement of problems; they should not be suppressed. *But if we tolerate contradictions, we shall be vanquished.* [italics added]" [23]

Mao's use of contradictions thus covers a wide range of his style in making decisions. He is quick to identify issues and he conveys an awareness of his own boldness in fearlessly bringing into the open conflicts and contradictions. He also uses the concept of contradictions to tame problems and make them benign. And he uses contradictions both to tease and to threaten. To some degree all of this could be a calculated style, which obviously works to the advantage of the great leader; yet there must also be something in Mao's personality that makes him employ contradictions so naturally. Later we shall have to search for the ambivalences which have enabled Mao to become skilled in utilizing the concepts of contradictions and the unity of opposites.

Approaches to Risk-Taking and Reason

Another important aspect of any leader's operational code is his approach to risk and his use of reason. How does he use reason as he faces the uncertainty of risk? Does he adopt the posture of judicious reasonableness to justify low-risk choices or does he modify the shock of high-risk decisions by enveloping them in a cloak of reasonableness? Or does he deny the importance of reason as he faces the uncertainty of risks and suggest that he has powers that exceed the limits of mere reason?

In recent years it has been customary to say that the Chinese Communists tend to be extreme in their rhetoric but cautious in action, particularly in the area of foreign affairs.[24] Some have observed that in contrast to the Chinese caution in foreign policy, Peking, under Mao's direction, has vacillated from revolutionary experimentation to periods of consolidation.[25]

Readily available evidence suggests, however, that Mao's vacillations and contradictions have not generally taken this form. Mao's own rhetoric, for example, has not been extreme, and to the extent that he has been inclined to use aggressive language, it has generally been directed against immediate foes, often people in his audience whom he has singled out for caustic and sarcastic attack. It would be very hard to find any occasion when Mao Tse-tung dressed up a cautious decision in inflammatory rhetoric. On the contrary, if there is a consistent element in the zigzags of Mao's decision-making style, it is that he has almost invariably chosen bold options, but presented them as eminently reasonable decisions.

From the time of his first decisions as a political leader in the Kiangsi Soviet period and then during the Long March, Mao has consistently been bold and novel in his choices. One has the impression that, unlike most decision makers with great responsibilities, Mao more frequently than not passes over possibilities to hedge against failure, and decides instead on unpredictable courses of action. Whereas most statesmen live with a vivid dread of the penalties for failure, Mao has been attracted to the potentially great payoffs that can come from success against long odds. While most executives crave certainty and only "reasonable" risks, Mao has taken great gambles as though it were only reasonable to do so.

Mao's willingness to take risks seemingly is associated with a sense of omnipotence that leads him to expect that nothing is final—there will always be another chance. Consequently, while he may have had doubts about the present, he has always had to look with optimism to the future, where he can expect to capture (or recapture) what is missing in the present. Thus, talk about catching up with Great Britain in fifteen years, or catching up with America "before I go to see Marx" was not idle boasting, but a genuine expectation that the infinite promise of the future could become reality (as fantasy once seemed to do in the past).

The full documentation of Mao's propensity for bold choices would require a complete history of the Chinese Communist movement, and therefore, we need here provide only a few typical examples. After the gamble of the Long March in the Yenan period, Mao acted with great boldness not only in pushing guerrilla warfare but also in risking a major ideological rectification campaign at the height of the Japanese War. Then, in his maneuvering with the Nationalists prior to the actual civil war, Mao at each turn in the negotiations refused settlements that a more cautious leader might have seen as providing reasonable security for later political struggles. Finally, he risked all in a gamble for total military and political victory. As soon as victory came, Mao again made the bold choice of "leaning to one side" and of going to Moscow for his prolonged negotiations with Stalin. A more cautious leader would have sent lesser officials to test the negotiating climate in Moscow. In domestic policies Mao, time after time, overruled the preferences for prudence among his colleagues and insisted on uncertain alternatives: It was Mao who personally pushed to speed up the tempo of land reform in 1950, who finally insisted on speeding-up collectivization in 1955, and pushed for communization in 1958. From the Hundred

Introduction: The Monkey and the Tiger

Flowers Campaign of 1956 through the Great Leap of 1958 to the Cultural Revolution in 1966, Mao repeatedly took tremendous risks. In foreign policy the record of Mao's bold decisions extends from his choice to enter the Korean War to his decision to invite President Nixon to Peking and to deal with a government that for twenty years he had been indoctrinating his people to regard as the ultimate evil.

Mao's propensity for making startling decisions distinguishes him from political leaders in general, and more specifically, from most other Chinese Communist high officials. One of the reasons why China has a debilitating succession problem today is that the political system has over the years overwhelmingly favored cautious actors who were able to survive because of skill in defensive maneuvering, in protecting their domains, and who did not have to aggressively build empires. Those who came to power with Mao in 1949 have generally cautiously sought to hold their own gains and not seek more. There has not been a great deal of mobility within Chinese officialdom and survival has gone with competence and not with success in climbing ahead of others. Although Mao has frequently spoken out about the need for cadres to take initiatives, to be constantly active, and not to slavishly adhere to dogma, his rhetoric has not altered the realities of power relationships or changed the fact that it has been Mao alone who has been free to practice high-risk decision making.

To a considerable degree, Mao has been able to mask his propensity for high-risk decisions by describing his choices as being self-evidently reasonable. There is little bravado or glorification of danger in Mao's statements of policy. Drama has been used to stimulate greater support for policies; but generally Mao defends his decisions with such reasonable language that he trivializes the very concept of risk.

Mao's style in the face of failure has been to withdraw,

often with an accompanying complaint about illness, or to ignore the losses and proceed as much as possible, as though nothing had happened, or, if finally cornered, he will either shift the blame to others or vigorously defend his actions in highly personal terms. During the early years of the Chinese Communist movement Mao took risks and had setbacks that put him out of favor with the Party leaders, and his response was to withdraw and recoup in isolation in the mountains of Kiangsi. These reverses were accompanied by health problems.[26] An impressive example of his capacity to shrug off serious failures was the way in which Mao dismissed the significance of losing Yenan to the Kuomintang at the outset of the civil war. Mao had risked war and then had lost his symbolically important base area that he had successfully defended throughout the entire war with Japan. By dismissing the loss as irrelevant and proceeding as if nothing had happened he was able to undercut the significance of the Nationalists' victory.

At times, however, Mao has not been able to ignore failure, as when his own colleagues have questioned the wisdom of his initial decisions. On these occasions he has combined hurt withdrawal with aggressive and highly personal defenses of his actions. His mood can be that of the misunderstood and mistreated leader who has done his best and is not appreciated, and in the traditional Chinese style, then declare that they can be rid of him, but then, in a more un-Chinese manner, he may add a threat to withdraw and fight back. Possibly, the classic example of this aspect of Mao's style was the "three sleeping pills" speech at the Lushan Conference on July 23, 1959, when he was under severe attack for the failure of the Great Leap and of the commune movement. Mao came into the hall and took the stage late in the evening and declared, "You have spoken so much; permit me to talk some now, won't you? I have taken three sleeping pills. Still I can't sleep." In a sense he was saying that he had tried to "withdraw" but could not so now he would have to fight back. And fight back he did, declaring that, "Nobody can be without shortcomings, even Confucius had his mistakes.* I have seen Lenin's own drafts that have been corrected pellmell. If there were no errors, why should he correct them?" As Mao rambled on he made it clear that he was ready to draw the line and force the issue, but in a mood of self-pity, "You have said what you want to say. . . . If you have caught me in the wrong, you can punish me. Don't be afraid of wearing tight shoes. . . . The fact is that you have all refuted me though not by name perhaps." Finally, Mao came to his not so veiled threat: "When I was young and in the prime of life, I would also be irritated whenever I heard some bad remarks. My attitude was that if others do not provoke me I won't provoke them; if they provoke me, I will also provoke them; if they provoke me, I will also provoke them; whoever provokes me first, I will provoke him later. I have not abandoned this principle even now." Mao coupled his threat with explicit allusions to how he was personally in the same class as Marx and Lenin. Then he ended on a note designed to shock: "Comrades, you should analyze your own responsibilities and your stomach will feel much more comfortable if you move your bowels and break wind" [27] [that is, make a clean slate of it].

On another occasion Mao's aggressive response to failure and criticism took the form of declaring to the Central Committee that, if they wished, they could take his wife and he would go to the hills again to raise another Red Army to oppose them.[28]

---

* This is only one of innumerable references by Mao to Confucius which have become extremely embarrassing to the Chinese Communist Party since the initiation in 1973 of the Anti-Confucius Campaign.

Close Control or the Delegation of Authority

A third consideration useful in arriving at a general under-standing of the operational codes of public men is their basic style in administration. Do they act as chief executives who maintain day-to-day control over all possible operations, or are they inclined to delegate responsibilities? If they do dele-gate responsibilities, how do they assert their own authority?

The boldness of Mao's decisions in many cases was en-hanced by his practice of not acting as a chief executive con-cerned with the day-to-day management of decisions. Mao's style, especially since 1949, has been to withdraw for periods, observe the processes of government, reflect on what should be done, and then suddenly to intervene with his own ideas. Mao thus vacillates between reigning and ruling, which has the effect of exaggerating the novelty of his decisions, since they generally do not follow directly upon the sequence of decisions that would normally flow from executive adminis-tration of policies.

In many respects, Mao's style is reminiscent of the tradi-tional role of Chinese emperors. For example, during periods of withdrawal Mao has quietly gone about the countryside inspecting at first hand the performances of lower officials, a practice similar to that of numerous emperors who sought first hand facts by employing disguises when away from court. At other times Mao's orders have taken the form of marginal com-ments on documents that he has been given to read, which, again, was a normal way for emperors to give commands.

This style of withdrawal and intervention has clearly ex-aggerated the fluctuations of Chinese politics for if, as Michel

55

Oksenberg suspects, "every important policy initiative over the past twenty years has been prompted by Mao," [29] then every intervention by him has, in some degree, interrupted the previous flow of routine administrative decisions. Because Mao plays many roles in government, when he returns from a phase of withdrawal, it is never certain at what point in the total process his new initiatives will be interjected. At one time he may return in his role as leading authority on agriculture, the next may be as chief ideologue, another time his concern might focus on military affairs, or his role might be that of strategist of foreign policy. Where the interjection comes sets priorities for the whole system as his new decision sends shock waves through the ranks of officials everywhere.

The style of reigning and ruling also contributes to the tendency of the entire governmental system to react dramatically to even the most casual intervention by Mao. Since he is not a part of the day-to-day process, any intervention becomes a major event which tends to stimulate widespread response throughout the ranks of the cadres. Sometimes the marginal comment Mao has made on a memorandum will be enough to stir massive bureaucratic reaction. At other times it is sufficient for him to issue cryptic slogans such as, "Agriculture is the base and industry the leading sector," or "Dig the tunnels deeper; store the grain everywhere; and don't seek hegemony." Mao himself claims that the exaggerated enthusiasm in spreading the communes in the summer of 1958 stemmed from a single word he gave to a reporter: ". . . A reporter asked me: 'Is the commune good?' I said, 'Good,' and he immediately published it in the newspaper." [30] Certainly the decision was much more complicated than this, but Mao was probably also right that the report of his one word sent out the signal to cadres throughout the land that they should step up the pace of communization.

Mao's style suggests a broad vision, concern for grand matters, preference for the abstractions of policy over concrete details, curiosity for particular details but not for the welter of facts basic to administration. His manner also reflects a man who trusts the world enough to feel that he does not have to dominate to have his way, and who is confident enough in his own judgment to feel he can safely override the decisions of those who are closer to the facts.

Yet, some qualifications are in order, for his vacillation between reigning and ruling also reflects Mao's apparent ambivalences about being alone: at one moment he seems to need privacy and to seek regal isolation, and at the next he tends to complain that others have isolated him and ignored his wishes. During the phases of Mao's withdrawals others must manage affairs, and as they concentrate on the tasks at hand, Mao sometimes seems to feel left out and complains that others are not speaking to him. For example, in October 1966 Mao protested, "On many things I was never even consulted. . . . Teng Hsiao-p'ing never paid me a visit." [31] He further noted that after 1958 Liu Shao-ch'i and Teng Hsiao-p'ing, who were then managing the Party, "treated me like their parents whose funeral was taking place," that is, showing formal deference but not speaking to him. Mao also once complained about being unable to be heard in the Peking area because the then mayor, P'eng Chen, controlled matters so completely that "no needle could penetrate, no drop of water could enter." [32]

Trusting Personal or Impersonal Relationships

Another closely related theme that helps to provide first approximations of leaders' operational codes is their preference for dealing with either formal and impersonal institutions or individuals with whom they have some personal ties. Some leaders feel most confident that their decisions will be properly executed if they are able to manage and orchestrate all the formal offices and departments executing policy. Other leaders feel comfortable only in dealing with an inner group of personally loyal followers. Mao Tse-tung clearly distrusts the impersonal relationships inherent in bureaucracies and seems to have a strong need to deal personally with those following his instructions. Mao's dislike of bureaucratism is too well known to need further comment, except to note that his hostility toward the impersonality of bureaucracies stems not just from the ways officials relate to the lower echelons of government but also from his frustrations at the top over commanding an impersonal structure. Mao constantly wants officials to be responsive not just to the people but also to himself. Consequently, even though he is not a line administrator and has not been a part of continuous day-to-day developments, he has often intervened to learn the names of lower officials, comment on their conduct, and thus convey the impression that he was personally informed about personnel.[33] In fact, his knowledge of lower functionaries must be quite spotty and based more on a review of names and performance records than on actual administrative experience.

Mao's dislike of impersonal relationships has also surfaced in the way he has impeded the institutionalization of much of the Chinese governing system, especially at the top level. In part, the problem arises from the fact that Mao wears many hats, and thus he understandably does not make in his own mind sharp distinctions among the various organs of decision making. On the other hand, Mao's erratic dealings with the cluster of formal committees, bureaus, and offices in the capital has tended to blur the lines of responsibility among them. The paradox of Mao's behavior in personalizing these official relationships has produced a vague, formless, and almost mystical concept of ultimate authority that is signified by the term "the Center."

All kinds of matters in China, from economic management to political control, are said to involve decisions of the "Center," but the Chinese never make clear what or who the "Center" is. Sometimes it seems that it is nothing more than the appropriate ministry in Peking, while at other times it appears to be the Politburo or its Standing Committee, but at still other times the "Center" can be the Central Committee itself. Lower-level officials speak always of the "Center" when referring to Peking, but they seem to have no concrete sense of precisely whom it is they are talking about.

Mao's preferences for diffuseness and lack of clarity in defining lines of authority, which have contributed to this peculiarly Chinese Communist concept, has spread since the Cultural Revolution from the capital to administrators throughout the land as the division of authority between Party and government has become less clearly defined. In particular, distinctions have become blurred between "revolutionary committees" and "Party committees," largely because in most organizations and jurisdictions the personnel of these two bodies are essentially the same, and the members, therefore, just as when Mao wears his many hats, find it difficult to differentiate their roles.

If we are to find the personal roots of Mao's administrative style, we will have to be sensitive to his feelings about responsibility and ask why it is that he seems never to want clear definitions of responsibility.

Popular vs. Elite Style

Another distinction in operational codes is the preferences of leaders for either open or closed decision making, in the sense of either welcoming broader participation or preferring to involve only a select few. Although, on the surface, the differences might seem to be those between a popular or democratic and an elite approach, such a simple classification is not possible. A leader may be inclined toward broad participation because it dilutes the influence of competitors and enhances his own importance, while the apparently elitist approach can be consistent with decisions favoring broad interests.

Indeed, in Mao's style the vacillations between involvement and isolation, and between action and seclusion seem to be a part of his ambivalences over faith in the views of the masses and a decided preference for secrecy associated with elite councils.

Possibly no major leader in modern times has a more rightful claim to populist sentiments, for glorifying the masses and seeing in them wisdom and strength. At the same time, no other major leader in the world has practiced governance in such seclusion. As a decision maker Mao has suggested that he can simultaneously be a spokesman for the masses and an isolated oracle. He professes belief in the value for policy makers of constant, day-to-day interactions with common people, yet his life style since coming to power has been one of mainly mixing with the powerful. Thus, he combines sympathy for the weak with personal identification with power.

In more concrete terms Mao's populism takes the form of favoring rural people and distrusting city life. Thus, the "people" are not in his mind an educated, knowledgeable population full of curiosity and diverse views, but rather, simple, rustic, hardworking, conforming peasants who are anxious to improve themselves through their own exertions. Mao's glorification of rural life and attitudes is consistent with his well-known faith in the superiority of human effort over technology and his distrust of formal learning. As we shall see, Mao has long attacked formal schooling and "book learning" for others while surrounding himself with books.

Mao's ambivalences about populist involvement and elitist seclusion have been translated into his dual political approach of championing the "mass line"—that is, the principle of learning from the people what they need and want and then bringing back to them whatever is possible—and the principles of a Leninist elite Party that has been carried to the ultimate extreme of making the entire Chinese decision making process one of the most secret in the world. Even supposedly open events, such as meetings of Party Congresses, are generally held in secrecy in response to surprise decisions of Mao and his few associates.

This feature of Mao's manner of decision making must again have roots in his personality, for his ambivalence seems to be extraordinarily complex. When he speaks of himself as being "alone with the masses" he seems to be clinging to his desire for isolation while identifying with a depersonalized public. Only by looking into his personality will it be possible to find explanations for his ability to idealize the people while protecting his own privacy.

Criticism and Conflict

A final dimension of any leader's style is his reactions to the conflicts inherent in politics and the ways in which he responds to attack and criticism. Some leaders are so self-confident that they rejoice in controversy and are impervious to personal attack. Others strive to rise above conflict and expect to be so respected that they will be spared direct criticism. Although great men tend to have large egos, there can be great diversity between those who value conflict or shy away from it, between those with thick and those with thin skins.

As with most dimensions of Mao's operational code, his style as decision maker appears to be based on ambivalence, for he has at one moment glorified conflict and welcomed clashes and confusion, while at the next moment displayed delicate sensitivities even to hints of criticism. Richard H. Solomon has documented extensively Mao's extraordinary readiness to take on fights, to rise above the traditional Chinese craving for harmony, and to accept fearlessly conflict and confusion.[34] Whereas most Chinese are anxious for order and dread disorder or *luan*, Mao seems to enjoy disruption and struggle.

Yet, at the same time, there is extensive evidence that Mao is hypersensitive to attack and senses even the most subtle hint of criticism. Instead of being a bruising fighter, he seems to be almost too thin-skinned for political life. Thus, Mao sometimes proclaims the value of having enemies, dismissing in an offhand manner the record of years of animosity, while at other times he bristles at even the most indirect suggestion of attack.

As early as 1939 Mao elaborated his view about the virtues of having foes in his short essay, "To Be Attacked by the Enemy is not a Bad Thing but a Good Thing."[35] In 1964 Mao recounted how a Japanese visitor sought to apologize for Japan's attack on China, but he had to interrupt to explain that without the war China never would have become an effective nation. "That is why I said to him (pause and smile) 'Should I not thank you instead?' " [36] On the other hand, the first sentence in Mao's *Selected Works* reads, "Who are our enemies, and who are our friends?" [37] In these opening words Mao echoes Lenin's proposition that the essential question for the Party must always be: "Who will dominate whom?"—the "Who-Whom" issue which was at the heart of Lenin's view of the world. [38] With Mao, as with Lenin, the issue of friend and foe has always bulked large whether he was analyzing political relations within the larger society or his most personal relations with others.

Mao's well-known hypersensitivity to criticism has revived the old Chinese cryptic style of using esoteric historical allusions for critical comment. Chinese politics was traditionally rich in the use of allegory and indirect forms of criticism and attack. Historically, Chinese ministers, hoping not to offend or provoke anger, frequently used subtle references to past examples as a way of communicating to their emperors. Under Chairman Mao, however, the use of historic allegory has reached previously unknown heights.

For example, at the start of the Cultural Revolution, Mao Tse-tung recognized subtle allusions to himself in the play, *The Dismissal of Hai Jui*, which depicted an emperor removing a popular minister from office. Earlier, in 1958, Mao spotted a reference in a publication of the Kiangsi Party School that seemingly identified him with Ch'in Shih Huang-ti, the first great tyrant of China who built the Great Wall, and he responded: "The rightist said: Why did Ch'in Shih Huang-ti collapse? Because he built the Great Wall. Now that we have constructed the T'ien-an-men, the great square in Peking, we are also supposed to collapse." [39] From that day on Mao, frequently and quite aggressively, identified himself with Ch'in Shih Huang-ti, and in 1973 in the Anti-Confucian Campaign, he insisted that the Legalists and Ch'in Shih Huang-ti should be held up as the great progressives of their day, in contrast to the "revisionist" Confucius.

By identifying himself with Ch'in Shih Huang-ti, Mao moved against the current of over two thousand years of Chinese history, for the first Ch'in emperor has always been thought of as a harsh ruler who opposed the humanistic tradition of Confucianism. At the Second Session of the Eighth Party Congress Mao Tse-tung held forth on an article in which a contemporary scholar had demonstrated that "respecting the modern and belittling the ancient is a Chinese tradition" and added the criticism that he should have cited the example of Ch'in Shih Huang-ti who exemplified that tradition. Lin Piao, who would become Mao's heir apparent before falling from grace and whose memory is now linked to the Anti-Confucius Campaign of 1974, interrupted Mao's observations to note that "Ch'in Shih Huang-ti burned the books and buried alive the scholars," a reference to his attack on the Confucian classics and their advocates. Mao instantly responded, "What did he amount to? He only buried alive 460 scholars, while we buried 46,000. . . . I once debated with the democratic people: You accuse us of acting like Ch'in Shih Huang-ti, but you are wrong; we surpass him by a hundred times. You berate us for imitating Ch'in Shih Huang-ti in enforcing dictatorship. We admit it fully." [40]

The contradiction in Mao between his apparent exhilaration over conflict and his sensitivity to criticism alerts us to an apparent ambivalence in his personality over the handling of aggression. Indeed, the likelihood that he has complex personal feelings about aggression is also suggested by his idealization of warfare. A man who has seen as much death and violence on the battlefield as Mao has, but persists, particularly in his poetry, in describing battles in highly romantic terms, would seem to be using idealization as a defense mechanism. In his poetry nearly every reference to violence is peculiarly benign: ". . . our red banners bound across the Ting River," [41] "The yellow flowers of the battlefield are unusually fragrant," [42] "At the mountain, the foot of the mountain, The wind will unfurl like a scroll our scarlet banner." [43] "Above us tower the mountains, And as we climb through the mountain pass, the wind unfurls our red banners." [44] Mao's imagery is certainly not that of realism about conflict when, in describing a specific battle, he writes:

> Two hundred thousand troops enter Kiangsi
> From the sky boils wind and smoke.
> We awoke a million workers and peasants to fight with one
>   heart.
> At the foot of Puchow mountain spreads an anarchy of red
>   banners. [45]

Or in another poem he writes:

> We sweep aside a thousand armies as easily as if rolling up a
>   mat.
> Someone is weeping,
> Sorry about the strategy of slow advance. [46]

Or,

> Once there raged a desperate battle here;
> Bullet-holes have scored the village walls;
> They are a decoration, and the hills
> Today seem still more fair. [47]

When Mao has tried to describe the suffering and hardship of war it becomes only a struggle against nature, not the violence of mortal encounter:

Introduction: The Monkey and the Tiger

"The Red Army fears not the trials of a distant march;
To them a thousand mountains, ten thousand rivers are
nothing;" [48]

But mostly he is inclined to make even nature pleasant, as with such imagery as "Our banners idly wave in the west wind," [49] and when he explicitly pictures the enemy, the mood is still benign as in "We shall call forth our courage and pursue the exhausted bandits." [50]

These traits of welcoming but also idealizing conflict and violence that have colored Mao's decision making point to elements in his private life we are now ready to explore. In looking further into the development of the private man, we shall be alert to clues as to why Mao developed a political style with the specific characteristics that we have noted in these general impressions of his operational code. What was there in his development that made him so given to extolling contradictions, so prone to high-risk decision making, so remote and yet so personally intense in governing, so distrusting of impersonal organizations and yet so aloof from colleagues, so worshipful of the masses and yet so eager for seclusion, and finally, so ready for conflict and confusion and yet so sensitive to the critical views of others? These are not random traits but rather seem to fit together as a part of a coherent whole that is only meaningful in terms of the coherence of Mao's personality.

This amazingly complex man was in part a product of his epoch, and in part a product of his reading, but he was also a man who was shaped by the forces that shape all men—his family and his peers.

PART TWO

The Private Man

"... there is no one who cannot be analyzed. If we believe that there is someone who can't be analyzed, we are believing in metaphysics."

Mao Tse-tung

CHAPTER

4

Home and the Mother

MAO TSE-TUNG'S birthplace is in one of the most fertile regions of Hunan Province, a province which Chinese characterize as the homeland of sturdy peasants, renowned scholars, and ambitious and crafty soldiers. The village of Shaoshan is in fact a series of hamlets lining a valley. Traditionally, Shaoshan was organized according to clans, and the Mao clan was the largest. Even today the majority of the families in the Shaoshan brigade have the surname of Mao. Indeed, in some respects it seems as though the old clan leadership has reemerged in the form of the brigade leadership.

When Mao Tse-tung was born on December 26, 1893, his father was just beginning his vigorous climb upward toward greater economic well-being. Mao Tse-tung's grandfather, who built the original segment of the house in which Mao was born, had been a poor and relatively unsuccessful farmer. It was his son Mao Jen-sheng who succeeded in raising the family to a position of leadership in the Mao clan.

The character of this setting is important for understanding the development of Mao Tse-tung. The environment was rural and isolated, some thirty miles from the county seat of Hsiang-t'an. Mao, therefore, grew up in an exceptionally quiet and remote setting, even for rural China. He would not have experienced as frequently as most Chinese peasant lads the thrill of visiting a market town, and therefore he probably never learned what most Chinese children knew: Next to the annual festivals, the most exciting and pleasurable thing in life is attending fairs and watching the movement and bustle associated with buying and selling in the marketplace. This typical dimension of Chinese life and culture was missing in Mao's childhood, and as an adult he has never shown great interest in economic matters or the human aspects of commerce and trading.

Instead, Mao Tse-tung grew up in a community in which almost nothing ever broke the daily routines and annual cycles. On the other hand, the folklore of his village was filled with tales of local and neighboring people who had left that region of Hunan to achieve greatness at the highest levels in China. This was the area that had produced a long line of great generals, and such great scholar-statesmen as Tseng Kuo-fan and Tso Tsung-t'ang, heroes of nineteenth-century Chinese officialdom's suppression of rebellion and banditry. Appropriately, the region has also had a long history of nurturing rebels and bandits.

Therefore, it was not presumptuous or out of the ordinary for a boy in Shaoshan to dream of doing great things. On the contrary, the road to achievement was well marked and it consisted of getting an education, becoming a scholar, and then moving into government. In a way Mao's childhood setting was comparable to those American small towns, particularly in the South, which seem so remote but which have reared a disproportionate number of senators and congressmen. Remote and isolated: These words capture not just the region but the personal character of Mao Tse-tung. Throughout his life, Mao has been removed from all others, even when in the vortex of action and conflict. In modern times, no major ruling figure has been so private in his ways, so limited in his public appearances, so remote from the daily speculations and the public moves of politics, and so isolated from councillors and advisors.

Chinese culture, ingeniously shaping conventions to surmount the realities of dense numbers of people and a consequent absence of privacy, has contrived in manner and style to normalize aloofness and personal dignity. Conduct that suggests inscrutability to the Western imagination may be for the Chinese no more than a defensive reflex, learned so as to protect the self from the bruising impact of too many people too close at hand. Even in agrarian China the villages are closely built and no one can be alone for long.

Mao's remoteness and isolation, however, goes well beyond, and is of a different order from, the conventions of Chinese culture. His isolation has been of both the inner spirit and his manner of action. In a culture in which the density of persons has compelled people to do private things in public, Mao has somehow always made his public acts seem to be private ones, and his private acts nonexistent. This quality of isolation and remoteness links the adult Mao to the boy Mao in his isolated home village. It runs all through Mao's life, and produces a strange confusion as to what is substance and what is spirit—much in the same way as Chinese landscape painting blends the terrestrial and the ethereal.

As he grew up, Mao must have sensed his family's steady advancement. His father, when only sixteen, had gone into the army to accumulate the necessary capital to pay off the grandfather's debts and to purchase back the family lands which had been sold to neighbors. During Mao's childhood the family fields expanded from fifteen to twenty-two *mou* and new rooms were added to the house so that in time it became the largest home in the hamlet. The impression of steady improvement must have been heightened because, while the house was divided and one segment occupied by another family, it was the Mao side that expanded with mud walls giving way to baked bricks and the thatched roof eventually being replaced with tile. The other family's quarters remained the same in both size and materials. This is why today the house, which has become a national tourist attraction, has an unfinished appearance.

The sense of the physical well-being of the scene of Mao's childhood was further heightened by the large pond in front of the house, and the pleasant wooded hills behind it. Mao mastered this environment and taught himself, some say as early as six, how to swim in the pond, and thus he began a life-long interest in an activity that few Chinese, especially peasants, ever learned. During World War II, less than 10 percent of Chinese troops in the elite divisions receiving American training knew how to swim. By developing this skill, Mao set himself apart from normal Chinese practices, and in doing so must have contributed to his growing sense of self-assurance. Mao was, of course, to use swimming as a way of communicating to all the world that he was fit and ready to hold command of China. Some years after his famous swim in the Yangtze that heralded the beginnings of the Cultural Revolution, Mao was to complain in a speech to Chinese officials that for thirty years he had ignored swimming and had had to work to regain his skill. His point at the time was that superstition and old folkways are easily revived in China, but that revolutionary progress must be fought for merely to hold its ground. Thus explicitly he linked his unique childhood skill with the concept of progress in China.[1]

Mao's confidence in himself was no doubt reinforced by being surrounded by relatives who treated his father as one of the most prosperous members of the clan. The community at that time consisted of only three hundred families—there are barely seven hundred today—and Mao grew up knowing by name all the people he met on any ordinary day. Later in life Mao Tse-tung was sometimes hypersensitive about the opinions that strangers might have of him, a tendency that, most likely, may have come from having learned so late how to conduct himself in anonymous relationships. As a boy, however, Mao was so completely at home in his community of relations and neighbors that, according to anecdotes, he was not in the slightest intimidated by adults, even in large numbers.

After leaving the security of his village and his schools Mao would at times show resentment over being unrecognized and would withdraw and display a degree of shyness completely inconsistent with a strong sense of self-confidence. The explanation may lie in the fact that the very experience of knowing everyone in the village of his youth made it uncomfortable for him to have impersonal dealings. In any case it is noteworthy that when, in later life, Mao met with strangers he customarily sought as early as possible to test their friendliness toward him. Whenever relations could exist only on an impersonal level, Mao tended to withdraw and drift away.

More important than the community setting in giving Mao Tse-tung a sense of self-assurance was his immediate family. Much has been written about the harsh authoritarian treatment Mao received from his father, and in due course we shall have to examine in some detail his relations with the person who was clearly the dominant figure in his childhood. But first we must note the total family context and his relations with the other members who each, in a way, contributed to building his apparently strong but ambivalent personality.

Mao Tse-tung was the oldest child, preceding his first brother, Mao Tse-min, by two years and his second brother, Mao Tse-t'an, by twelve years. In the same year that Mao Tse-t'an was born, 1905, the family adopted a daughter, Mao Tse-hung, the child of a clan member who was financially distressed.[2] In addition, the grandfather lived in the household during Mao's childhood. Since he had been a failure and had conspicuously depended upon his son to revive the family fortunes, the grandfather was not a domineering figure and thus did not seem to deserve the traditional Chinese reverence for elders. Rather, he seemed to be living testimony to the prospect that each generation of the Mao family could expect to surpass the last. His role in the family involved helping to look after young Mao, and in turn he was someone Mao learned early to humor and bend to his will. Furthermore, since the grandfather was not a strong personality, he could not have significantly reinforced the image of authority of elders in the family. Rather, he might have dramatized to the young Mao the notion that those with the highest legitimate authority may not have much power in reality, thus contributing to the development of Mao's confidence in his ability to manipulate authority figures.

This extraordinarily weak position of the grandfather was possibly the least typically Chinese feature of the Mao household. Customarily grandfathers were the center of attention, often figures of commanding authority. Yet Mao barely mentioned the existence of his grandfather. In allowing this situation to exist, Mao's parents acted in a strangely un-Chinese fashion. Neither in their own conduct toward the grandfather nor in their instruction to their children as to how they should behave toward him did they manifest the cardinal Chinese value of reverence for one's forebears. This is significant, for it suggests that Mao's parents did not observe a fundamental practice of Confucian tradition. They were striving and aspiring parents, but they failed to grasp the fundamentals of respectability in their culture—fundamentals that even the most insensitive *nouveau riche* of the Treaty Ports would have understood. They failed, as did their son, to manifest the proper spirit of filial piety.

The weakness of the grandfather's position also meant that, aside from his domineering father, Mao Tse-tung was from a very early age the central figure in his family. This is obvious from Mao's account of his childhood where he always sees himself as the key actor rather than a slightly removed observer. Mao constantly dwells on his own relations to others and largely ignores their behavior toward each other. Of his relationships the most important, in his own eyes, was that with his mother. There must have been something very special in that relationship, and unquestionably Wen Ch'i-mei gave much to her firstborn son and made him feel that he should be special, but she may have also taken something away from him, which he was never to recapture, when she had to divide her attentions with the later children.

Mao Jen-sheng's wife came from a nearby village, had a very pleasant face in the "pear-shaped" tradition of North China,[3] and was plump.[4] Physically Mao resembles his mother more than his father. Wen Ch'i-mei was illiterate, gentle, generous, easily moved by the sufferings of others, a devout Buddhist, and a believer in all local superstitions. She was completely dominated by her husband, came from a poorer family, and since she had received no education, she respected greatly the little her husband had obtained.

Yet as a result of giving birth to a son, Mao Tse-tung, Wen Ch'i-mei had found fulfillment in her life. In terms of the Chinese culture of her time, she became a woman of some significance in the community because her first child was a son and even more so after she had had two more sons. She had a warm, nurturing disposition and was supportive of her first son who had done so much for her just by being born. She surrounded the young Mao with a mixture of indulgence and awe.

Although Wen Ch'i-mei never directly challenged or openly offended her husband, she constantly risked his displeasure by supporting, siding with, and sharing secrets with her son. In so championing her firstborn she shielded him from the extraordinarily harsh pressures to which the oldest son was exposed in traditional Chinese culture. She also strengthened him so that he could fully cope with his situation. In Chinese families, the oldest son in surviving the pressures put upon him, often became an intensely inhibited and rigidly conforming personality. Or he broke under the strain and became completely self-indulging, especially once the control of the parents was removed by death. Wen Ch'i-mei's warm and generous nature made it possible for her to enlarge for Mao Tse-tung many of the psychological advantages of being a firstborn son.

Mao was appreciative of the kind and sympathetic character of his mother, whom he saw as "ever ready to share what she had." [5] He was able to communicate easily with her, and, very significantly, he seemed to feel that he knew her and loved her more than her husband did. First, he sensed, and rejoiced in, his natural inclination to side with her against his father, and once he lost all fear in confronting his father, he was elated with his ability to mobilize his mother to his side in opposing his father.

In his early years he was attracted to the one area of his mother's special interest, her devout worship of Buddha. Mao later talks of how his mother "gave her children religious instruction, and we were all saddened that our father was an unbeliever. When I was nine years old I seriously discussed the problem of my father's lack of piety with my mother. We made many attempts then and later to convert him but without success." [6] We shall return to reflect on the significance of a nine-year-old having such concerns for his father, but here our interest is in the extent to which the young boy identified with his mother and felt that he shared with her a concern over a flaw in his father. Seemingly, he had resolved his oedipal problem not by identifying with his father or by achieving early autonomy, but rather by making the most of his mother's generous disposition and identifying with her in fancying that he had to yield like her to the cruel and harsh demands of the father—a possible source of the element of femininity in his character. This manner of Mao's oedipal solution could lead him to suspect that others might be seeking to sway him improperly, and hence make him highly sensitive to the possibility that others must be a threat to him.

Thus Mao paradoxically combined self-assurance with a sensitivity to the possibility of enemies—a useful combination for a politician of revolution.

The fact that Wen Ch'i-mei was apparently an unusually devout woman and had a theology that distinguished between believers and nonbelievers also meant that she gave her children a system of beliefs in which there was a logic of causality that went beyond immediate physical cause and effect. From her Buddhism, and her elaboration of superstitions, Mao must have gained his first conscious understanding that a hidden order in fact existed beyond the appearances of accidental events. Earlier as an infant, he must have sensed, from the reliability and predictability with which his mother responded to his expression of needs, that there was order in the universe and he was the center of it.

His mother's ability to juxtapose a world governed by doctrinal religious forces and an earthy, practical world may have contributed to Mao's capacity to place events in which he was involved in a larger, historical context. This was an ability that would become even more pronounced after he found such great pleasure in reading, but even before this development Mao had already demonstrated a larger time perspective, an appreciation of the value of delaying gratifications, an awareness of the inevitability of death, and the possibility of a hereafter—all themes that might have emerged from exposure to his mother's sense of religion.

As Mao's clashes with his father increased in intensity, he became more aware of his ability to manage his mother as an ally. In speaking to Edgar Snow, Mao jokingly used Communist political terminology to refer to his leadership in the family. "There were two 'parties' in the family. One was my father, the Ruling Power. The opposition was made up of myself, my mother, my brother and sometimes even the laborers. In the 'United Front' of the Opposition, however, there was a difference of opinion. My mother advocated a policy of indirect attack. She criticized any overt display of emotion and attempts at open rebellion against the Ruling Power. She said it was not the Chinese way." [7]

Mao's mother was only partly correct; for it was also she who was not acting in "the Chinese way." She was solidly in the mainstream of Chinese culture when she opposed "any overt display of emotion," and she was also in the tradition when she favored indirect actions. On the other hand, for the mother to act so explicitly in league with the son and to discuss with him alternative strategies in opposing the father's authority was not common. Traditionally, the father's authority was supposed to be absolute and severe; the mother could comfort the disciplined son but she usually did not go further and plot with him to challenge the authority of the father. In Chinese culture authority was presumed to be monolithic and thus could not be properly divided between father and mother. Thus, the obligation of the father to be aloof and alone in his authority, the mother's obligation to be more intimate, and the severe limits to ultimate communication between husband and wife provided some scope for crafty children to play off father against mother and exploit the advantages of an apparently divided authority. There was, however, less room for such action than in most Western cultures.

It is true that Chinese culture recognized the henpecked husband and the strong-willed wife who in shrill and abrasive language denounced the failings of any and all members of her family. There was also the classic strong-minded but apparently passive Chinese wife who quietly managed family affairs and kept her own counsel. Wen Ch'i-mei's conduct was exceptional in that she was meek, gentle, withdrawing, inclined to indirect action, but also willing to plot actively with her son.

One of Mao's biographers, Hsiao San, who knew him as a boy and benefited from long conversations with him, has described Mao's mother more as the traditional passive but strong Chinese woman. He writes: "The father as family head was very severe toward the children and was not very considerate of his wife either. The mother opposed this kind of family administration, but did not resist it openly. She resorted to gentle persuasion and passive resistance. Sometimes the father ate good food alone and gave the leftovers to the mother. But the mother had self-dignity and would not eat the food." [8] Such a description would seem to be more in character with Chinese behavior. Yet what is important psychologically is that Mao pictured his mother as actively supporting him, and that he believed he could manipulate her behavior. He saw her not just as his defender but also as one whom he could force to defend him.

All of this could suggest that Mao's mother had indeed been very responsive at an early age to Mao's wishes and so made him feel that he was extraordinarily precious. Such a hypothesis might suggest that she gave him a deep sense of self-assurance, especially with respect to conflict situations. In return for all of these positive gifts from his mother, Mao seemingly was ready to describe her as a wonderful person who was selfless. This interpretation would also help to explain why Mao was so self-assured in attacking his apparently severe father: His mother's reassurance had not only made him self-confident but had made him feel that in fighting his father he was protecting his mother.

This view of Mao as having had a strong, nurturing and reassuring mother is consistent with much of the evidence. Yet there are some episodes which suggest that the relationship may have been more complex, and that Mao may have had some deep anxieties as to whether his mother was reciprocating his own feelings toward her. At times his behavior seems to suggest that he was testing her feelings for him and that he was even ready to hurt her.

A hint that Mao might have deeply valued his mother but also been ambivalent about her feelings toward him can be seen in his behavior at the time when he ran away from home after his teacher had been harsh with him at primary school. As was common in traditional China the experience of attending school represented for Mao exposure to an authoritarian situation in which there was no immediate source of comfort. The young Chinese child was customarily indulged and in many ways pampered, certainly by the mother if not the father, until he experienced the shock of school.[9] The contrast between early indulgence and harsh demands tended to make even more vivid the disciplinary commands of the school master. Mao tells us that he, at the age of five, when he was required to work in the fields, was exposed to his father's harsh discipline. But, even so, the experience of school came as a shock to Mao, particularly when he was physically punished. As a result of some episode at the school, the accounts differ—Mao's report to Snow was that it happened when he was ten and that it stemmed from his teacher's practice of beating him,[10] other sources say it happened when Mao was only seven and he was rebelling against the old-fashioned Chinese tradition of requiring students to stand while reciting their lessons [11]—Mao expressed his hurt and tried in turn to hurt his parents by running away. It was not an effective effort in that he never went more than eight *li*, a little over two miles, from home. What is revealing is that he heard his mother crying, which apparently comforted him, and finally he returned "because it occurred to him that his mother would have no one to defend her." [12]

An act of defiance was thus combined with testing to determine how much he was loved by his mother—and also, as we shall see, by his father. By the act of apparently placing himself in a dangerous position and of experiencing loneliness, he learned that he could also offend others. He learned that he could strengthen his self-assurance by discovering how readily others worried over him and missed him. Mao Tse-tung was aware of what he had accomplished. "After my return to the family, however, to my surprise, conditions somewhat improved. My father was slightly more considerate and the teacher was more inclined to moderation. The result of my act of protest impressed me very much." [13]

Our suspicion that the relationship between Mao and his mother must have been complex and contradictory stems in part from the fulsomeness of Mao's praise for his mother and his protestations of his love for her. And yet he admitted that his constant fights with his father "hurt" his mother. The details of these clashes will be discussed in Chapter 6, but it is significant that Mao recognized he could hurt his mother by fighting with his father, and he seemed to have rejoiced over his record of confrontation with the father.

In searching for the nature of the "monkey" in Mao's spirit we are led to wonder about what ambivalences may have existed in what Mao has claimed to be an absolutely ideal relationship. Indeed, the very intensity with which Mao has idealized his mother, makes us wonder whether he was not using idealization as a defense mechanism against very strong inner feelings that he would like to deny. We would be inclined to speculate that any underlying ambivalence in Mao's feelings toward his mother would stem first from her having given him her undivided attention—nurturing him, feeding his sense of moral worth—and then, probably with the birth of the second son when Mao was just two, seemingly having to withdraw her total love—abandoning him, dividing her affections among others.

As we would expect there is nothing in the direct relationship that cannot be seen in an ambiguous light once the postulate of ambivalence is made—the test of the plausibility of our hypothesis must await examination of Mao's attitudes toward his siblings, the emotional character of his clashes with his father, and above all his treatment of his wives and children. Behavior cited as proof of Mao's dedication to his mother can also be seen either as idealization or as attempts by Mao to prove to his mother that he remained deserving of her undivided affection. For example, shortly after Mao emerged from his prolonged phase of drift and disorganized living—a moratorium phase that will be discussed in Chapter 7—he re-established relations with his family, obtained the necessary support of his father to go back to school, and then in an ostensible act of generosity and consideration for his peasant mother, invited her to visit the big city of Changsha where he was at school.[14] Yet, psychologically, he may have really wanted to impress his mother with how successful he could be even without her love.

The plausibility of the thesis that Mao experienced both a period of strong nurturance and affection from his mother and the trauma of feeling that she had abandoned him is reinforced by what happened at the time of her death when Mao was at last finding himself at school. Mao has said, "In my last year in school my mother died, and more than ever I lost interest in returning home."[15] Yet we know that Mao returned home frequently for "rest" periods, once, shortly after his mother's death, because there exists a photograph of Mao, his father, brother, and a senior clan relative taken at that time.* The spirit of the picture is completely middle class: The father looks like an affluent Chinese merchant in his silk jacket, long robe, and silk cap; the elder relative seated beside him is similarly dressed; between them is a table on which stands an ornate clock, a flower arrangement and two Western style cups; the third son, standing by his father, is dressed in a Sun Yat-sen tunic; while Mao is dressed in a traditional Chinese long gown. And it is Mao alone who has a black band of mourning

* This picture can be seen following page 130 in the photo section.

pinned to his sleeve. One would not guess it to be a picture of a family of peasants.

While still in mourning Mao revealed, through a psychologically telling poem, a key to his personality: he communicated unmistakably his suffering, possibly even rage, that his mother's love had been distant and not especially his.

"In Memory of Mother" [16]

Of my mother's high virtues, her philanthropic love must come first.
The far and the near, the close as well as the distant were equally cared for.
Her loving and understanding, kind and gentle nature moves all.
The power of her love springs from sincerity and honesty.
There was never a lie, never a deceit.
Her mind was attentive and sophisticated, logical and reasonable;
Never was a plan miscalculated, nor a thing overlooked.
When I was ill, she would hold my hands with an aching heart and anguished soul.
I write this for you all, so that you will strive to be your best.

Coming from a man who has always been quite precise in articulating the flow and direction of sentiments, these words must give us pause, for emotions seem to be systematically reversed. The exact opposite of what is said seems patently intended. When he speaks of "the far and the near, the close as well as the distant" being "equally cared for," is he not really saying that as the firstborn, as her son, he was somehow not especially loved by his mother? What might be a compliment in one context becomes a barely veiled criticism in the context of the mother-son relationship. In short, the poem tells of being abandoned because a mother's love has been given as much to others as to oneself. When Mao says that there was "never a lie, never a deceit," he seems to be expressing what he deeply wished might have been. The act of reflecting on the possibility of deception seems so disturbing that in the next line Mao has to pull away from the realm of emotion and interject two lines about his mother's ability to reason, plan and calculate. Yet is he not also saying that what his mother did to him by not reserving all of her affections for him was fully intentional and planned by her? What happened was not accidental but calculated. Do we have a hint here of Mao's abiding suspicion that reasoning and planning are as masks for covering deceptions in the realm of the emotions. In the next line Mao tells us that he knew, possibly unconsciously, that through "illness" he could recapture full attention and affection, and that he could punish those who should feel guilty for abandoning him—and, as we shall see, Mao frequently throughout his career became ill when he felt mistreated and ignored. Finally, in the last line he draws a curtain over personal emotions and protects his sentiments by the cloak of impersonal public morality.

The mother had originally given him security, but she had also taught him that human sentiments could not be counted on to endure. To protect against future disappointment it was necessary to generalize rather than ever again particularize affection. Having once been "abandoned" it was necessary to protect one's emotions by thereafter always being the first to disassociate oneself from any engagements of sentiment.

Mao's poem thus provides a clue that a central theme in his life is possibly that of abandonment, both as a danger which he always had to be on guard against and as a device which he could use first to protect himself. We shall want to test the validity of this theme as we examine Mao's approach to intimacy in other contexts, and especially in the ways he treated his wives and children and the pattern of his friendships with colleagues.

In terms of the public Mao, we may have here a partial explanation for Mao Tse-tung's extraordinary sensitivity to the issues of loyalty, revolutionary commitment, and treachery.

The distinctive combination of first receiving warm nurturance and then experiencing abandonment would also help explain Mao's amazing appreciation of the importance of human emotions and affect in motivating people, his sense of both the possibilities for using affect and the danger that passions will fade. Out of his probable longings for the fantasized ideal self, which his command of his mother's total attention once gave him, Mao may have derived his deep insight into the potency of wishing in most people, and he translated the need to wish into a reverence for willpower. Mao sensed the linkage between the once known bliss of completely commanding one's universe and the belief that anything can be accomplished if willed enough; but he also experienced doubts, and indeed a deep fear, that one could be tricked into losing one's mastery by the false emotional pretensions of others. These early experiences may thus have prepared him for public life, making him inordinately sensitive to the craving for security and bliss of the masses of people, the urge for utopia, and the longing for emotional expression; all of which provide the leader with the possibility of holding out hope for those who are otherwise hopeless but who have not lost the unconscious memory of an innocent dependency that was indistinguishable from complete mastery. Yet while preaching to others about the efficacy of willpower, Mao has always suspected that emotions will not last, disappointments are likely, and that personally he must not allow his wishes to dominate his own actions.

This understanding of the potency of affect but distrust

of its durability is a central theme characteristic of Mao's political style. Time and again he has been able to reach out and evoke tremendous outpourings of emotions among the Chinese people; time and again he has shown that he doubted their ability to maintain their emotions; and time and again he has been able to shift from emotional policies to cold pragmatic programs without the slightest sign of personal involvement. The dual themes of abandonment and the manipulation of affect thus seem to be a part of the heritage Mao gained from his mother who also gave him the self-assurance to seek to be the master rather than the victim.

Mao's private response was to appreciate the importance of affect in human affairs but never again to allow himself to become emotionally dependent upon another. His goal thereafter was to seek self-sufficiency. No one could ever love him quite as much as his mother had, and yet since she had broken his trust he must expect that all others who pretended to loyalty would also violate his trust.

Further confirmation of the thesis that Mao's relationship with his mother was critical in forming his basic character will come as we examine his lifelong history of relations with women: In adolescence he was aggressively resistant to any romantic associations; he obliterated differences in the sexes but treated girls as subordinates; his first attachment came only when he was nearly twenty-seven years old; and most significant of all, he never had an enduring husband and wife relationship.

Mao's poem seems to reveal not only his distrust of affect but also his tendency to use idealization as a defense against the threat of his feelings. By idealizing his mother, and making her relevant to all the world he is able to reassure himself that his own feelings are correct and he is then able to deny that he has any negative feelings towards her.

An important test of our concept that Mao was traumatically affected by a sense of being abandoned by his mother would be the ways in which he treated his younger brothers and sister. In Chinese culture, as in most, the loss of a mother's attention is legitimately compensated for by encouraging the older child to find new objects of affection and by allowing him some degree of command over, and responsibility for, the younger siblings who otherwise compete for the mother's love. Therefore it is appropriate next to examine Mao's relations with his two brothers and a sister and to ask why they apparently did not provide him with the satisfactions Chinese culture usually reserves for the oldest son.

CHAPTER

5

Brothers and Sister

WHEN Mao Tse-tung was
approaching two and was just beginning to talk, his mother
gave birth to her second son, Mao Tse-min. For the village of
Shaoshan, the event could not have been as dramatic as when
Wen Ch'i-mei gave birth to her first son, Mao-Tse-tung, but
there still must have been great excitement on the arrival of a
second son in the Mao household, and everyone who knew
the family must have made the point that Wen Ch'i-mei was
a special person because of her great good fortune in producing male children.

Of Mao's feelings about this, we have some evidence
from his later description of his childhood in his autobio-
graphic report to Edgar Snow. One of the most extraordinary
and psychologically revealing oddities of Mao Tse-tung's
reminiscences is that he refers to his first brother in only one
sentence and never mentions his younger brother and sister

who were twelve years his juniors. The one reference to Mao Tse-min occurs in the statement (see above page 78) about organizing a "united front" against his father. Basically, throughout his autobiography Mao pictures himself as an only child who alone had to cope with his father. Furthermore, we have not been able to find another single public utterance in which he expressed strong positive feelings about his brothers and sister.

This is the more striking in view of the relative openness of Mao's references to his hostility toward his father. It might have been easy to account for this strange void if the brothers and sister had gone their separate ways as soon as Mao left home, but this was not the case since all three came to violent deaths by execution as the result of their family connections with him.

Such silence on the part of Mao about two brothers and one sister who paid such a high price for their commitment to him provides us with psychological evidence that Mao may have unconsciously resented their intrusion into his world, and experienced a sense of abandonment by his mother. The circumstances are clear, but we can only infer the psychological reactions. Yet it seems safe to surmise what must have happened because we can find so much evidence throughout Mao's subsequent life that he was thereafter hypersensitive to the matter of abandonment—the breaking of affective ties—and emotionally he always remained bitter about anything that resembled being ignored.

For example, we have Mao's extraordinary statement about how hurt he was when he felt he was being ignored by those he admired when at the age of twenty-six he served as a librarian at Peking National University. Mao had just graduated from a provincial normal school, and through the personal intervention of his favorite teacher, he was fortunate enough to become assistant librarian at the most prestigeous university in the country. Indeed, his teacher introduced him to Li Ta-chao, one of the most illustrious professors at Peking University and one of China's leading intellectuals who subsequently helped found the Chinese Communist Party, and who was at the time university librarian as well as dean of the social science faculty. Objectively, much seemed to be going for the young Mao, who was now suddenly near the center of Chinese intellectual life, yet he speaks bitterly of being ignored. "My office was so low that people avoided me. One of my tasks was to register the names of people who came to read newspapers, but to most of them I didn't exist as a human being. Among those who came to read I recognized the names of famous leaders of the renaissance movement. . . . I tried to begin conversations with them on political and cultural subjects, but they were very busy men. They had no time to listen to an assistant librarian speaking a southern dialect." [1]

In later years on repeated occasions in the Party, Mao showed that he expected to be the central figure, that he did not appreciate the need to struggle for power but rather expected as a natural right to be above peers, and when he was not so received he tended to withdraw into periods of silence and isolation, and then subsequently would explode with bitterness. The Chinese Communist Party has had its ups and downs, but Mao's have been even more extreme. For example, the outside world learned of the degree to which Mao's influence had declined after 1958 in the wake of the failure of the Great Leap only when years later he bitterly told of how "There were many things about which they did not consult me. . . . Teng Hsiao-p'ing never consulted with me about anything since 1959. . . . I could do nothing about the high targets. I came to Peking to hold a conference. You hold one for six days, but I could not even hold a one-day conference." [2] He then graphically said he was ignored by Liu Shao-ch'i and Teng Hsiao-p'ing who treated him "like one of their parents whose funeral was taking place." Mao's analogy is to the traditional Chinese funeral at which there is much show of deference and respect for the departed, but also ritualized wailings and not infrequently a barely disguised sense of relief over the end of parental authority and the beginning of autonomy. As such the statement may seem to reflect the sentiments of an aging Mao faced with the prospect of his own death and of being thereafter revered in ritual, but ignored in substance. Yet, there may be a connection between being ignored, and death and birth; for the beginning of knowledge about the blankness of death can come from a vivid awareness of birth, for birth teaches that existence and nonexistence are not far removed from each other. The arrival of a competitor can also evoke wishes for his disappearance or fantasies of revenge through one's own disappearance. At the least the experience of the birth of a younger sibling can make vivid the reality that each life has its terminal point, for to learn how sudden is the beginning of life is to sense the prospect for an equally sharp end. The older child, aware that life in his family had proceeded in its routines before the birth of the brother, and possibly wishing that it could again be that way, may also be struck with how easily the world could ignore his own birth and death. What had been vital to him, his own preciousness, might suddenly seem to be utterly insignificant for others. Such subjective learning about one's own significance from the objective experience of the birth of another will be even more powerfully sensed if the individual had wished that the brother would return to the state of nonexistence.

In short, the peculiar vividness with which Mao has frequently mentioned his sense of being a lonely and unappreciated wanderer in this world may, in some undetermined measure, be related to the trauma of losing the security of his mother's undivided attention with the birth of his brother. Mao developed into a man who combined such characteristics as: expecting leadership as a natural right; resenting any need to compete for power or attention; being easily embittered on being ignored, highly sensitive to the historical phenomenon of his own life; and furthermore, having an acute sense of detachment about himself, able to speak easily and vividly of loneliness, of passing through this world, and of his own death. All of these traits seem to suggest that he did experience in a rich form all the psychological potentialities that can be the intense experience of an oldest child on the arrival of another.

Before pursuing further Mao's relations with his brothers and sister, we must first take note of how the Chinese culture of his time expected brothers and sisters to behave toward each other. We have been making much over the trauma that Mao may have experienced, but to appreciate the significance of what seem to have been his reactions, it is necessary to understand the extent to which Chinese culture extolled the positive and ignored the negative aspects of being a firstborn son. Possibly no culture has made more of the importance of the order in which brothers and sisters are born than the Chinese. Although legally the Chinese did not practice primogeniture, they have always appreciated that the personality of any individual is likely to be decisively shaped by his order of birth. Chinese do not speak in terms of just the two categories of brothers and sisters, but rather they will indicate how many older brothers, younger brothers, older sisters, younger sisters they have, thus always explicitly placing themselves in their own distinctive rank in the family. By customarily indicating with such precision one's place in relation to older and younger brothers and sisters, the Chinese tend to emphasize a quality of individuality, while still giving priority to the collective, a tradition that is strangely missing in the West where individuality is supposedly valued over the collective.

In contrast, in the West the legal concept of primogeniture was accepted as the easiest method of avoiding impossibly difficult decisions, but in actual judgments of personal character the tendency has been to minimize the importance of the relative age of siblings. In spite of substantial empirical evidence that firstborn, middle children, and last born tend to be essentially different, Western theories about personality development generally treat all individuals as though they remain in identical circumstances as they pass through the same stages of growth. Among the Chinese the question of birth order is the natural starting point in judging an individual's likely personality.

As the oldest son and brother, Mao Tse-tung was expected to assume a number of life-long responsibilities. As the oldest son his father had to treat him in certain special ways and expect of him certain obligations, matters that we shall examine when discussing his relations with his father. As the oldest sibling he was expected by everyone, not only in his family but also in the clan and the community, to bear responsibilities for his two younger brothers and sister.

The responsibilities of the oldest brother were traditionally not considered onerous by the Chinese who tended rather to idealize the concept of brotherhood and to extol the presumed intimacy of fraternal relations. Next to filial piety the most esteemed relationship in Chinese culture was that between the protecting, helping older brother and the appreciative, loyal, dependent younger brother. A basic moral presumption of the Chinese was that between brothers there could be only respect, understanding, and unbreakable bonds of loyalty. Whereas the Chinese might acknowledge that behind this idealized version of purity and filial sentiments there might be a basis for tensions between sons and fathers that had to be overcome by formal training, the Chinese tended to expect that the brother-to-brother bond was a more natural and spontaneous one.

Needless to say, the Chinese could not escape in practice the natural ambivalences of brother-to-brother relations. The potentialities for rivalries were, in fact, peculiarly great in the Chinese family because the parents could legitimately cast the oldest in a responsible role while indulging the younger. Furthermore, the culture did not insist upon "fairness" or equal treatment of all children. On the contrary, Chinese parents were given considerable freedom to demonstrate which of their children were their favorites and which got on their nerves. The traditional Chinese concept that authority could respond to whim—indeed, that it could blatantly acknowledge favorites and reward those who sought its support—was based in part on the well-established practice of fathers keeping their children guessing as to who at any moment was the favored, and of rewarding the child who was the current cause of parental happiness.

The effect of all this was often to create tension among siblings, and particularly among brothers, both as a result of latent competition for parental favor and the strain of trying to maintain the idealized pattern of older brother-younger brother relationship, one of the five cardinal human relationships in Confucianism. Indeed, the usual pattern in families was for brothers to drift apart once their common parental authority disappeared. However, the Chinese realistically understood that sibling tensions could be reduced by giving each child his or her distinctive rewards and obligations.

Traditionally, in Chinese culture the shock of the arrival

of a second child was presumably mitigated for the elder child by immediately giving him greater responsibility. He was promptly taught that he could always be secure in his unassailable role of oldest son, and that he would always have certain advantages and quasi-parental obligations. Thus as he lost the undivided attention of his parents, he was supposedly compensated by receiving a new special status in the family. Furthermore, as soon as he was able and certainly before he went to school, he would be called upon to look after the younger child, manage and even discipline him. One of the most common sights on the traditional Chinese social scene was that of an older child carrying a younger one on his or her hip while playing with others.

The older child was thus encouraged early to avoid picturing himself in competition with his younger brother, and to see himself instead in a premature parental relationship to the younger children. This encouragement for psychic maturity was further accelerated by the father's urging his son to imitate his work practices and to learn as early as possible the skills and techniques associated with his occupation.

With these features of traditional Chinese culture in mind, let us return to what apparently took place in the Mao family as young Mao experienced the arrival of his brothers and sister. The birth of Mao Tse-tung's first brother barely two years later and that of the next almost a decade later meant that the spacing of the children did not bring Mao the traditional psychological rewards of becoming an older brother. The first brother came when Mao was old enough to have experienced the joys of the undivided affections of his mother but before he was mature enough to have assumed the quasi-parental role; and by the time the second brother and the sister appeared he was too old to be thrilled by flattery but mature enough to be assigned onerous tasks.

Both the timing of the arrival of the siblings and the intensity of Mao's original feelings about his mother's love for him must have contributed to the decisiveness with which Mao Tse-tung utterly rejected all of the mechanisms that Chinese culture had provided for easing the role of oldest brother. The evidence clearly suggests that Mao rebelled more intensely and effectively against the Confucian fraternal role than against the filial role. He rejected absolutely the responsibilities of oldest brother and refused the perquisites of a premature parental role.

In this process he also threw aside the possibility of identifying with his father and his occupational activities.

In Mao's descriptions of his relations with his father, as we shall see, he constantly insists that his father made harsh and authoritarian demands on him. Yet viewed from the perspective of traditional Chinese family relations, it is possible to see many of these presumed "demands" in a different light, and indeed to recognize many of them as efforts of a father to help his son accept both his filial and fraternal responsibilities. For example, Mao claimed that "My father wanted me to begin keeping the family books as soon as I learned a few characters. He wanted me to learn to use the abacus." [3] In Mao's version his father was grossly mistreating him, but other Chinese might have interpreted the father's actions as efforts to help his oldest son discover the pleasures of a premature adult life. After all, the father was encouraging the son to perform activities that, once mastered, would have insured the son's advancement beyond the professional attainments of the father. Doubt is cast on Mao's interpretation of his father's intentions since the second son did not rebel against the father's encouragements, and, as we shall see, he became a qualified bookkeeper and accountant, and ultimately he was to be one of the most skilled economists in the Communist movement.

The Private Man

In rejecting the responsibilities of the oldest son's role, Mao also declined its traditional rewards that included the pleasures of being allowed to manage and supervise the younger children. It is no doubt significant that the adult Mao, while anxious to be the leading figure, has never found gratification from the detailed management and administration of the activities of others. His concept of leadership has been to provide broad policies without performing as a functioning executive. Similarly, the adult Mao has shown great interest in the development of youth, but his concern has always been with the forming of policies, the making of statements about the importance of different forms of educational policy, and never with the actual supervision of young people. He chose the profession of teaching for which he trained himself, but he never assumed the continuing responsibilities of a classroom.

All of these propensities of Mao Tse-tung tend to reinforce the suggestion that he strongly rejected the obligations of the oldest brother, and in doing so he relied on idealization—the same defense mechanism that he employed to deal with the trauma of the loss of his mother's undivided love. It is therefore not surprising that in early adolescence Mao balanced his rejection of real fraternal responsibilities with a quest for an idealized sense of fraternity. By the time Mao was old enough to assume the duties of oldest brother, he was absorbed in reading romantic histories and the stories of the *Shui Hu Chuan*,[4] which idealized the fraternal camaraderie of sworn blood brothers. Mao's reading gave him a sense of participation in fraternal relationships without the degree of responsibility that was expected in his role as oldest brother. Much has been written by those who have explored Mao's intellectual growth about how the young Mao developed a feeling for rebellion, revolution, and warfare from his favorite childhood reading of the romances of old China. It seems likely, however, that Mao gained more than just a fancy for rebellion from his reading; in his emotional development, he came upon an atmosphere of idealized fraternal equality that could provide an escape from both immediate responsibilities and deeper feelings of guilt.

After Mao Tse-tung left home, in his relations with his schoolmates, and later with comrades in the Communist Party, he seemed to be constantly in search of new fraternal ties in which he could be the elder brother, but without either Confucian obligations and responsibilities or anything analogous to the threat of competition with younger siblings for attention and affection. His search was for a new form of fraternity that would have all the positive sentiments of the outlaw brotherhood without the strains and latent competitiveness of the actual brother-to-brother relationship. This exalting of a selfless spirit of brotherhood was to be a dominant theme in an aging Mao's struggle to maintain in China the appeal of revolution he had once known. As a septuagenarian Mao's preoccupation became the importance of instilling in Chinese youth the exhilaration of fraternity which he had sought in revolutionary activity throughout his singularly lonely life.

As a political leader, Mao's private propensity to employ the defense mechanism of idealization of fraternal bonds made it possible for him to communicate to a responsive generation of Chinese that he could offer them a pure vision of a new society in contrast to the hyprocrisy surrounding the old Confucian norms and the artificiality of its brother-to-brother standards. In rejecting the obligations of his own family position, Mao was able to dramatize a new kind of family that had extraordinary appeal for a society ready to seek some alternatives to its conventional morality.

For generations of Chinese much of the mystique of the

robber band and the rebel clique, depicted in such popular novels as the *Shui Hu Chuan*, lay in the spirit of innocent and tension-free camaraderie that seemed to capture a truer sense of brotherhood than the stiff and morally demanding Confucian concept of brotherhood based on stern rules of mutual obligations among brothers. The appeal of such novels was that they portrayed among supposed outlaws an intimate style of personal relationships that manifestly was more genuine and praiseworthy than the orthodox Confucian virtues. This spirit of revolutionary brotherhood, which Mao first discovered in novels and then sought not too successfully to realize in his associations in the early Chinese Communist Party, has been a vital element in the appeal of Mao Tse-tung for the Chinese people. Most Chinese, having experienced the demands of Confucian norms and knowing that there should be an ideal sense of brotherhood, can appreciate in varying degrees the tension-free ideal that Mao suggests should be possible. This purer, less artificial, more of the free spirit and less of learned etiquette ideal of brotherhood has meant so much to Mao that he would have it be precious to all young Chinese. Out of the resonance of his own personality he came to believe that once young people experience the joys of such an un-Confucian, competition-free brotherhood, they would, as he did, never want to lose that spirit. Of course, they would always hold precious the source that had made the new fraternity possible.

In late 1975 Mao's startling denunciation of the *Shui-Hu Chuan* as being an excellent "negative example" of "capitulationism" provides further evidence that he in fact has been using idealization as a defense mechanism to guard his quiet feelings about brotherhood. Under political stress he was able to turn against his presumed loved novel and in his old age admit that there has in fact been something essentially fradulent in his lifelong idealization of the comradeship of that bandit band.

We must, however, return to our analysis of the private Mao to see whether the facts in his treatment of his brothers and sister support our conjectures about the pattern of his emotional development after he became aware of his abandonment by his mother. Mao's extraordinary silence about his brothers and sister becomes even more significant as he describes many clashes with his father over issues that would have affected his brothers and sister as much, if not more, than himself. For example, Mao reported to Siao-yu that when he decided to go to school, his father first asked how he could pay his expenses, and when Mao showed his father that he had the necessary savings, his father then said, "If you leave home I shall be a laborer short. Who will help me work in the fields when you are gone? You tell me I will have nothing to pay, but you forget I will have to pay another laborer to take your place. You know, my son, I cannot afford to do that." [5] Finally, Mao borrowed from a relative enough to cover the wages for a replacement for himself. From this account one gets the impression that Mao was able to leave home to get further education only after overcoming unreasonable opposition from his father. If such were the father's views then, presumably it would have been even more difficult for the second and third sons to leave, since the father would have been even more dependent upon their help.

It is, therefore, extremely significant that Mao's two brothers each in his turn left home for further schooling at about the same age that Mao did. Unfortunately, neither of them ever reported on whether they felt that they had had to overcome parental opposition to follow in the oldest son's footsteps. It is conceivable that Mao succeeded through his struggles to break his father's will, and this eased the way for his younger brothers, but according to Mao's own testimony his father never mellowed and to the end remained incorrigibly stubborn. The objective facts remain that at exactly the same stages in their respective lives all three sons left home to advance their education; even though this meant that when the youngest left, the elderly father, still running his farm and enterprises, had to manage alone.

The three sons did not, however, follow autonomous routes on leaving home, for Mao Tse-tung was to have a powerful influence on their careers, and as we have said both his brothers and sister were to come to their violent ends because of his connections with them.

It is somewhat difficult to appraise the psychological character of Mao's later relations with his brothers and sister because of the very strong ethic in Chinese Communism for leaders not to disclose their family affairs. This tradition of ignoring private and personal matters goes back, of course, to Bolshevik practices, but it was no doubt given reaffirmation in the Chinese movement because of certain marital matters that will soon be discussed. The articulated rationale for the Chinese was that all Communists should rise above nepotism and therefore they should never hint at family considerations. The practice of secrecy about family relationships has, however, led in some cases to suspicions that behind silence there may have been acts of favoritism, and even of the opposite—abandonment.

In any case, we know that Mao influenced his brothers' careers but we do not have any public expressions of his sentiments about their fate. A recital of the main facts in the two younger brothers' lives does, however, help to put Mao Tse-tung's behavior into a clearer perspective.

The second brother, Mao Tse-min, not only followed his older brother in search of a better education in the provincial capital of Changsha, but one year after Mao Tse-tung helped to found the Chinese Communist Party he was persuaded to end his schooling and become one of Mao Tse-tung's first recruits in trying to organize workers in the Anyuan coal fields.

Apparently, Mao Tse-tung was not reluctant to exploit his authority as older brother to get Tse-min to work for him. In less than a year's time, however, Tse-min rose on his own within the Party when he moved to Shanghai. For the next three years he distributed propaganda in cities along the Yangtze. Then, Mao Tse-tung, an instructor at the Peasant Movement Training Institute in Canton, apparently enticed Tse-min to join him. Tse-min finally came and joined the fifth class to be trained, but Mao Tse-tung had just left that assignment before he arrived.

After the Communist forces had moved to Wuhan with the Northern Expedition in 1926, Mao Tse-min became the editor of the *Min-kuo Jih-pao* (Republican Daily). By this time the second brother was practically the equal of the older within the ranks of the growing Party. When the Wuhan government collapsed Mao Tse-min tried to flee but he was captured by Kuomintang forces. How he then gained his freedom is a mystery that has never been resolved, but he finally arrived at Shanghai where he again worked in the underground propaganda division of the Party. Again he was arrested, and again released for no apparent reason. At this point, when acute strains existed within the Party between those at the Shanghai headquarters and the guerrilla bands Mao Tse-tung was organizing, Mao Tse-min slipped out of Shanghai and joined his brother in Kiangsi. For a period the two worked closely together, and Tse-min participated in the Juichin conference at which Mao Tse-tung was elected chairman of the Chinese Soviet Republic. In the years thereafter, Mao Tse-min followed his talent in the area of economics and public finance. While Mao Tse-tung was rising to the political-military leadership of, first, the Kiangsi Soviet and then the Long March, Mao Tse-min took over the more pragmatic problems of financing the Communist movement. He thus became for the Communist Party what his father had wanted Mao Tse-tung to be for the family enterprise in Shaoshan.

Once the Communists settled in Shensi and Kansu, Mao Tse-min helped to organize their paper currency and general finances. In 1938 after the Japanese War commenced, Mao Tse-min's health gave out and he was sent to the Soviet Union for treatment. On his way he was delayed in Sinkiang by Governor Sheng Shih-ts'ai who insisted that he serve as provincial commissioner of finance. By 1943 Governor Sheng had decided that the Soviet Union was likely to lose the war and turned against all the Communists he had once invited to his province. Mao Tse-min was apprehended and on September 27, 1943, was executed. After the Communists came to power, four men who were presumably involved in the execution of Mao Tse-min were themselves executed and Tse-min became an honored martyr in Sinkiang. Mao Tse-tung never himself said anything publicly about the life and death of Mao Tse-min, a competent and capable man who had a distinguished revolutionary career in his own right, and who did not depend upon his older brother for what he accomplished.

Mao Tse-tung's youngest brother was only four years old when Mao left home, yet he too followed in the tradition of his two older brothers. He was thirteen when his mother died, and a little over four years later he left home to attend school. In this case the school was one which Mao Tse-tung had established in Changsha two years after he had helped to found the Communist Party. The Self-Education College was in fact a channel for recruiting members to the new Party, and thus by bringing his brother into the school Mao Tse-tung took a direct hand in recruiting his youngest brother to Communism, as he had done the year before with Tse-min. Mao Tse-t'an worked rather closely with his eldest brother. In 1927 he was the messenger who helped bring Chu Teh's remnant forces to Mao Tse-tung's headquarters in Kiangsi.

This liaison role is of interest since traditionally in Chinese politics principal figures often used their brothers as middle men in delicate negotiations on the assumption that brothers were prima facie deeply loyal to each other. Thus, Mao Tse-tung used his brother in a traditional fashion, but in doing so put Tse-t'an in a dangerous situation in which the older brother could not effectively protect him—a most untraditional act.

During the period of the Kiangsi Soviet Mao Tse-t'an was assigned to administrative record-keeping in connection with land reform. At the time Mao Tse-tung was out of favor with the Party leaders in Shanghai who were in contact with the Comintern, and in making their case against Mao Tse-tung they charged that he was favoring his brother. The fact that his two brothers were active in the same mountainous base area provided grounds for suspecting nepotism. It is not clear whether Mao was reacting against such charges or whether other considerations prevailed when in the fall of 1934 it was decided that Mao Tse-t'an should be left behind while the rest of the leadership in Kiangsi took off with the main army on the Long March. Over 120,000 men and a handful of women, including Mao Tse-tung's wife, broke out of their mountain retreat and set out on the great adventure that would end in Yenan with only 10,000 survivors; and those who were left behind included the aged, the sick, and Mao Tse-t'an. He was instantly captured and executed. Mao Tse-tung may have been practicing a new, more impersonal morality; he probably was experiencing the exhilaration of a new form of fraternity and camaraderie—Mao was later to say that his "health and happiness were never better than during military campaigns." But what is certain is that according to traditional Chinese standards he had failed as the older brother to protect the younger brother.

Lastly, there is the tragic story of Mao's adopted sister, Mao Tse-hung. Four years before Mao left home to advance his education, and shortly after the birth of his youngest brother, his parents decided that they needed a daughter who in time would be able to help the mother in the house and be a comfort in the parents' old age. It is significant that Mao himself has never spoken of this decision of his parents, which must have suggested to him that they were not entirely satisfied with their natural offspring.

Significantly, Mao Tse-tung never had a true brother-sister relationship with his much younger adopted sister. In traditional Chinese culture the brother-sister relationship tended to be very gratifying, secure, and sympathetic. With his sister the boy had none of the latent competitiveness inherent in his relations with his brother, and since there were no demands of sexuality the relationship had a degree of pure innocence and openness that was lacking in the husband and wife relationship. The fact that Mao was so much older than his adopted sister meant that he essentially grew up without knowing what it meant to live on a day-to-day basis with a female of his own age, a matter to which we shall return when we come to the place of women in his life.

Mao did, however, see his sister from time to time as he visited his home, especially after his mother's death. In 1925, when Tse-hung was twenty and Mao was thirty-two, he returned from his revolutionary activities for a period of "rest." At that time his relations with the Party were not entirely happy, and he was frustrated over not receiving greater recognition. His father was weak and within two years of his death, and the only person who now remained with him was his adopted daughter. At this juncture Mao asserted his influence as older brother and recruited his sister to join him in returning to organizational work among the peasants and workers of Hunan. She was soon caught up in underground work, but periodically returned to the family home. By this time Mao had gone on to Canton, but he left his wife and his sons with his sister and father in the family home in Shaoshan. However, the security of the ancestral home was no protection for the wife and sister when, in 1930, the Kuomintang authorities became aware that Mao's family was left unguarded while he was in his mountainous retreat in Kiangsi. The two women were arrested and executed.

It can be argued that up to a point Mao's actions were consistent with customary Chinese practices. Chinese normally exploited family ties for a blend of reasons which ranged from the belief that one can only trust a family member to the highly pragmatic fact of their utilitarian availability—in a sense relatives are around to be used. In later years, for example during the Cultural Revolution, Mao did not hesitate to use his wife, Chiang Ch'ing, and their daughter to help him politically, presumably because he felt he could trust them. Possibly, as some people have suggested, Mao left Mao Tse-t'an behind because he felt he needed a trusted representative among those who had to stay on in Kiangsi—yet he must have known that the odds for survival for those obviously identified with his cause were exceedingly low. Possibly, as others have argued, he was reacting against charges of his political opponents at the Shanghai Party headquarters that he had succumbed in Kiangsi to nepotism—yet to allow his brother to be killed merely to counter criticism of nepotism seems a bit excessive. Edgar Snow reports that Mao looked after the children of his two brothers, as would be the Chinese custom; on the public record we only know that he had contacts with one of Mao Tse-t'an's sons, and this is only from a conversation with that nephew which as we shall shortly see reveals a rather distant relationship.

Thus, in spite of some superficial appearances it is, in fact, impossible to pass off Mao's relations with his brothers and sister as typically Chinese. The most telling reason is his failure to shelter them from the risks of his public life. The brutal executions of Mao Tse-tung's two brothers, sister, and wife, and the death of his oldest son in the Korean War brought the violence of revolution into Mao's personal life. His official biographers have said that these deaths only made Mao a more determined and sincerely dedicated revolutionary. He has in fact remained largely silent in public, but he did once talk to Edgar Snow of these family losses and his conversation reveals a more complex pattern of reactions. His reflections on the violent deaths of so many of his family members led Mao not to bitterness or self-pity but rather to a psychologically sophisticated wonderment as to why he alone should have been spared death.

> At dinner Mao mentioned that both his brothers had been killed. His first wife had also been executed during the revolution (1930) and their son had been killed during the Korean War. Now, he said that it was odd that death had so far passed him by. He had been prepared for it many times but death just did not seem to want him. What could he do? On several occasions it had seemed that he would die. His personal bodyguard was killed while standing right beside him. Once he was splashed all over with the blood of another soldier but the bomb had not touched him.
> "Was that in Yenan?"

In Yenan, too. His bodyguard had been killed during the Long March. There had been other narrow escapes. According to laws of dialectics all struggles must finally be resolved, including man's struggle for life on this earth.

"Accidents of fate which spared you have made possible perhaps the most remarkable career in Chinese history."

After a moment of reflection Mao said that I knew he had begun life as a primary school teacher. He had then had no thought of fighting wars. Anyway, events did not move in accordance with the individual will.[6]

Frequently individuals who have experienced disasters in which they were inexplicably spared while their dear ones were killed first pass through a period of feeling guilty for being alive, but in time they are compelled to rationalize this emotion and arrive at the conviction that their survival may prove that they are somehow special. This sense of being charmed gives them a sense of omniscience and invulnerability. They come to the conclusion that indeed "events do not move in accordance with individual will," and therefore they personally are destined for success and can take greater risks than others.[7] Given the evidence that Mao, in his youth, must have had guilt feelings about his relations with his siblings, it is not surprising that, by the time they were killed, he was capable of transforming whatever further feelings of responsibility and guilt he may have had into wonderment about his own invulnerability. The experience of psychic abandonment by his mother, who had previously given him the basis for narcissism, thus set in motion a dynamic process of emotional development, so that by the time violent death in fact came to his siblings Mao's control of his own affect was nearly complete. He already had been hurt too much by an earlier sense of abandonment, and he had been forced to overcome his ambivalence toward his competing siblings, so that by the time their actual deaths occurred his emotions were deadened. His commitment by now was toward a new and idealized spirit of fraternity, and new concepts of authority and justice.

To understand the quality of Mao's moral indignation about authority and justice we must turn to his relations with his father.

CHAPTER

6

The Father

ALTHOUGH his shadow has already crossed the path of our investigation, we have delayed introducing Mao Tse-tung's father until we had met the other members of his family, for Mao Jen-sheng was such a domineering figure that had he walked onto the stage earlier it would have been difficult to perceive the nuances in the other more subtle family relationships. The crude forcefulness of the father and the bitter reactions of the son have been so publicized by Mao Tse-tung that all of his major biographers have acknowledged that he must have been profoundly influenced by his supposedly tyrannical father. The crucial importance of the father in forming attitudes toward authority is also propounded by all conventional theories of political psychology.

Mao's father obviously did play a major role in his personal and political development; but we must ask in what degree and in what ways the flow of influence ran between father and son. According to all accounts Mao's father, Mao Jen-sheng, was a "rough autocratic man for whom existence was measured by the gap between buying cheap and selling dear [and] he embodied the narrow grasping prejudices of the poor peasant once removed." [1] In Mao's own words, his father was a "severe task master," a "hot-tempered man" who "frequently beat me and my brothers," and "gave us no money whatever and the most meager food." [2] He was certainly not a popular figure in his community. He was a short, thin man who seemed an unlikely father to his tall, full son. But what Mao Jen-sheng lacked in physical appearance he more than made up in his steadfastness of purpose, his single-minded ambitiousness, and his shrewd sense of how to advance his family's well-being.

We have already noted how Mao Tse-tung claimed that he had to fight against his stubborn father in order to leave home at sixteen to advance his education, but interestingly, the two younger brothers, without any apparent difficulties, left home when they were about the same age. It may, therefore, be significant in appreciating how Mao Jen-sheng treated his sons to note that he left his father when he was sixteen. Mao Jen-sheng's purpose was not to get more education—he was apparently content, or at least reconciled, to barely enough education to be able to read elementary materials—but rather he left home in order to help save his family from bankruptcy. Under his father, Mao's weak grandfather, the family was forced to sell land merely to survive. If the Mao family was ever to recoup its fortunes and advance within its clan-dominated community it needed capital. Mao Jen-sheng was willing to do what might be needed, but at that time in China it was not easy to find jobs in cities for wages which could be saved and remitted to the home village. He therefore was forced to take what in the Chinese social scale was a lowest of positions—he enlisted in the army. According to the Chinese saying, "Good iron is not used for making nails, and good men do not become soldiers." Yet in the Mao family both father and son found that through armies they were each to achieve their different ambitions: For the father a few years of service provided enough savings to bring the family out of debt, establish a small grain trading business, and marry a bride from a nearby district who would bear him three sons; and of course for the son, armies were to provide him with a way to change the nature of Communist revolution and a vehicle to reach the height of political power in China.

Mao Jen-sheng devoted himself to expanding the family land holdings from fifteen to twenty-two *mou*, improving the family house, running a small rice mill and buying and transporting grain to Changsha and other cities. All of this required extra hands and there were therefore usually at least two laborers who lived and ate with the family.

Mao Jen-sheng expected everyone in the household, except the grandfather, to work for the family, and of course we know that Mao Tse-tung deeply resented these demands and felt that he was cruelly mistreated. His chores included both physical work and managerial responsibilities. As soon as Mao Tse-tung had learned as much at school as had his father, he was expected to keep the family books.[3] When not working on the books, he was assigned farm tasks. It is hard to judge how exhausting these may have been; we do know that at one time he was required to carry baskets of manure and his quota was fifteen—not a particularly hard assignment as even Mao admits when he tells of how quickly he completed the work and then, hiding behind a tree reading, he was discovered by his father who severely scolded him because he assumed that he had not finished his work.[4] Another time we know that Mao had to pick berries—in this instance Mao again provoked his father's displeasure because his younger brother covered a much larger area, but one where there were few berries while he concentrated in a small area where there were many berries, and therefore the father assumed that the oldest boy had done less than his proper share.[5] (The fact that Mao did not argue in this instance but seemed to have derived private amusement over his father's lack of understanding gives us one of the first hints of the extent to which Mao saw himself as superior to his father.)

The father forced Mao to perform tasks that the latter found socially distasteful. For example, the young Mao was required to make the rounds of the neighborhood to collect money for the eggs and chickens that the father had sold. Mao seems to have found the job of asking others to pay him peculiarly distasteful and became angry at his father for putting him in what he considered an awkward position.[6]

When we keep in mind the excruciating pain which middle-class American boys experience when asked, for example, to mow the lawn, we must be careful about dismissing too lightly the possibility that Mao did suffer mental anguish from the demands of his father. But compared with what was then, or even today, expected of boys in rural China, Mao's chores seem completely routine. From all the evidence we have it is impossible to show that Mao's father made him work any harder than was normal in that society.

Yet, Mao Tse-tung's account of his childhood makes the unqualified charge that his father mistreated him. In fact it may be difficult to discern what precisely was troubling Mao because, like most Chinese, he has felt it necessary to exaggerate any possible physical causes of suffering since his culture provides him with so few ways to express psychological or spiritual suffering. Mao is driven, for example, to trying to claim that his father refused to nourish him, even asserting that he received neither eggs nor meat.[7] However, in the same account Mao provides great details about how much rice the family consumed, and how much it sold; and in doing so he employs calculations indicating that everyone consumed the same amounts, and that his "family ate frugally, but had enough always." [8] No doubt Mao's statement about his receiving inadequate food is not to be taken literally, but rather as the way in which one must seek to communicate a sense of having been mistreated in a culture that stresses the importance of oral gratification and pleasures of depending upon and receiving nurturance. Moreover, the adult Mao has so many oral characteristics that he must have received care typical of Chinese who are well above the poverty level. We also know that a boyhood friend reminisced with the seventy-nine year old Mao Tse-tung about the pleasures of various Hunanese dishes that must have been associated with some of his earliest childhood memories.[9]

Whatever the problems of the charges of mistreatment, there is no uncertainty about Mao's willingness to express hostility toward his father. In recounting his childhood to Edgar Snow he made the bold statement of his feelings toward his father: "I learned to hate him." [10] In any culture it is a cause of wonder for a son to say openly and without qualification that he hates his father, but in Chinese culture this is especially shocking. Indeed, it is revealing that in the Chinese version of Mao's autobiography these words were left out, apparently because they were too strong for either Mao's admirers who translated and published the Chinese edition or because these admirers judged the Chinese public would be horrified at the idea of any leader having such feelings about his father.

Thus, regardless of the facts of how his father treated

him, the important psychological consideration is that Mao chose to publicly depict his father as a harsh and oppressive man. Indeed, it is Mao's theory, and not that of any psychoanalytically oriented historian, that he learned the spirit and tactics of rebellion in his childhood battles against his allegedly cruel father. Throughout his life Mao has claimed that his arguments with his father profoundly affected him, and even in his old age he would come back to the theme. For example, in his seventy-eighth year, in a conversation with the Prime Minister of Japan, Mao Tse-tung, with no apparent relevance to what had gone before, suddenly referred to his father's treatment of him, and just as suddenly dropped the subject:

> CHAIRMAN MAO: Do not drink too much Mao-tai. It will hurt you.
> PRIME MINISTER TANAKA: I hear Mao-tai is 65 proof, but I really enjoy it.
> CHAIRMAN MAO: It is not 65 proof, but rather 70. Who gave you the wrong information? By the way, there are too many ancient things in China. It is not good to let old things bind you. When I was a child, my father was very harsh with me, and I rebelled against him. It is said in the Four books and the Five Classics of Confucianism that unless parents love their children they cannot expect their children to respect them. I asked my father why he was unkind to me. Not to change the subject, but you seem to have a rough time in elections in Japan, don't you.[11]

Over the years Mao in various settings referred to his struggles with his father. Increasingly, they became joking remarks that might suggest some limits to the intensity of his problem. During the Cultural Revolution, for example, he told a Red Guard detachment that they should be a little less violent and only physically hurt those who truly deserved punishment, and then he added with a smile that, of course, his father would have deserved "the jet ride treatment" (a Red Guard practice of making a victim kneel and then pull his arms out behind to his back as with the wings of a jet).

The particular issues which Mao says he fought over with his father have stayed with Mao, and long after his father died, Mao persisted in trying to prove that he was right and his father wrong. Specifically, there were two dominant issues: first, the father's charge that Mao was lazy and lacked willpower, and second, the father's view that the son spent too much time with useless and impractical books. There would seem to be an uncanny connection between these two issues and Mao Tse-tung's ultimate political style and his historic contribution to Chinese Communism. Rarely in political psychology do we seemingly have such a clear case of a man who in his public role acts out his childhood battles with his father and compulsively seeks to prove his father wrong. The historic consequences of the two issues are that Mao Tse-tung will be remembered, possibly above all else, first for his unbounded faith in the supremacy of willpower, in the superiority of human exertions over machines and technology, and his obsession with the virtues of manual labor, especially important to young people; and second, of course, for having produced the Little Red Book that supposedly contains the answer for all mundane problems.

The father denounced the son for his desultory, lazy ways, his lack of will and determination; and the son grew up to turn Marxism on its head by glorifying voluntarism and human willpower in the historical process. The father wanted his son to work in the fields and make his education practical, all of which the son deeply resented, but then the son in his turn has made millions of Chinese youths leave their cities and homes to spend their lives in rural work; and, of course, he has insisted that all education in China must be "practical," "utilitarian," and not just interesting and imagination provoking. The father ridiculed the son's fascination with books because he said they were of no practical worth; and the son grew up to write the book which more than any other has been idolized by more people for its practical worth. The connection between the father's treatment of the son and the son's subsequent behavior seem so utterly plausible as to be supported by the logic of common sense without the need for any refinement of psychological theories.

Indeed, it is quite possible that the story of Mao's passion for rebellion, his belief in the sovereignty of willpower over technology, and his devotion to ceaseless revolutionary striving can be traced back to the problem he obviously had with his father. There are, however, certain troublesome facts that cast doubts about these admittedly plausible theories and that demand exploration for possible alternative explanations. Not the least of which is the obvious ease and even relish with which Mao talks about his problems with his father. If the trauma of the experience had been as severe as he has suggested, would he have found it so entertaining to talk about it in later years? Moreover, Mao's attitudes toward authority and rebellion took far more complex forms than can be covered by such a simple explanation. For example, instead of a blind hostility toward authority, Mao learned from his fights with his father that hate and love are not far removed from each other, and that conflicts can be constructive, creating positive bonds between adversaries. Also, Mao clearly discovered early that there was little risk in challenging authorities, particularly if one could claim moral superiority. Mao had no hesitation in confronting the first authorities he met once he left home, something he probably would have been more inhibited in doing if he had been intimidated by his father. If Mao's father was as uncompromising as Mao has said he was, then it is strange that Mao developed such confidence in his own abilities to triumph by carrying controversies to extremes beyond the point to which others are prepared to go.

By his own account Mao's rebelliousness enabled him to compel his father to be more "considerate" of him, and suggests that his father was not an uncompromising disciplinarian. In order to gain perspective on Mao's relations with his father, we need to keep in mind some further characteristics of the typical father-son relationship in traditional China. We have already noted the centrality of filial piety in Confucian ethics. In practice Chinese fathers were customarily harsh and demanding of their sons. Certainly, Chinese fathers and sons often clashed, and an atmosphere of bickering and verbal conflict pervaded many devoutly Confucian households. One of the principal reasons for generational tension was, paradoxically, a view about human nature that also contributed to the extolling of filial doctrine: The Chinese, far more than traditional Europeans, believe that the ultimate character of a person is determined by conscious parental influences and not by heredity. Chinese parents, unable to relax with the notion that their offspring might be naturally endowed with desirable qualities, felt the need to be eternally vigilant in their efforts to compel their children to grow up in the right way. If parents detected any flaws in the child's behavior, they could take no comfort in the thought that it might be a mere passing phase; they felt compelled to scold and harass until virtue and correct behavior prevailed. Thus the very self-consciousness of Chinese parents about the potency of their influence, and their refusal to ascribe significance to accident and heredity, meant that if they were at all ambitious for their young, they could give them no peace of mind.

These considerations, combined with traditional Chinese culture that allowed for very few ways of expressing affection within the family, meant that the principal way in which a Chinese father displayed his concern for his son was to be tireless in compelling him to improve his habits. We have already noted that, whereas Mao complained of his father's demands that he work at the bookkeeping, it is possible that the father was seeking to advance his son, and, by giving him manly responsibilities while still a lad, he was trying to groom Mao to be a responsible and effective person.

Thus, up to a point Mao's father apparently treated him in much the same way as other Chinese fathers of his generation treated their sons. The question is why Mao seems to have resented so much his father's demands that he work for the family enterprise. In most Chinese families sons appreciated their duty to contribute to the collective well-being of the family. Since they accepted an unquestioned obligation to do what they could for the family as a whole, they generally did not imagine that they were being exploited, as Mao did, for the advantage of the father alone. We have the hint here that Mao not only found it difficult to identify with the father and with the traditional role of male heir, but also was not fully committed to the collectivity of the family.

Mao was quite explicit in speaking of his interest in dividing his family in order to isolate his father, and win over his mother. Mao's description of his clashes with his father invariably contained some mention of how during these incidents his mother agreed with him or displayed sympathy for his sufferings. His fights with his father thus served to bring him closer to his mother. He sensed that she saw him as a heroic figure and the moral superior of his competitor, his father.

Thus, conflict with the father became a device for trying to recapture the happiness that once was his when he felt he completely owned his mother. Although he pictured himself as risking much and being in grave danger, the conflicts usually turned out to reassure Mao of his own superiority. Mao seems to have gained from his struggles with his father a sense of ego, an understanding of the tactics of bluff and challenge, and an insight that those who are willing to quarrel with each other must also have positive feelings for each other. We can sense how he felt strong enough to challenge his father from the following incident he recounted to Edgar Snow: "When I was about thirteen my father invited many guests to his home, and while they were present a dispute arose between the two of us. My father denounced me before the whole group calling me *lazy and useless*. This infuriated me. I cursed him and left the house. My mother ran after me and tried to persuade me to return. My father also pursued me, cursing at the same time that he demanded me to come back. I reached the edge of a pond and threatened to jump in if he came any nearer. In this situation demands and counter demands were presented for cessation of the civil war. My father insisted that I apologize and *k'ou-t'ou* if he would promise not to beat me." [12] From this Mao concluded: "Thus the war ended, and from it I learned that when I defended my rights by open rebellion my father relented, but when I remained weak and submissive he only cursed and beat me the more." [13]

There seem, however, to be several other points worth noting. First, the issue of laziness and idleness that triggered dramatic emotions between father and son. Second, there is young Mao's remarkable self-assurance in being willing to make a scene before company; he was, of course, an actor who loved an audience. This suggests he appreciated that his father was more restrained by social inhibitions than he. It was not just that he was more willing to quarrel than others, but he was less constrained by any feelings of the inappropriateness of time and place. Third, there is the implausible bluff of self-destruction and the notion that one can threaten another by indicating a willingness to risk damage to the self. Since Mao had known how to swim from an early age it was not a credible bluff that he was about to drown himself. Throughout his life, Mao has made much over his prowess as a swimmer and several times in his old age when faced with severe challenges he has dramatically taken to public swimming. Mao's father, of course, knew that his son could swim and so he could not have worried about his son hurting himself. Rather, the father must have been defeated by the humiliation of having a son who could so shamelessly misbehave in front of guests. The confrontation thus could not have been so physically violent or extreme as Mao suggested in retrospect. Both father and son must have appreciated the symbolic rather than the actual significance of the scene: The son was testing to see if the parent truly valued him, and the father was compelled to yield precisely because he was not as harsh and unfeeling as Mao liked to picture him. Mao admitted that he learned much from his conflicts with his father. Referring to the above incident, Mao said, "At the same time it probably benefited me. It made me more diligent in my work; it made me keep my books carefully, so that he should have no basis for criticizing me." [14]

Mao's credibility in his claims of mistreatment by his father is further weakened by the fact that Mao in later years upheld his father's values and never sought to justify contrary ones. For example, in the winter of 1914 when Mao had finished his period of drift and "moratorium" and was working for his degree at the Normal School in Changsha, he wrote in some class notes,

> It is human nature to indulge in pleasure and to hate toil, and laziness is the source of all evil. Laziness will make a peasant.

abandon his fields, a worker his compass and squares, a trader his wares, and a scholar his study. With his trade abandoned, a person has no means to make a living, and this will lead to his own destruction and the destruction of his family. A lazy nation is marked first by lack of progress, next by retrogression, then by decline, and finally by its downfall. How dreadful! It is therefore said that laziness is the source of all evil.[15]

Later in these same notes Mao added the observation that, "A young man must have vitality and vigor, otherwise slackness will arise. Therefore, laziness is the grave of life." [16] Not just the sentiments, but the very words seem to be those of his father. Could a boy who was deeply rebelling against his father on precisely this issue of laziness have uttered such thoughts only five years later?

If we assume that Mao was in some degree trying to test the love of his parents for him in these conflicts with his father, then it follows that the conflicts were essentially played out as emotional confrontations in which Mao could assert his superiority over his father because of his greater control of his emotions. In Mao's descriptions his father was constantly losing control of his passions, and indeed he usually left his emotions so unguarded that the son could easily manipulate them. In Chinese culture it is widely assumed that people who cannot control and mask their emotions are easily dominated by others. That is why children, whose emotions are constantly getting ahead of their calculations, must be deliberately teased so that they will learn to be more careful about showing their feelings. We know that Mao's mother made a point of teaching him to control his feelings at all times. "She criticized any overt display of emotions." [17] By controlling his own sentiments and by provoking his father to lose his grip on his emotions, Mao was able to demonstrate to his mother that his father was not a proper model in his behavior, and that in the relationship between father and son it was the son who was mature in spirit and the father was really the child.

All of these considerations suggest that, rather than being completely intimidated by his father and developing a deep hostility toward him, Mao Tse-tung sensed that his father was vulnerable, that he could prove his moral and emotional superiority over his father, and that he could manipulate his father because he understood better the ways of controlling and influencing emotions. How was it possible that Mao as a child had such superior control over his emotions? We must assume that the answer lies in the domain of the after effects of his feeling of abandonment by his mother. Having once suffered that traumatic hurt, Mao thereafter would be cautious about exposing his feelings. And his experience with his father reinforced his later refusals to commit himself emotionally to any other relationship.

Conflicts with his father could briefly reassure him of his inherent goodness, particularly since they provided a brief opportunity for sensing that he was a hero in his mother's eyes, but in the end such conflicts were also profoundly frustrating because after they were over the cold reality was that he had not, and could not, recapture his mother's undivided love.

Thus, the basic lesson Mao Tse-tung must have learned from his fights with his father was a dual one: First, it can be beneficial to provoke intense anger and emotional outbursts on the part of others. But second, one must not in fact become emotionally involved. If one is to influence others through their emotions, one may pretend to outbursts but actually one must be unfeeling, and, in Mao's own words, never appear to be "meek and submissive." [18]

These considerations bring us to the important conclusion that Mao Tse-tung's remarkable capacity to manage political controversy came not only out of his experience with "successful" arguments with his father but, at a deeper psychological level, from the total psychic dynamics of his family relationships that made him exceptionally adept at shielding his affect, especially in confrontation situations. This basic ability to control one's emotions in conflicts is, of course, invaluable for political leaders in any culture, but it is particularly significant for a leader in modern China. In Confucian China, as in many traditional societies, the culture repressed aggression, and the social norms favored harmony and the suppression of controversy. Disagreements were muted, etiquette governed relations to the point that emotions would not disrupt life. The worst fear in Chinese culture was that aggression might surface, producing confusion and social disorder.[19] As long as Chinese society had the coherence of the Confucian order there were few situations in which aggression was legitimate. But with the breaking down of the old order there was both an increase in anxieties, producing greater tendencies to express aggression, and more competitive situations that stimulated conflict and hence a need for new ways to express aggression legitimately. In most modern societies in which interests must compete, conflicts are contained by the institutionalization of adversary roles, such as those of lawyers and legislators. In most transitional societies and certainly in modern China, it has been exceedingly difficult to accept adversary practices because people have had little experience with apparent conflicts that are not also filled with aggression. Therefore, in modern Chinese politics, men involved in conflict situations have tended to manifest considerable aggression, which in turn has often reduced their effectiveness. Among Chinese leaders, Mao Tse-tung stands out as one who not only can engage in controversies without being emotionally confused but can exploit controversy and then put it aside when it no longer is useful. Having learned from his experience with his mother and then his father to suppress his emotions and not allow his affect to become engaged, he later had little trouble controlling his feelings in political controversy.

It is ironic that Mao Tse-tung achieved the emotional bases for playing a modernist role out of his family experiences because in nearly all his arguments with his father he was prepared to use traditional positions. We have mentioned earlier how Mao at the age of nine was "saddened" because his father was a "nonbeliever," and he discussed with his mother how to "convert" his father, but for his efforts he was only "cursed" by his father. By the time Mao was in school he was using the Classics and Confucian quotations to criticize his father's conduct. Mao essentially used traditional standards of morality to criticize his father's behavior.

In this respect Mao's experience was quite different from that of countless self-conscious Chinese youths who came of age in the two or three decades after Mao did. In the early twentieth century untold numbers of Chinese boys, exposed to currents of the modern world sought to "convert" their fathers to new ideas, and when failing to do so, became contemptuous of them. Sons wished they had fathers who were not "old-fashioned." The former, admiring the new trends, could only despise the latter and see them as weak and incapable of mastering the modern world. Like Mao the young felt they were justified in their hostility toward parental authority, and they easily accepted the virtues of rebellion, which they conceived of as a morally superior and almost pristine enterprise. Mao, however, was not the restless modernist opposing a timid traditionalist father, but instead, his sense of moral superiority was of the old China of both Buddhism and Confucianism. Thus his rebellion was not the easy one of merely being younger in a rapidly changing world and hence unallied with what was receding and dying. Mao challenged the old on its own terms, and he discovered that the old was not as imposing or fierce as it pretended.

Possibly, the reason that Mao as an adult was so extremely confident that the old could be brushed aside in China was that he had never "lost" the argument for the new as against the old with his father. As we shall see, Mao has always remained strangely ambivalent about the past of China; sometimes he has seen values in it, at other times he has felt it should and could all be swept aside, and at still other times he has been depressed with the tenacity of the old, but he has always been willing to use allusions from the past to bolster his arguments.

As with so many of the paradoxes and ambivalences in Mao's character, we can find support for our interpretations of them in Mao's own words. It is appropriate now to go back to the full conversation between Mao Tse-tung and Prime Minister Tanaka, a few remarks of which we quoted at the beginning of this chapter. What first might have appeared on the surface as unrelated thoughts will now seem more coherent.

> CHAIRMAN MAO: (speaking to Premier Chou and Prime Minister Tanaka) Did you finish your quarrel yet? Quarrels are good for you.
>
> PRIME MINISTER TANAKA: We have had amiable talks.
>
> CHAIRMAN MAO: Truly good friends are made only by quarrels.

Mao Tse-tung then referred to banqueting and the dangers of too much drinking of Mao-tai. At this point the conversation continued with Mao's comments about the existence of "too many ancient things in China," his own rebellion against his father, and his observations about the Japanese elections (see above, page 116). The rest of the conversation follows:

PRIME MINISTER TANAKA: I have experienced eleven general elections during the past 25 years. I have spoken on the street a lot, too.

CHAIRMAN MAO: Speaking on the street is a tough job, please take good care of your health.

PRIME MINISTER TANAKA: In Japan you cannot appeal to the people unless you speak on the street. Under the existing system you cannot be elected without making street speeches.

CHAIRMAN MAO: How is the parliamentary system?

PRIME MINISTER TANAKA: It has its problems too.

CHAIRMAN MAO: Japan certainly has a lot of problems, doesn't it? Street speaking must give you a hard time." [20]

From our analysis we can now see that instead of random jumping about from subject to subject there is coherence in Mao's observations that seem to express some of his most deeply held sentiments. We find in his remarks stark ambivalences. On the one hand, there is his belief in the value of quarreling in the making of friendships; on the other, his dislike of competition and his sense that the morally superior should be acknowledged automatically as authorities. Similarly, there is the ambivalence over the old being "binding" and yet a willingness to cite the Classics in defense of his own position, which has made Mao both a rebel against and an example of Chinese values. Quarreling with his father provided Mao with a way of gaining from his father an indication that he cared for and loved his son; it made it possible for both his father and his mother to acknowledge his superior virtues that should put him above the need to compete with others, such as his brothers and sister, to prove the legitimacy of his own will. Mao's sense of his own goodness that he gained from his exceptionally warm and loving mother made him assume that if he could only focus the attention of others on what was his true self they would have come to appreciate also his inherent goodness. He therefore constantly needed the attention of his father which he was able to gain through their conflicts. Each conflict seemed to have the double pay-off for Mao of reaffirming both his moral superiority and his father's feelings for him. This was not a father who ignored his son or was uninterested in his development. The father was as absorbed with his son during his lifetime as Mao has been with his father throughout his later life.

It was thus the blend of a strongly nurturing and sympathetic mother, a demanding father who in the end could be bested and shown to be less morally good than his son, and a generally supporting larger family and community context that combined to implant the basis for Mao's search for the charismatic role. In that role the bringing together of the heroic and the benign, and the beloved and the aloof, and above all, the powerful and the moral captured the key elements of Mao's personality as shaped by his family.

Mao's conflicts with his father provided him with more than just a means for strengthening his sense of self-esteem, reviving his feelings of narcissism, and reassuring him that his mother had been wrong in abandoning her total commitment to him. The conflicts were also tests of the issue of manliness, for they generally involved a confrontation between physical prowess (the "tiger") and intellectual cleverness (the "monkey"). In their relationship the father was clearly cast in the virile, physical, masculine role, and the son sought supremacy by being the clever "scholar," the user of words, the almost feminine figure. Yet the son admired physical strength, dreamed of violent activities, and identified with heroic actors who went well beyond his father in the role of soldier and warrior. In contrast to the father's demand for physical activity, productive labor, and utilitarian preoccupation, the son sought the release in literature, the escape into books, and the world of fantasy and imagination.

The father was vigorous and always active for a purpose, and he saw the son as lazy, weak, and ineffectual. As Mao later said: "Against his charge that I was lazy, I used the rebuttal that older people should do more work than younger, that my father was over three times as old as myself, and therefore should do more work. And I declared that when I was his age I would be much more energetic." [21] In time he was to make physical exertion the ultimate test of moral worth, but as a child his response had to be the superiority of intellectual over physical activities. Mao acknowledged that he was "the family scholar." [22]

Yet, as the "scholar," Mao again sought the safety of ambivalence. He could excel in the Classics, quote them back at his father to make his own moral point, yet he also declared to his father that he "disliked the Classics" which his father believed to be of utilitarian value because "he had once lost a law suit" [23] when his opponent used a telling Classical quotation. Instead, Mao preferred romantic novels and popular histories; and thus even as the "scholar," he sought to show his detachment from the serious, the responsible, the "tiger" (which in part he was) and his preference for the light, the imaginative, the "monkey" spirit.

We have here an important hint that Mao's incessant search for the security of ambivalence reflects a fear of commitment with respect to both emotions and thought. Mao's resistance to affectual demands, his need for emotional detachment was matched by a reluctance to make serious intellectual commitments. As we shall see, his self-esteem was easily reinforced by playing the role of the "intellectual," by reading widely but showing always some disdain for what he read, by suggesting that the popular, the "vulgar" is the superior of the

Illustrations

Mao's birthplace in Shao-Shan: The secure world of his childhood.

The room Mao was born in: Note the photographs
of his mother and father on the wall.

Mao (far right), his two brothers
Mao Tse't'an (left),
Mao Tse-Min (center),
and his mother.

At his mother's funeral: From left to right:
Younger brother Mao Tse't'an, father, uncle,
and Mao, wearing black mourning band.

Mao Tse-tung (fourth from left) with classmates at the Hunan First Normal School, about 1917.

The young radical Mao
at the beginning of his career (1919).

Mao's first wife, Yang Kai-hui,
and their two sons Mao An-ying
and Mao An-ch'ing (standing).

Mao and his third wife, Chiang Ch'ing,
at the time of their marriage.

Mao in Different Roles

As party intellectual (1923).

As soldier (1937).

As young orator (1938).

As old orator (1945).

As writer.

Reading.

Mao in Different Roles

Mao in military action.

Comrade Mao Tse-tung and his close comrades-in-arms.
All, in varying degrees, were at one time abandoned by
Mao. From left to right: Chu Teh, Chou En-lai, Ch'en
Yun, Liu Shao-ch'i, Chairman Mao, Teng Hsiao-p'ing,
Lin Piao.

respected. Eventually he was to suggest that even his most off-hand remarks along with his most ambitious thoughts were of the same class as the works of the great Karl Marx.

The division between the physical and the intellectual was very real for Mao, given the substance of his relations with his father. Very early the son learned that he could use words to counter and demean the vitality and human energy of the father. The dichotomy between the cerebral and the physical became the difference between the inherently superior and the self-evidently inferior.

Mao thus learned early that he could and should use his book knowledge and his scholar's status to counter the authority and power of his father. The idea that it was inappropriate for his father to ask him to engage in physical farm labor because he was destined to become a scholar survived Mao's childhood and reappeared in his behavior at the time of the Revolution of 1911, which overthrew the Manchu Dynasty. At that time he was nearly eighteen and a student at Changsha. "I decided to join the regular army . . . my salary was seven dollars a month . . . of this I spent two dollars a month on food. I also had to buy water. The soldiers had to carry water in from outside the city, *but I, being a student, could not condescend to carrying*, and bought it from water peddlers" [24] (italics added).

At the same time, however, Mao clearly envied physical prowess and was far from prepared to honor without qualification the scholar's role. For example, at the very time Mao felt it beneath him to carry water he also rejected the position of the scholar that was then available to him when he joined the regular army rather than a student corps: "Many students were now joining the army. A student army had been organized . . . (but) I did not like the student army; I considered the basis for it too confused." [25]

The Private Man

Instead of a sharp fork in the road that might have led Mao away from the world of his father's commitment to physical activities and into unqualified acceptance of intellectual activities, Mao almost as soon as he left his father began to repeat his father's arguments. We have already observed the passion Mao expressed in his class notes from 1914 when he declared that "laziness is the source of all evils." [26] In one of the first essays he published while still a student he linked physical fitness and vigorous activity to national development, and argued that the weakness of China was that its people were lazy and lacking in vitality. Mao's readiness to champion the importance of physical fitness must have reflected a not uncommon adolescent ambivalence. Although his father spoke of the importance of effort, it was the son who was physically the better; he could swim and his father could not; and thus in spite of his difficulties in putting his energies together, he knew he was, in truth, physically his father's superior. (Except, of course, when it came to the important difference of being able to command the attention of his mother.) Hence, Mao could not, with others, deny for himself the advantages of praising physical prowess.

It has not been just a youthful Mao who repeated his father's arguments. One can almost hear his father speaking in the words Mao used to a conference in Hangchow on December 21, 1965.

> It takes a total of 16, 17, or 20 years to reach the university, from primary school, and in this period one never has the chance to look at the five kinds of cereals, to look at how workers do their work, how peasants till the fields, and how traders do business. In the meantime, *one's health is ruined*. Such an educational system is harmful indeed. I said to my child once: "when you go to the countryside tell the poor and middle peasants: my papa says that *one who goes to school for several years*

becomes more stupid as he reads more books. Ask your uncles and brothers and sisters to be your teachers and learn from them." As a matter of fact a child, until he is seven when he goes to school, has a great deal of contact with society. When he is two years old he learns to speak. *At three he knows how to quarrel with others*. As he grows older he picks up a little hoe to dig in the earth imitating the adults in labor [27] (italics added).

Later we shall return to Mao's ambivalences about intellectual pursuits and physical activities as we examine his use of ideals as an ideologist and his approach to power as a manager of affairs. Here we need only emphasize that Mao's ambivalences about both books and physical actions and his vacillations over the relative value of each appear to have been rooted in his more fundamental ambivalence about his relationship to his father. He found ideas and words useful in countering his physically more active father, yet he also learned that it was the strong, simple man who always in the end had the ultimate claim to his mother's attentions. Mao in his father's presence had to defend himself against the awesomeness of the efficient, activist parent. Mao did so by both claiming that when he grew up he would be even more energetic and by retreating into the wonderworld of books, and especially fictionalized histories.

There is evidence that Mao thought of himself as physically weak and therefore shortly after leaving home he engaged in programs of physical fitness and sought to harden himself by living close to nature. Undoubtedly, this was related to not only his lifelong obsession with health matters but also his extraordinary record of recourse to illness whenever his self-esteem was severely damaged.

Over the years repeated reports have consistently exaggerated the severity of Mao Tse-tung's health problems. In part, the widespread belief that Mao has had serious medical troubles was encouraged by the frequency with which Mao did have physical difficulties whenever his political fortunes were down. On some occasions, for example, when Mao missed the Second Party Congress because he was at home "resting," there is no evidence of any physical symptom of illness. When Mao was out of favor with the Central Committee and dropped from the Politburo after his failures in the Autumn Harvest Uprisings he became seriously ill and needed hospitalization for a variety of complaints.[28] These physical difficulties came on the heels of the Party leadership blaming Mao for being over zealous and cruel in carrying out a purge in Fukien. Shortly after Mao purged Kao Kang, the first of the top leaders to be abandoned after victory, he apparently became ill and Liu Shao-ch'i had to give the principal speech for him at the Fourth Plenum of the Seventh Central Committee.[29] Shortly before Mao initiated the Cultural Revolution he was being squeezed from power and reportedly had health problems.[30]

For whatever it is worth, Soviet authorities report that there was an apparent correlation between Mao's health and the stress he felt in dealing with Stalin. They claim that the reason why Mao spent nearly three months in Moscow shortly after his great victory in conquering all of China in 1949 was that he had repeated physical difficulties: specifically, they claim that in meetings he would become pale and apparently lost his power of speech—the very thing that made him the master of his father.

In contrast to incidents of health problems when faced with political challenge, we have Mao's personal testimony that his health was never better than when he engaged in military campaigns. Thus Mao easily vacillated between exalting in the heroic glow of physical prowess, which fed his narcissism, and utilizing physical disabilities to recapture attention, as we learned from his poem to his mother.

Sentiments About Justice

We are about ready to follow Mao Tse-tung as he left his family and learned to deal with peers and new authorities, but before we leave his relations with his father, there remains a final dimension of how Mao's concept of justice was affected by the strains between himself, his father, and his brothers and sister. The problem of coping with parental authority in the context of sibling relations is generally a powerful factor in shaping people's emotional feelings about justice. Most individuals learn as children what in time become almost instinctive modes for dealing with authority. They usually discover in the context of relations with parents and siblings that a powerful shield for protecting themselves is the manipulation of concepts of justice. Many also discover that they can use arguments of justice not solely for defensive purposes, but that they can exploit the concept to inhibit and even hurt others.

Differences in approaches to justice reflect both individual and cultural differences. Some people seem to have learned from their particular family situation that they have to fight constantly if they are to get "fair" treatment, while others can be more relaxed since they expect that justice will work automatically. Younger children often are intensely sensitive about being ignored and not receiving equal treatment, while older children are more likely to sense injustice because parents are too demanding of them.

Precisely because family patterns are so culturally distinctive, there also tend to be quite different approaches toward justice from culture to culture. For example, in American culture the concept of justice is intimately tied to requirements of equity in treatment: Authority must be even-handed, everyone should be treated alike, and there must be rigid adherence to established rules.

Generally, American children cling to the idea that all siblings should be treated alike, are quick to resent or exploit any manifestations that another has received more, and expect to win the day if they can show that their parents have been "unfair," have shown favoritism to another, and have not acted according to their own precepts. American parents often feel helpless in trying even to articulate any basis for special treatment since fairness is so closely associated with instant equity. In contrast, in British culture "fairness" is related more to discretion and understanding of what is called for in particular circumstances. Children want whatever special treatment may be due them, and rather than asking for the constraints of explicit rules they believe that they will be better off by getting, and giving, civility. Quite a different pattern seems to exist in French families where children see little merit in everyone having to adhere to all the rules and are remarkably tolerant of arbitrary punishment. Whereas American children experience great suffering over being punished for something they did not do, French children are reportedly more stoical, accepting silently such punishment because they can easily remember other things they did wrong that went undetected: Therefore justice prevails as long as punishments and wrong doings are seen as being in approximate balance.[31]

These cultural variations may help to give perspective on both Chinese practices and Mao Tse-tung's particular experiences. As we have already noted, in Chinese culture authority was expected to act according to whim, parents could assert their power by playing favorites, and children could expect to be treated well, which was better than obtaining mere justice, if they could learn to effectively manage their parents' emotional state. Chinese children generally knew that they risked becoming the defenseless targets of uninhibited parental wrath if they provoked them by intimating that they might be unjust merely because all the children were not being treated alike. Children generally accepted differential treatment because they knew that in time their turn for special treatment would arrive. In the short run one could always hope to be a favorite in return for good conduct, while in the long run each child could expect his or her particular period of special treatment. At a comparable state or age one should expect appropriately comparable treatment, and thus the younger child could look forward to growing older and eventually becoming the oldest left in the household. During their lifetime the parents were expected to treat the children differently, but with their death each child would receive an equal share of the estate, and what had been the favored position of the oldest son was modified as equity prevailed in the end.

Chinese children hoping to influence their parents employed a wide variety of tactics that ranged from seeking to humor, flatter, honor, impress or submitting docilely to their commands. Their object was either to soften their parents' hearts or to shame them by asking for pity for their mistreatment. Thus in Chinese culture the concept of justice was usually associated with depicting authority as bad spirited and one sought justice by appealing for pity for mistreatment.

Mao Tse-tung's political success has depended in part upon the remarkable degree to which he shared this cultural feeling about the tie between pity and justice. At the same time, Mao developed certain idiosyncratic feelings about justice that strengthened his skills in using the concept politically.

Mao certainly shared with the Chinese of his generation the notion that by elaborating in great detail one's own sufferings at the hands of authority and by asking for pity one was in fact expressing an appeal for justice. It is significant that an elderly Mao, more than twenty years after coming to national power, became convinced that young Chinese would have little commitment to the revolution unless they were constantly exposed to horror stories of those who suffered prior to his rule. Pity for others presumably can produce appreciation of the merits of existing conditions.

Mao's concept of justice has been consistent with traditional sentiments in the extent to which he has tended to personalize injustice as the work of bad spirited people. Although in Marxism Mao supposedly committed himself to a materialistic interpretation of history in which justice and injustice were the workings of impersonal forces, in fact Mao has persisted in dwelling on the evil motives and the sinister characteristics of landlords and other enemies. Instead of the operations of the feudal and capitalistic systems inherently causing injustices, Mao has always tended to emphasize the bad moral qualities of the individuals of political classes.

While Mao Tse-tung has shared the traditional Chinese view that the prime source of justice and injustice must be authority, he has been extraordinarily blind to other possible sources. Specifically, Mao has been relatively insensitive to the possibilities of injustices in peer relations. As we have noted, Mao has always had little to say about his brothers and sister, and he was never particularly sensitive to the possibility that as oldest brother he could have been the cause of injustice in their eyes. Within his family it was only his father who was accused of injustice, and in later life it was generally only holders of power who could cause injustice. Although Mao was to suffer in his own peer relations with classmates, he persisted in thinking of teachers and especially headmasters as the principal cause of injustice.

In linking only authority to injustice Mao developed early the tactic of countering the injustice of an immediate superior by appealing to a higher but abstract concept of justice. Mao tells us that on many occasions, "I quoted to my father the Classics"; "I told my father that the Classics said . . ."; "My father could not answer when I mentioned the Classics." [32] Mao in an almost Western and non-Chinese manner played off one authority against another. At the same time, however, he put himself above all authorities by declaring that, "I hated the Classics." [33] In part he rejected the Classics because they were "too binding"—but, since it was their very "binding" quality that made them useful for Mao in controlling his father, his hostility was in fact to the idea that he himself should be bound by what could bind others. In later years Mao was to look for new ideologies that might serve the same function which the Classics did in controlling his father, but in the end he never found any system, including Marxism, to whose authority he would completely submit himself. His own will had to remain the ultimate source of justice.[34]

Mao's capacity to combine a sense of moral superiority over his father and an ability to appeal to abstract authority, which he himself defined, did not, however, bring Mao to the role of the peacemaker or precocious dispenser of justice in his household. Often bright children who find that they have an aptitude for legalistic argumentation seek to dominate their families by being a perpetual voice of reason who can excel over adults in determining what is right and wrong in any situation. As the oldest son Mao could easily have assumed such a role and proved his superiority by managing disputes and calling upon the other members of the family to "talk out" their differences.

Instead of using this approach to reason, Mao Tse-tung clearly preferred the opportunity for expressing aggression legitimately which his claims to justice gave him. Any injustice, whether to himself or to others, justified outbursts of hostility. In a sense his aggressiveness toward the "unjust" father relieved him of anxieties over his abdication of responsibilities as older brother.

The combination of the virtuous, narcissistic self, expressing strong and hostile emotions against "injustice," provided the basis for a romantic approach to fighting evil. Mao Tse-tung, much like the medieval knights of Europe, could idealize the thrills of aggression as long as it was done as a justification for fighting injustice.

The intensity of Mao's belief that his father was "unjust" seems related to a feeling that his father had failed to appreciate him and had not given him the special treatment he longed for after he lost his mother's sole attention. He no doubt was anxious that he was not as physically strong and active as his father expected him to be. Whenever he could express his superiority, in his arguments about morality and justice, he was also free to express hostile emotions. All of these considerations combined to give Mao the feeling that he could criticize, challenge, manipulate, and even exploit his father without any feelings of guilt.

Mao's description of leaving home suggests that he essentially broke with his father, whom he was, however, prepared to accommodate when necessary to obtain funds. Mao, therefore, sought to deny dependency, claimed that he was responding to an awakening sense of social justice, and yet took from his father what he felt was his due. In turning to Mao's experience as an adolescent leaving home, we need to keep in mind that Mao persisted in identifying himself as his father's son, indeed his only son, when it came to the family estate. Precisely what happened after his father's death is obscure, but we do know that Mao assumed possession of the entire family property in Shaoshan and used the rents he collected to support his revolutionary activities. His wife, his sister, and the wives of his two brothers continued to live on the estate, and it was here that his wife and sister were apprehended before their execution by the Nationalists. With respect to the estate, Mao once depicted himself as a typical landlord whose peasants were intensely loyal to him and respected the legitimacy of his property rights even when they could have benefited from its confiscation. ". . . I heard the tale that the local peasants believed that I would soon be returning to my native home. When one day an airplane passed overhead, they decided it was I. They warned the man who was then tilling my land that I had come back to look over my old farm, to see whether or not any trees had been cut. If so, I would surely demand compensation from Chiang Kai-shek, they said." [35]

A total review of Mao's relationship with his father from the time of their early quarrels, through his attempt to convert his father, to his attitudes about his father's estate reveals a consistent note of ambivalence. He resented the dominance of his father, but he also felt superior to him. He was aware of his ability to outwit his father, but in doing so he must have also sensed guilt. The test of our interpretation of Mao's experiences with his father must come later when we examine both his own use of authority and his manner in performing the father's role. We need only suggest here that Mao's refusal to assume the responsibilities of being a father towards his own sons, and his preference for playing the abstract role of father of the new China, indicates the degree to which he must have appreciated the vulnerability and the untenable position of a father confronted with a rebellious son. He had learned early that his father could not "win," and therefore, psychologically, he was incapable of ever allowing himself to be trapped into the responsibilities of a father.

In testing ideas about the effects of Mao's early family experiences against the kind of family setting he created when he became a husband and father, we must observe how Mao reacted to the authority of teachers, the competitiveness of the school environment, and the opportunities for fraternal friendship or hostile self-assertion as he moved out of his family setting and became an increasingly autonomous individual. To some degree these outside confrontations with authority, discipline, and peers reinforced the sentiments and the defense mechanisms that Mao had developed in his relationship with his mother, his brothers and sister, and his father. Yet there was also growth and modification of behavior as he increasingly had to deal with choices as to what he was to make of his life. To complete the circle of Mao's private life from dependent son to independent husband and father we must next consider the modifications of a lonely adolescent away from direct family influence, the stimulus of knowledge and travel, and the demands of political awakening and career choices.

Students and Teachers

THE STORY of Mao's leaving home, as he has recounted it, was a mixture of defiance of his father's will, a quest for knowledge, and a response to the heightened sense of social consciousness of the time. At the turn of the century, it had become common for Chinese boys to leave home when they were in their mid-teens. Fathers often sent their sons out to seek their fortunes. Indeed, of the generation of Chinese leaders, both Nationalists and Communists, who were either on Mao's Politburo in 1949 or were closely associated with Chiang Kai-shek at the time he withdrew to Taiwan, slightly over three-quarters had left their family homes and were boarding at schools by the time they were seventeen.

When Mao reached the age when young Chinese of his generation were expected to give up complete family dependency and seek a greater degree of autonomy his father agreed that he should leave home, not for more schooling, but rather as an apprentice in a rice shop "with which he had connections." Again the father clearly thought that he was helping his son to a better life than his had been, but a life within the context of Shaoshan.

Mao rejected his father's proposal in favor of more formal education. In the culture of the time the alternatives did represent significant forks in the road, yet it is important to recognize that the difference was not one in which education was perceived as being less practical than service as an apprentice. For Chinese of the times, schooling was regarded not as a mere intellectual or liberal arts experience but rather as a means to open doors to definite career advantages. Education was a matter of practical investment, by an individual or more likely by his family or even his clan; and therefore the quest for more education was universally interpreted as signifying strong motivations for higher material successes.

Years later when Mao had established himself as the leader of the Chinese Revolution he spoke emotionally of his dissatisfaction with his rural school and of his desires to get a better education. Yet his words and his reasoning mask whatever his motivations were because they seem to jump from immediate provocations—"My father naturally opposed me. We quarreled about it, and finally I ran away from home" [1]—to some very lofty considerations which seem to reflect the same propensity for idealization which we observed in Mao's writings about the death of his mother.

Specifically, Mao tells of three events which he claims wakened his sense of social consciousness and national humiliation. It is significant that Mao later claimed that "These incidents, occurring close together, made lasting impressions on my young mind." [2] Yet Stuart Schram in carefully identifying, dating and clarifying the incidents revealed that they took place over several years, from the time he was still at home to two years after he had left for school.[3] With respect to the first incident Mao clearly exaggerated when he said that it "influenced my whole life."[4] Schram has determined that this was an incident in which a Hunanese official by the name of Huang Huang, who, frustrated in his political ambitions, attempted in 1904 to assassinate some important imperial officials gathered at the provincial capital to celebrate the birthday of the Empress Dowager.[5] This politically motivated act of personal revenge became in Mao's memory a dramatic morality play built around a food riot during famine conditions. The riot was sparked by the governor who told a delegation begging for relief, "Why haven't you food? There is plenty in the city. I always have enough."[6] According to Mao's memory, a good official, supported by a righteously indignant population, clashed with the bad governor and might have won the day if the Emperor had not "disliked" the virtuous official. A new governor was appointed who then arrested and beheaded the leaders of the rebellion, displaying their heads on poles "as a warning to future 'rebels.' "[7] According to Mao, most of his fellow students were sympathetic with the "insurrectionists," but his personal reaction was different from theirs, for "They did not understand that [the rebellion] had any relation to their own lives. They were merely interested in it as an exciting incident. I never forgot it. I felt that there with the rebels were *ordinary people like my own family* [italics added] and I deeply resented the injustice of the treatment given to them."[8] Apparently, the youthful Mao had transformed the undoubtedly confused account of official intrigue into a profoundly moving incident involving "the people," whom he pictured as "ordinary" like his "own family." This is not the last occasion in which Mao shows strange ambivalences about the class or social identity of his family.

The Private Man

In the second incident his father was the target of a form of food riot: Rice was short in the district, but his father as a rice merchant was exporting grain to the capital for even better prices. "One of his consignments was seized by poor villagers" and, according to Mao, his father's "wrath was boundless. I did not sympathize with him." But, very interestingly for a future revolutionary, he adds: "At the time I thought the villagers' method was wrong also." [9]

The third incident involved a conflict between members of a secret society, the Ke Lao Hui or Elder Brother Association, and a landlord. The latter sued and won his case in court, but the members of the society refused to "submit" and withdrew to the mountains, built a stronghold, and instigated a revolt. The landlord spread the story that they had "sacrificed a child" as a part of their ritual of initiating insurgency, whereupon he called for troops who eventually captured the leader and beheaded him.

The psychological significance of these stories by a leader, who was striving at the time he recounted them to legitimize his own attempts to mobilize poor peasants and fight against government troops from mountain strongholds, hardly needs elaboration. Less psychologically self-evident is what connection Mao felt might have existed between his awakening sense of social consciousness and his decision to get more education. Implicit in his recounting of what he did is the idea that people concerned with social injustice will "naturally" seek more education. Yet, of course, Mao, the political leader, would in time become identified as the world's spokesman of the view that formal education inevitably deadens the student's social awareness and that the young must be removed from classrooms and exposed to farm and factory life if they are to gain political consciousness. In citing his own rebellion against his family and his sympathy for those suffering social injustice as explanations for why he took the initiative for more education, Mao failed to make clear whether he thought more schooling would make him more aware of social injustice or more knowledgeable about what to do to counter injustice, or even possibly that schooling would give him the social station from which he could be more effective in bringing about changes.

In any case, the ambivalences about education that have characterized Mao's political views were clearly present in his own initial decisions about education. Also we find that Mao had to idealize on a grand scale the rationalizations he felt appropriate for his decision to leave home for school. This tendency to jump from unpleasant private considerations to impersonal obligations is even more dramatically evident in another set of explanations Mao gives for wanting more education. He tells of reading a book, *Sheng-shih Wei-yen* (*Words of Warning*) written by a wealthy Shanghai comprador, Chung Kuang-ying, who wanted to reform China by advocating parliamentary government and to end foreign humiliation by employing Western technology to revitalize the nation. Mao claims that the book ". . . stimulated in me a desire to resume my studies." And then in the next sentence he says, "I had also become disgusted with my labor on the farm." [10]

With respect to what actually happened, it will be remembered that Mao made his first move by running away from home, living with an unemployed law student, and studying mainly the Classics. Then, he returned home for a brief stay before finally getting his father's support to attend a Western influenced higher primary school (junior high school) in his mother's county of Hsiang Hsiang. Mao was now sixteen and living twenty miles from home. He had given up the security of his rural community, but he had not ventured far afield, for his world was still a familiar one; the people spoke the same dialect, were a part of the rural culture of Central China, and he was among his mother's people. Indeed, he was even going to school with one of his cousins. In discussing Mao's relationship with his mother we have already observed his occasional practice of claiming native roots in his mother's county, and apparently this is what he initially did in order to gain admission to the school. (But then, when he discovered that it was not necessary to be a native of Hsiang Hsiang, he corrected the record.) We do not know how close he was to his cousin or his cousin's family, but apparently, after he started boarding at the school, the cousin was still interested in him and provided him with books that expanded his interest in the modernization of China. At the time, Mao thought his cousin (who had introduced him to the writings of Liang Ch'i-ch'ao, the essayist of the reform movement at the turn of the century) was "very progressive," but he said later the cousin became a "counter-revolutionary," a member of the "gentry," and joined the "reactionaries" in 1925–27, the years when Mao was active in Hunan investigating the possibilities of peasant-based revolution. In reporting about his cousin Mao seems to be suggesting that they either drifted apart, or possibly had a political falling out at the time when he was recruiting all possible members of his family in his role as Communist organizer.

Mao's vagueness and his suggestion of distance from his relative's family is significant in that by the mid-1970s, when Mao was the aged leader of China, his reported eyes and ears in the Foreign Office was the Assistant Foreign Minister, a woman by the name of Wang Hai-jung who has been identified as the granddaughter of Mao's cousin; that is, the great granddaughter of Mao's mother's older sister. Apparently, Mao maintained ties with his mother's family in spite of suggesting that their relationships were distant.

All of this is of special interest in the light of Mao's ambiguous account of leaving home which seems to confuse whether it was he who was abandoning his family or his family who abandoned him. Mao claims credit for striking out on his own, but by playing down the fact that his father financed not only his expenses at the Tungshan school in Hsiang Hsiang but also all his subsequent education, Mao seems to suggest that his family had abandoned him. In describing his problem at school he pictures himself as a lonely, almost "orphaned" child who succeeded eventually but only by his wits and willpower, the precise qualities his father rebuked him for lacking.

The awkward, unsure manner in which Mao at the very outset aggressively challenged classmates, teachers, and even the headmaster suggests that he was indeed feeling a sense of abandonment and needed to draw attention to himself to prove his goodness and virtues, especially to those with authority. His soon to be friend and fellow student, Siao-yu, has described vividly the confusion, hostility, and bold daring which characterized Mao's behavior on his arrival at the Tungshan school. He approached the janitor and gateman, demanded admittance, created a scene when the students present laughingly said that he didn't know how things were done, and finally attracted the attention of the Headmaster.[11] As so often in Mao's life, confrontation produced a scene of tension into which stepped that ubiquitous figure of Chinese culture, a mediator, who in striving for compromise, invariably helped legitimize Mao's extreme position. After the Headmaster of the Tungshan primary school had refused Mao's request for admission on the grounds that he was unqualified, Mao persisted in asking for admittance until one of the teachers intervened to propose that he be given a chance to prove himself on a trial basis. Admission under such terms did not produce acceptance by the other boys. Indeed, the new school adventure was an intense period of loneliness for young Mao, for it is evident from both what Mao and some of his schoolmates have said that he did not have an easy time making new friends.

There were several dimensions to his social difficulties at this stage of his life. First, there was the unnatural fact that Mao was some six or seven years older than his classmates, yet academically less well prepared than they. In traditional China there was no strong sense of age cohorts, and children of all ages frequently mingled together as they learned from a single stern taskmaster who was likely to be the only teacher available. The concept of systematic schools with progression through grades and instruction by several specialized teachers was a Western importation that was just taking hold at the turn of the century. But take hold it did, and very quickly, so that by the time of the Revolution of 1911, the Chinese were already developing the concept of classmates as intensely intimate friends to whom one would have special ties for the rest of one's life. Few cultures have traditionally valued the concept of friendship more highly than the Chinese, and therefore it is quite understandable that they should have so readily imputed to the concept of classmate such deep and abiding sentiments of friendship. In time the Chinese concept of classmate evoked powerful notions about mutual obligations, shared happiness and a lifelong relationship that would become more rather than less intimate with time.

Mao Tse-tung's experience with a modern style school occurred in the first decade of the century when the concept of peer cohorts was just beginning to dominate Chinese youth culture, and therefore the fact that he was so much older than his classmates was not unusual enough to make him outlandishly conspicuous. Mao himself never mentioned the obvious fact that he was so much older than the other pupils, but one who knew him as a student, Siao-yu, tells of how the other students regarded him as a country boy with exaggerated ambitions who was much too old to be in only the sixth or seventh grade.[12] Indeed, when Mao first arrived at Tungshan even the janitor sensed that he was completely out of place and maybe out of mind, in his demands to be accepted as a student. He was already sixteen years old, and furthermore he was large for his age and could be easily taken for at least eighteen or nineteen. The students who first saw him at the school, and who were ten to twelve, thought he was of university age and sensed he would be a menace in their schoolyard.[13]

In light of the contrast between Mao's relations with his parents and those with his younger brothers and sister, it is not surprising that at school he focused on and was more successful at gaining the attention and favor of his teachers than the friendship of his classmates. Mao himself admits that he had "never before seen so many children together," [14] and he clearly was as unsure of his role as they were of what to make of him. Nothing in Shaoshan or in his family setting had prepared him for the interplay of peers. He immediately revealed that he was extremely thin-skinned, completely unaccustomed to being teased, and that his only response was to bully back. The ease with which children six years his junior were able to intimidate him and make him feel like a crude and dull-witted peasant tells much about Mao's vacillations between self-assurance and uncertainty among strangers, the latter being a completely new experience for him.

Mao himself has had two explanations for why he had troubles with his classmates. First, "I was more poorly dressed than the others. I owned only one decent coat-and-trousers suit. . . . Many of the richer students *despised me because usually I was wearing my ragged coat and trousers*" [15] (italics added). Second, "I was also disliked because I was not a native of Hsiang Hsiang. It was very important to be a native of Hsiang Hsiang and also important to be from a certain district of Hsiang Hsiang. There was an upper, middle and lower district . . . I took a neutral position in this war. . . . Consequently all three factions despised me. I felt spiritually very depressed." [16]

In speaking about his classmates' attitudes toward him Mao reveals a degree of hypersensitivity to their opinions that stands in contrast to his self-assurance in his relationship to his family. The young man who left home with such confidence was suddenly undone by children years younger than himself. Mao's sensitivity to matters of dress and his precocious concern about social gradations suggest how deep were his anxieties about being accepted. Mao's subsequent training in Marxism may have made him boast that at sixteen he could recognize that "There was an upper, lower and middle district, and the lower and upper were continually fighting, purely on a regional basis. Neither could become reconciled to the existence of the other." [17] What is not attributable to Marxism, and far more revealing, is Mao's feeling that because he was not a part of the controversy and entirely out of the social situation, he was "despised" by everyone.

Thereafter, Mao revealed remarkable sensitivity to both social gradations and to being the object of scorn. In addition to his statements about how he perceived others' views about him at the Tungshan primary school, we have his testimony that when he was Assistant Librarian at Peking University his "office was so low people avoided me" and for most people "I didn't exist as a human being," and the important intellectual figures of the day "had no time to listen to an assistant librarian, speaking a southern dialect." [18] Mao's sensitivities about being "despised" and "looked down upon" thus extended from his first experience at a large school to his first job after graduating from normal school.

Mao's manifest suspicions that others had such scorn for him tends to support the presumption that he had some inner doubts about his own worth, doubts that must have been deeply implanted when he felt his mother had abandoned him and when his father proved impervious to his son's hostility toward him. Thus, we see in this first experience in a new setting Mao's reenactment of the drama of his family relationships. Troubled that others could not appreciate his basic goodness, he was predisposed to place people in hierarchical order, presuming that those at the top were contemptuous of those beneath them. Power gradations were already important to him, and he did not appreciate being left out of the topmost category. Even more important, he was "depressed" by being the complete outsider, the one who came from beyond even the "lowest district" and spoke with an outsider's accent.

Mao's reaction was to strive to prove his worth by seeking to impress his superiors with evidence of his intellectual and moral worth and to seek the respect of his juniors by demonstrating his courage and his capacity for aggressive hostility.

Just as Mao's account of his childhood omitted all details of his relations with his brothers and sister, so his description of his experience at Tungshan, beyond noting that the other children despised or ridiculed him, tells little about his relations with classmates. Others, however, have recounted incidents from that time suggesting that his behavior was consistent with what it had been at home in Shaoshan. He had learned at home that it paid to be outspoken and hostile toward his father while seeking to dominate his mother and his brothers and sister. At Tungshan school, when he had disagreements with his teachers, he boldly sought to win the students to his side. When he had troubles with the student leaders in his class, he directly challenged them and looked for support from the younger students. He did not hesitate to express anger or to escalate small incidents into major confrontations that he would then carry to the brink of physical violence and even a complete break in personal relations.

Siao-yu tells of Mao becoming deeply embroiled in arguments with his history teacher and his classmates over his beloved *San Kuo Chih Yen Yi* (*Romance of the Three Kingdoms*) passionately insisting it was accurate history, while they scornfully dismissed it as only embroidered accounts of events and personages in history. Mao's response to his difficulties with the history teacher was to try to get all the other students to agree that he should be dismissed. He carried the issue to the Headmaster and when he was rebuffed he immediately challenged this authority figure.[19]

Mao's style of attack was to suggest something irregular in the relations of his enemies. He accused the Headmaster of protecting the history teacher because they were "cousins," which everyone knew they were not. Then when one of the boys openly challenged Mao and supported the Headmaster, Mao instantaneously accused him of being the nephew of the Headmaster, which of course he was not. He also accused all the boys of being cowards for not siding with him, denying the possibility that they might honestly disagree with him. Furthermore, he singled out the one student with whom he had come the closest to having a real friendship and denounced him as a "traitor."

Throughout his public life, time and again, Mao has had remarkable political success by relying upon this identical approach in conflicts with colleagues. He has ignored the substantive merits of issues and reformulated the problem into a question of personal courage and loyalty. When he first employed this method in his family, his mother had always sought to bring people together in order to maintain the solidarity of the family, and his father had always retreated from any irrevocable extremes. Thereafter Mao was usually saved in the end by the forces of circumstances that compelled others to endure his behavior rather than risk shattering whatever group solidarity might exist. At Tungshan school the students had to go on living with each other, and they could not allow their conflicts with Mao to compromise their goal of getting an education. Later it was the value that others placed in the Party and the goal of the revolution that made them accept Mao's wishes rather than risk greater destruction.

At the same time, while challenging the authority of his teachers, he also sought to prove to them that he was a superior person both morally and intellectually. Just as in his relationship with his father, he expected that his act of rebellion would bring attention and better treatment. According to Mao's own perception of what happened: "I made good progress at this school. *The teachers like me, especially those who taught the Classics, because I wrote good essays in the classical manner*" [20] (italics added). Again, we find Mao admitting, without appreciating the irony, that his personal strength lay in precisely the area his father had encouraged, the study of the classics.

During the first months when he was on probation at the Tungshan school, Mao displayed those truly outstanding qualities of intellectual concentration and physical endurance that were to mark his later period of high creativity. He easily convinced his teachers that he should be allowed to stay on for the full year. Paradoxically, however, as he became more secure in the new setting, his relations with his classmates and even with his teachers were increasingly filled with tensions and open conflicts.

The Private Man

Apparently what happened was that as Mao gained self-assurance from his success with his teachers, he needed to remind them that they had been wrong about him. And in his relations with his classmates he was now ready to strike back at his tormenters. In doing so he naturally exploited the fact that he was bigger, stronger, and intellectually more developed than they were, and thus he came to take on the distinctive aggressive, almost bullying style that has at times characterized many of his personal relationships.

While Mao's behavior during his year at the Tungshan school provoked enemies among his schoolmates, there is evidence that he was still seeking fraternal ties. As the oldest student in the school, he seemed to be groping for a more effective older brother role than he had with his brothers. Whereas in his own family Mao had monopolized the attention of his parents and had felt no need to be protective with his younger siblings, he discovered at the Tung-shan school that it was possible to learn from younger people and in return he could provide protection. This was his first halting step toward the spirit of comradeship that he idealized from his favorite novels, particularly the accounts of blood-brotherhoods among the heroic bandits of the *Shiu-hu Chuan*. But few of his classmates accepted him, for most were afraid of his "violent temper." [21]

At the same time Mao's intellectual world was rapidly expanding, and his knowledge of politics grew. In general he seemed to have a positive view of those occupying the ultimate commanding heights of Hunan affairs. He later confessed that he considered the Emperor as well as most officials to be "honest, good and clever men" who "only needed the help of K'ang Yu-wei's reforms." He was at the time also "fascinated by accounts of the rulers of ancient China: Yao, Shun, Ch'in Shih Huang-ti, and Han Wu-ti." He began to learn "foreign history" and geography. He first discovered America in an article that told of the American Revolution and that contained a sentence he long remembered: "After eight years of difficult war, Washington won victory and built up his nation." He was excited by a book called *Great Heroes of the World* which told about Napoleon, Catherine of Russia, Peter the Great, Wellington, Gladstone, Rousseau, Montesquieu and Lincoln.[22]

Thus we have the strange situation of a sixteen-year-old boy learning about the world of great men and politics from sources designed for eight-to-ten year-olds. He could not have been very well informed because he tells us that he only learned of the death of the Empress Dowager two years after the event, and was not to see his first newspaper until he was nearly eighteen.

There was thus a strange contradiction in Mao's learning experience at this critical stage of his development. On the one hand, he was learning second hand about a much larger world that was, according to the texts, utterly benign and filled with model leaders. At this point in his life he had not made a connection between his own means of dealing with authority and enemies and his views about the workings of politics and history. On the contrary, history was for him a great drama filled with heroic figures and even the contemporary scene in China was populated by "good and honest" men.

There is conflicting evidence as to why Mao left the Tungshan school: One source states that it was because of the unpleasantness of his personal relations, another that he wanted to experience the excitement of a larger place, the capital of Changsha. According to Siao-yu, "The feelings of fear and animosity which he had stirred up in the Tungshan school were so strong that Mao finally decided to leave for good. One fine day, he packed up his simple belongings and set off on foot for Changsha, the capital city." [23] Presumably this is how

The Private Man

Mao at one time talked about why he left Tungshan, and it is consistent with how he pictured his leaving of home. Yet in his later account, as reported to Edgar Snow, he said,

> I began to long to go to Changsha, the great city. . . . It was said that this city was very big, contained many, many people, numerous schools, and the *ya-men* of the governor. It was a magnificent place altogether! I wanted very much to go there at this time, and enter the school for Hsiang Hsiang people. That winter I asked one of my teachers in the higher primary school to introduce me there. The teacher agreed, and I walked to Changsha, exceedingly excited, half-fearing that I would be refused entrance, hardly daring to hope that I would become a student in this great school. To my astonishment I was admitted without difficulties.[24]

Whatever the reason, Mao was becoming more self-assured in his behavior. He was ready to take on a larger world, partly because he may have found his immediate one disagreeable. Yet there was still nothing to indicate in what direction his search for personal and career commitments would lead.

Chinese society at that time had institutions that were truly remarkable in reinforcing the self-confidence of those who were even moderately adventurous. As Mao indicated, he was ready to go to a big city, but he was anxious to be accepted at a school that parochially accepted only students from his mother's county. In those days, in the provincial capitals of China, there were various organizations seeking to counter the anonymity of large cities by looking after the interests of people from the same counties or clans. Similarly, in the national capital and in the larger cities of Shanghai, Canton and the like, co-provincials would find associations that would help them establish contacts and protect their interests against a potentially hostile world.

In the big city Mao still maintained his links with other rural people and was not plunging into the unknown. The community guilds helped to smooth the transition to urban life so that immigrants could continue the social practices and customs of their communities. Consequently, the mood of the new migrant usually was passive and appreciative. But Mao Tse-tung spent only six months in the upper primary school (ninth grade) in Changsha before dropping out to support the Revolution of 1911 that overthrew the Manchu Dynasty. Even during those spring and summer months of 1911, while registered at school, he was absorbed in learning about provincial and national politics. He read his first newspaper and learned that there were living heroes and martyrs, not just those in history books.

Mao was rapidly learning about national events. In the early fall of 1911 he wrote his first political article, which he posted on the wall of the school. Years later during the Cultural Revolution of 1966–69 Chinese students as Red Guards, in seeking to capture the revolutionary experiences of Chairman Mao, also engaged in writing large character wall posters. Mao's article was a rather innocent proposal that his three heroes of the day should be made President, Premier, and Foreign Minister of a republic. The Red Guards of his old age were to make more shocking revolutionary proposals.

Mao was becoming an activist who wanted to go beyond words to acts in support of his new-found anti-imperial and pro-republican sentiments. In one of his first political acts he and a friend forcibly cut off the queues of over ten boys. During the Ch'ing Dynasty Chinese were expected to wear queues as a sign of their subjugation by the Manchus. Near the end of the dynasty Chinese nationalism sometimes took the form of cutting off one's pigtail as an act of defiance of the tradition and the authorities. According to Mao, "One friend and I clipped off our pigtails, but others, who had promised to do so, afterwards failed to keep their word. My friend and I therefore assaulted them in secret and forcibly removed their queues, a total of more than ten falling victim to our shears." [25]

The incident caused considerable controversy. Mao admitted that he had to argue about it with an older student from a nearby law school who held that, according to tradition and the Confucian Classics, one's body belonged to one's own parents and therefore one could not destroy even one's hair without parental permission. Mao claimed that he was able to silence his opponent by developing a "counter theory on an anti-Manchu political basis." [26] This is the first indication of Mao's belief in the supremacy of political justifications over others.

No doubt the temper of the times accelerated Mao's increasing political awareness. Whereas his classmates enjoyed the excitement of the crisis that erupted in the Revolution of 1911 and applauded the fall of the Imperial system, Mao took the upheaval much more personally and felt that he ought to be a participant in these history-shaping events. Changsha was the scene of some military activity in October, 1911, but Mao Tse-tung's description of the uprising is, according to Stuart Schram, "largely fictional." [27] Politics clearly was taking hold of Mao's imagination and distorting his perceptions in a romantic way. He tells of viewing his first battle and of seeing bodies in the streets, as "landlords and merchants" opposed the revolutionary fervor of the "poor."

The Revolution of 1911 provided Mao with his first introduction to army life. The experience was less relevant in shaping his ultimate interest in military matters and far more significant in revealing Mao's persisting ambivalence toward education and the place of students in society. In the excitement of the events students in Changsha and from elsewhere in Hunan organized a "student army," a quasi-military organization dedicated to supporting the Republican forces and to denouncing, if not fighting, any lingering Imperial remnants. Mao tells of how he rejected the idea of joining such an army because he "considered the basis of it too confused." [28] Apparently he could see that such an organization would be effective neither militarily nor educationally. Undoubtedly, he was also influenced by the fact that his experiences with fellow students had not been happy and therefore he felt little attraction toward a group in which others might share a sense of camaraderie from which he was excluded. His immediate classmates were still far younger than he, and he would have had little chance to know the older students who must have been the natural leaders.

Therefore, Mao Tse-tung took the extraordinary step of enlisting in the regular army of Li Yuan-hung who had thrown in his lot with the anti-Manchu forces. Mao's actions seemed to deny his student identity, yet once within the army he reasserted his student status and claimed special privileges, such as refusing, as we have noted, to carry water for himself. [29] Just as in his family setting where he had both scorned and exploited his role as its "scholar," so now he was doing the same by rejecting what the students were doing while assigning them special characteristics. Needless to say, Mao's attitudes about the separation between the roles of soldier and student were to undergo radical changes in time, but his ambivalence about education remained.

Mao's army experience, which only lasted six months, reinforced his sense of being special. He had time to read all the newspapers and journals he could get his hands on, while most of the ordinary soldiers were illiterate. He realized that most of them were "mediocre, and one was a rascal." [30] He did like a miner and an ironsmith, and he says that he "became on friendly terms with the platoon commander and most of the soldiers. I could write, I knew something about books and they respected my 'great learning.' I could help by writing letters for them or in other such ways." [31]

Although Schram is probably right in doubting Emi Hsiao's claim that Mao's military experience led him to conclude that "in China the army is the key to political power," [32] it is true that Mao did not find army life unpleasant, for he was for once unambiguously superior. Indeed, he was so exhilarated that he wrote to several classmates about his expanding political thoughts, but only one responded. It was in this personally satisfying and exciting atmosphere that Mao first read about socialism to which he claims that he was completely won over. In fact, it was to be several years before he made any deep commitments to the principles of socialism, but he undoubtedly developed a political outlook on the subject which he associated with his satisfying experiences as an "ordinary" but obviously special student-soldier.

Mao's first military experience lasted only half a year because the military phase of the Revolution of 1911 was brief and it appeared that Sun Yat-sen and Yuan Shih-k'ai were about to work out a common approach to building a Chinese republic.

After leaving the army Mao did not immediately return to school. Instead, he entered a phase of drift and indecision. His early excitement about politics seems to have spent itself and left him in a depressed and uncertain state. The prospect of returning to classes with children much younger than himself was unappealing, but without the structure of teachers and peers to struggle against, Mao seemingly lost all sense of purpose. He had no desire to return home; he had no career skills; he lacked political connections. He had been in the middle of events, but now they had moved beyond him, leaving him emotionally deflated and without motivation.

In this state of disorientation he seems to have entered that phase of "moratorium" that Erikson has identified as a critical phase in the process of maturing, a period of detour of some kind, a time during which psychic growth can catch up with physical development. Most societies have in varying degrees institutionalized such a phase of life by not holding young people fully accountable for their acts even though they are recognized as being physically mature. According to Erikson, during the moratorium the young person often develops some skill or technique that will subsequently become central to his identity or give him the necessary sense of discipline so that he will be able to employ more effectively some other faculty or skill. Luther's moratorium was spent in the monastery; Freud's monastery was his medical and scientific training; G. B. Shaw spent his moratorium in a business house; Darwin spent his in medical training and the two years aboard the *Beagle;* for Winston Churchill it was the Indian army. Erikson suggests that the common pattern of the ideological innovator is one of coming upon his life work without prior planning or design. Disciplined training is in one area, and creative innovation in another.[33]

Mao entered such a period of indecision after he left the army in 1912. Years before Erikson identified the concept of "moratorium," Robert Payne noted such a period in Mao's life and commented: "There appear very often in the lives of men who later become revolutionaries periods of intolerable poverty and indecision. Uprooted, without money, suddenly confronted with harsh necessity, they withdraw into themselves while at the same time, in order to live at all, they take on the most menial occupation. So, Hitler painted his postcards and became a paperhanger, Chiang Kai-shek became a bartender and Lenin a proofreader." [34]

The lack of purpose in Mao's life left him exposed to drift with whatever currents came his way. He had just discovered the newspaper and it became the center of his existence. If there was anything the uncertain Mao respected at that critical juncture in his life, it was the power of the printed words he read in the Changsha newspapers. At that time Chinese society was beginning to adjust to the potentialities of the mass media; and although Mao was on the receiving side of the new technology of mass communications, the communications relationship between the future leader and Chinese society was being established. When we come to analyze Mao's role as political spokesman and ideologue, we will want to remember that the man who became so skilled in using the printed word to stir the emotions of a nation was once the boy who found in the mass media comfort for his emotions when he was in a state of uncertainty.

Mao read any newspaper in Changsha, but he was most excited by the segment which was most designed for personal appeal—the advertisements. As a young man adrift he seemed helplessly eager to be captivated by any appeals directed his way. We must not, however, exaggerate the idiosyncratic extent of Mao's interest in newspapers and advertisements, for, at that time in Chinese history, the very idea that there could be daily printed communications was startling to most Chinese of rural origins. The average Chinese felt there must be something special, endowed with both appeal and authority, in newspapers, and for Mao, their attraction was intense, possibly because he had no other diversions. We shall want to delay discussing the singular fact that the young Mao, at this time and for several more years, had no association with women or girls, but we need to note here that he was thus unaffected by the distractions that engage the psychic energies of most young men.

Mao is remarkably frank in describing how easily he was swayed by what he read in the newspapers. He was staying in a cheap rooming house and what little money he could borrow from friends he put into buying newspapers.[35] As he reports,

> I did not know exactly what I wanted to do. An advertisement for a police school caught my eye and I registered for entrance to it. Before I was examined, however, I read an advertisement of a soap-making "school." No tuition was required, board was furnished and a small salary was promised. *It was an attractive and inspiring advertisement* [italics added]. It told of the great social benefits of soap-making, how it would enrich the country and enrich the people. I changed my mind about the police school and decided to become a soapmaker. I paid a dollar registration fee here also.[36]

It was not entirely accidental that Mao was attracted by the police school, for he had apparently had some trouble with the military police during his army service.[37] Nor was soap-making so completely nonpolitical for he had read in Liang Ch'i-ch'ao that "the one thing which China needed to learn from the West was the importance of cleanliness and sanitation." [38]

However, neither of these choices held Mao's interest for long, for soon thereafter he was inspired by "an alluring advertisement of [a] law school, which promised many wonderful things." [39] A friend also pressured him to join the advertised school. ". . . finally I wrote to my parents, repeated all the promises of the advertisements, and asked them to send me tuition money. *I painted a bright picture for them of my future as a jurist and mandarin* [italics added]. Then I paid a dollar to the law school and waited to hear from my parents." [40]

This capacity to imagine himself at one moment a lowly policeman or soap-maker and the next as a high government official testifies to Mao's groping state of mind. Anything was possible, but there was no scale of preferences. Thus what was attractive on one day could be outdone by the appeals of the next. This was not an alienated individual, hostile to any established careers. He was willing to accept power and position if he could only decide what he wanted to be.

Yet before he followed through on the idea of law school, Mao says, "fate again intervened in the form of an advertisement for a commercial school." [41] The very way Mao tells of what happened makes explicit the extent to which he saw himself as a passive figure being manipulated by the alluring modern world associated with the media. Most Chinese would attribute such twists and turns to "fate" or "luck," but for a Mao Tse-tung, believer in historical materialism and the doctrine that "there are no accidents," to do so suggests the degree to which he had been at loose ends. Thus, the vision of being a mandarin gave way to another friend's argument that for China ". . . what was most needed were economists who could build up the nation's economy." [42] Yet, hardly had he enrolled in that school when he read another advertisement "describing the charms of a higher commercial public school." [43]

It is important to keep in mind that Mao's difficulties revolved around no more than the choice of high school, even though to him the problem was fundamental not only to his own future life but also to the well-being of his country. These frequent vacillations confirm that he was in a state of moratorium, and his search for a career in law, business and even soap-making suggests in its own way that the youth of Mao's generation was convinced that China must find its way into the essentially bourgeois modern world and escape from the decadence and purposelessness of China's declining Confucian traditions. To the extent that these possible choices of schools suggested any ambitions for himself or his country, they were that both would realize the ideals of what can only be called Western middle-class culture. Mao wished to be modern and he wanted even more for China to be able to stand up among the modern countries of the world.

Furthermore, the commercial school had additional appeal, for as Mao said . . . "[I] wrote to my father of my decision. He was pleased. My father rapidly appreciated the advantages of commercial cleverness. I entered this school and remained—for one month." [44] The reason for Mao's withdrawal was that most of the courses were taught in English and at the time he barely knew the alphabet. It is strange that at this point in Mao's life, given his personal commitment to modernizing his country, he did not do what most Chinese of his generation with similar ambitions did and try to learn English or another foreign language. Instead, Mao speaks of his lack of knowledge of English as an absolute given and not as a matter that might be altered by effort. Indeed, Mao's whole approach to the learning of English is most revealing, for in many ways he indicated that psychologically he wanted to grasp all that a command of English would have provided, but at the same time he did not want to expend the energy necessary to learn a new language or to forsake the one language he knew and excelled in, Chinese. He wanted to be a modernizer; but he did not want to acculturate to Western ways nor to humiliate himself in the eyes of others by being once again a "beginner." In time, Communism was to represent the unique solution he was seeking, namely, modernization without Westernization. Through Communism he could achieve moderni-

The Private Man

zation, which he first saw as coming from the West, without giving up his less cosmopolitan and more Chinese-rooted sense of identity.

Unable to cope with the English language commercial school, Mao, in an erratic shift in direction, abruptly enrolled in a highly traditional middle school where he devoted himself to learning classical Chinese and most of all enjoyed reading Imperial edicts and the commentaries of the great Chinese emperor, Ch'ien Lung. Anachronistically, he found a home in the world of traditional Imperial authority at its grandest and most incisive heights precisely at a time when that Imperial system had just collapsed and, of course, when he himself had just been a member of the Republican forces which stood against all that the old system represented. For a youth professedly looking for a career, this was an unlikely school; for an aspiring student who had denounced the Classics and admired only modern knowledge, his behavior was indeed unaccountable, except as an example of moratorium behavior. The reading of the Chronicles and the Ch'ien Lung Commentaries lasted six months, and after they were finished Mao found nothing more in the school that interested him.

Abruptly, then, he said:

. . . I left the school, and arranged a schedule of education of my own, which consisted of reading every day in the Hunan Provincial Library. I was very regular and conscientious about it, and the half-year I spent in this way I consider to have been extremely valuable to me. . . . During this period of self-education I read many books, student world geography and world history. There for the first time I saw and studied with great interest a map of the world. I read Adam Smith's *The Wealth of Nations*, and Darwin's *Origin of Species*, and a book on ethics by John Stuart Mill. I read the works of Rousseau, Spencer's *Logic*, and a book on law written by Montesquieu. I mixed poetry and romances, and the tales of ancient Greece, with serious study of history and geography of Russia, Armenia, England, France and other countries.[45]

Unquestionably, Mao's mind was expanded as he read such Western classics in translation, though one cannot judge just what he absorbed from it all. The search for knowledge, the compulsive drive that took him daily to the library at its moment of opening and held him there until closing time, and the sense that he was accomplishing much and finding great satisfaction in reading were all probably more significant for his personal development than were the particular ideas he came across in the books he read.

It was a way of acting with self-discipline at a time of aimlessness. It also strengthened his deep feelings of ambivalence about books. Clearly he had found here a means of escaping from his sordid surroundings, a way of putting aside his uncertainties over what he should do with his life, and a way to avoid all the problems he still had in dealing with peers. Books also gave him a sense of status—he was still a "student"—and books sheltered him from criticism. He read what he chose and did not have to be in any sense "tested" or react to challenges of others. Yet precisely for all of these reasons, and moreover because his apparent mastery of so many books was so easy, the experience in the Changsha Public Library must have strengthened his sense of self-assurance, and at the same time made him contemptuous of books. The experience consolidated a pattern in Mao's life: He would never again be far removed from books and whenever possible he would surround himself with them; yet at the same time he would freely denounce the utility of books and decry the abstract unreality of intellectual pursuits.

The six months that Mao spent in his self-imposed regime of daily reading also took his mind away from the vexing questions about what he should do with himself. He was still living at a guild hall for people from Hsiang Hsiang district so he was not entirely alone in the city. Indeed, it does appear that at this time Mao was becoming more adept in establishing male friendships, but he continued to have no contact with females. For the first time Mao tells of friends who influenced him and to whom he listened, rather than "friends" who did his bidding as had his younger classmates at school.

His living situation was not, however, entirely pleasant. The young men in the guild hall were divided between students, of whom Mao, of course, considered himself to be one, and soldiers, or ex-soldiers without jobs. "Students and soldiers were always quarreling in the guild house, and one night this hostility between them broke out in physical violence. The soldiers attacked and tried to kill the students. I escaped by fleeing into the toilet, where I hid until the fight was over." [46]

Mao's passive mood at this time was striking. Only shortly before he had been exhilarated by scenes of conflict at the time of the Revolution of 1911, and throughout his earlier years he had never been far from a fight. Even more striking, only a year or so later when Mao had finally committed himself to a normal school, he took the lead in organizing the students in physically resisting the occupation of their buildings by soldiers who were seeking quarters. His friend Hsiao San told Robert Payne:

> It often happens that soldiers will receive orders to take over colleges for barracks. Our own college received an ultimatum. Mao immediately sprang to its defense. He took charge as though he had received the sanction of the Ministry of War. He drilled the students and professors. His orders, even to the senior professors, were instantly obeyed. He sent out students to buy arms and medical supplies. We kept the soldiers out, and Mao remarked : "This is the first time I have taken military command." He seemed to know it wouldn't be the last. [47]

His need was not so much for authority but rather the need for an instantaneous response by others to his own feelings.

The difference in Mao's behavior during these two clashes between students and soldiers tells us something about the state of his "moratorium" at the two times. Also, when he returned to school he was again in a structured situation in which he was years older than his classmates and his teachers saw him as someone out of the ordinary.

Mao's period of intensive library reading came to an end partly because his father refused to send him more money for such activity. Economic realities and the need to leave the guild hall drove Mao back to reading advertisements. Mao reports, "Meanwhile, I had been thinking seriously of my 'career' and had about decided that I was best suited for teaching." [48] It is interesting that Mao arrived at this decision while in a state of suspension. He was not in a school setting at the time, and it was mainly pressure from his father that was driving him back toward school. He had not yet met a teacher who greatly inspired him, as he would later. Yet to the extent that Mao ever achieved a career identity outside of politics and revolution, it was as a teacher. He was to maintain that identity and reassert repeatedly his professional claim to being a teacher throughout his later years. After coming to power, educational policy became one of his special domains, and he has constantly projected himself into debates over educational matters. Although Mao's confidence in his own judgment was great in almost all matters, he always felt that he was especially qualified to talk about educational policies and practices—and consequently he often felt compelled to express shocking and unorthodox ideas, often as mere dictums without need for justification.

Having decided that his career should be teaching Mao

was attracted by an advertisement for the Fourth Provincial Normal School in Changsha. "I read with interest of its advantages: no tuition required, and cheap board and cheap lodgings." [49] Then Mao makes a very interesting confession which shows how far he was ready to go to make friends: "Two of my friends were also urging me to enter. They wanted my help in preparing entrance essays. *I wrote my intention to my family and received their consent* [italics added]. I composed essays for my two friends, and wrote one of my own. All were accepted—in reality, therefore, I was accepted three times. I did not then think my act of substituting for my friends an immoral one; *it was merely a matter of friendship*" [50] [italics added].

Not only did he not think the act immoral, but his experience seems to have made him contemptuous of examinations and academic requirements. In the light of what he did in the spring of 1913, we may be able better to appreciate what seemed to be a startling statement by Mao when he was seventy. At that time he told a conference of educators, "The students should be allowed to whisper to each other in an examination or to *sit for examinations under the names of other candidates* [italics added]. Since you have given the correct answer, it is a good thing for me to copy it. Whispering to each other or sitting for an examination under the names of other candidates *could not be practiced in the open in the past* [italics added]. This can be done now. It is all right for me to copy what you have written because I do not know the answer. We can try this." [51]

The fact that Mao on entering the normal school both sought to help friends and wrote to ask for his parents' permission suggests that he was emerging from his "moratorium" experience. His greater sense of self-assurance made it easier for him to relax with others rather than to terrorize them as he had done earlier.

In the fall of 1913 the Fourth Provincial Normal School was combined with the First and Mao found himself in the elite school of Changsha. The normal school was not a college or university, but it did have standards that put it above the usual high school or middle school. Its graduates were presumably qualified to teach not only at primary and secondary schools but also at middle schools.

Someone with Mao's intellectual capabilities should have had no trouble with the subjects taught at the First Normal School, but Mao had strong likes and dislikes, and what he disliked he did not do well. He said later,

> There were many regulations in the new school and I agreed with very few of them. For one thing I was opposed to the required courses in natural science. I wanted to specialize in social sciences. Natural sciences did not especially interest me, and I did not study them, so I got poor marks in most of these courses. Most of all I hated a compulsory course in still-life drawing. I thought it extremely stupid. . . . Fortunately, my marks in social science were all excellent, and they balanced my poor grades in these other classes.[52]

The mood of rebellion was still there, but Mao also showed constructive dimensions. He was ready to accept the influence of some teachers. His search for friendship continued. This took the form of Mao inserting an advertisement in a Changsha newspaper asking for "young men interested in patriotic work." [53] He was now prepared to be a leader who could attract to himself people of his own liking. Mao did not settle, however, for merely informal ties of friendship: he soon transformed his group of friends into a formal society, the

Hsin Min Hsüeh Hui or New Peoples' Study Association, which was to become a significant focus for student politics in Hunan with a national reputation. He was able to make the necessary adjustments to his surroundings to stay in school for five years and finally obtain his degree. The paradox should not be lost: The younger Mao seeking leadership needed to formalize relationships; the older Mao asserting leadership denounced all formalized relationships.

Possibly these may have been the happiest years of Mao's life. He was steadily achieving greater recognition. By the time he graduated he had found an enthusiastic patron in the most sophisticated and Westernized teacher in the school, Professor Yang Chen-ch'i, who was to sponsor him for a job at the library at Peking University, provide him with contacts with leading intellectuals of the country, and whose daughter was to be Mao's wife.

We have arrived at the point where we must ask about Mao's relations with women, and this means that we are ready to begin to complete the cycle of the private Mao by seeing what kind of a family he created when he moved from being a son to being husband and father.

CHAPTER

8

Wives and Children

ALTHOUGH there is scant
information about many aspects of Mao Tse-tung's life, the
most obscure area is probably that of his relations with women
and his role as father. We have already noted how he idealized
his mother, which we presume was his defense against not
being able to monopolize her affections. Within his family he
never had close associations with his sister and grew up primarily with male companionship. His early school years were
devoted to competition with classmates among whom he was
the biggest, strongest, and most ambitious boy in the class. At
the same time Mao had continuing health problems, and as an
adolescent he revealed anxieties over his own manliness and
his physical endurance.

While at the Changsha Normal School, Mao Tse-tung
surrounded himself with a group of intense, "serious minded"
boys who had "no time to discuss trivialities." Mao himself

has described his own earnestness and that of his friends and of how "they had no time for love or 'romance' and considered the times too critical and the need for knowledge too urgent to discuss women or personal matters." Mao bluntly stated:

> *I was not interested in women* [italics added]. . . . Quite aside from the discussion of feminine charm, which usually plays an important role in the lives of young men of this age, my companions even rejected talk of ordinary matters of daily life. I remember once being in the house of a youth who began to talk to me about buying some meat, and in my presence called in his servant and discussed the matter with him, then ordered him to buy a piece. I was annoyed and did not see this fellow again. My friends and I preferred to talk only of large matters—the nature of men, of human society, of China, the world, and the universe! [1]

Thus, it is Mao himself who points to the union between his lack of interest in women and his scorn for the practical details of living. The key to the linkage was his need to employ idealization that encouraged romanticism over abstractions of history and the human condition. His psychic energies, directed away from sex, focused on the use of words and the creation of social ideals. Instead of seeking the exhilaration of imagining himself the ideal and the hero in the mind of some particular girl, Mao at that time sought the emotional rewards of thinking of himself as a hero of history. Just as when he tried to express himself over his mother's death and had to employ idealization to make her a person of universal importance rather than of private attachment, so when Mao came to the natural age of interest in sex, he found it hard to focus on the particular, preferring the security of the general and the abstract.

Along with his denial of interest in sex the adolescent Mao took an enthusiastic, and even compulsive interest in body building and physical toughening. Engaging in what they called "body training," Mao Tse-tung and his friends tramped through fields and over mountains in the cold of winter and the heat of summer. They swam in cold waters in November, stripped away their clothes to run about in the rain, and slept on the open ground even after the frosts had arrived. This phase of being "ardent physical culturists" also involved scorn for personal grooming. Mao allowed his hair to grow longer than was customary at the time, his clothes were untidy, and his appearance unkempt. During these school years, and even more during the summer vacations when Mao and a friend wandered as vagabonds throughout the province, much as American youth hitchhike and backpack, Mao seemed to be trying to deny any element of the feminine in him. Adulation of the masculine and the physical permeates Mao's essay on "The Study of Physical Culture," which he wrote at this time and which became his first published article.

> Exercise should be savage and rude. To be able to leap on horseback, and to shoot at the same time; to go from battle to battle; to shake the mountains by one's cries, and the colors of the sky by one's roars of anger; to have the strength to uproot mountains like Hsiang Yu and the audacity to pierce the mark like Yu Chi—all this is savage and rude and has nothing to do with delicacy. In order to progress in exercise, one must be savage.[2]

This earnest romanticism about social and historical matters, humorless concern for great issues, contempt for private and practical concerns, wanting to test the body in the wilds of nature, hiking and camping, and seeking danger and discomfort, being conspicuously scruffy and of ungenteel appearance, and above all, of denying all interest in personal

romance and sex—this syndrome has been frequently manifest among late adolescents during different periods in Europe
and America. It was, however, unusual behavior for youth in
Central China in the second decade of the twentieth century.
Chinese culture was just beginning to evolve new norms to
match the new phenomena of boarding schools and colleges,
of dormitory life and of large numbers of boys and fewer girls,
living away from homes in a new peer group culture. These
exciting experiences made it possible for them to indulge
briefly in the illusion that they could in fact escape from the
otherwise all pervasive demands of authority of traditional
China. Among Chinese students there was equal craving for a
more vigorous, vital, and active style than the reserved Confucian tradition allowed and more idealistic, romantic aspirations than adult realities encouraged. The decay of the Confucian order evoked among young Chinese more than the
normal adolescent awe of both action and ideals.

From the time missionaries introduced boarding schools
and dormitory life there had been in Chinese student life an
unusually high incidence of idealistic appeals and moral uplift.
The state supported schools and colleges followed the missionary traditions of almost daily assemblies and ceremonies
of self-dedication and of assigning to teachers the obligation to
develop character among their students. Even the most secular
institutions did not separate intellectual and moral development. Peer group cohesion was generally so strong that any
teacher who sought to concern himself only with intellectual
instruction often found that he had little authority in the
classroom, while those who could appeal to the latent idealism
of the students were generally more accepted.

While Mao Tse-tung was still in school, the awakening
Chinese youth had not yet focused on the ideals of nationalism, as they did later after the shock of the Versailles settle-

ment in 1919 and the subsequent May Fourth Movement. During Mao's school days youthful idealism hovered between dreams of a new and more vital society, and wishes for more satisfying standards of private conduct among the liberated youth. More specifically, the new culture of dormitory life made it easier to legitimize abstract national ideals, which could be easily expressed as the search for power, progress and opposition to foreign infringements, than to define new norms for relations between the sexes. In most societies modernization in the social sphere has meant that an increasing proportion of the population accepts the social conventions of the most progressive elements of the small liberal components of the upper class. In China, however, the upper class that had broken from the taboos of tradition had not evolved new patterns of social life acceptable to the emerging modern educated classes. The end of Confucian proprieties had brought widespread corruption and immorality without creating a significant liberal-minded elite element.

The vanguard of modernizing Chinese youth thus continued to follow an innocent and essentially puritanical code of private conduct while asserting that they were being more free and unconstrained in their relationships. Both boys and girls insisted that they were ready to boldly make their own decisions, but almost invariably their choices still indicated modesty and limited freedom in sexual relationships. The sexless relationship of boys and girls in China, which caused worldwide comment after the Communists came to power, and which has been widely interpreted as a sign of revolutionary dedication, actually had its origins in the culture of university students of Mao's generation, and was firmly established by the late 1920s and early 1930s.

Mao Tse-tung thus belonged to the early generation of modernizing Chinese who wanted to fashion new styles of social life. They accepted the idea that women should be freed from the arbitrary restrictions of archaic custom and allowed to follow professional concerns. Their romantic ideal was individual choice in place of the parentally arranged marriage. Until marriage, however, there would be complete purity in relations, for as boys and girls had greater opportunities to mingle their conduct toward each other would be as brothers and sisters. The idealistic young Chinese seemed anxious to prove to the older, and in their minds corrupt, adult generation, that if they could be released from traditional constraints, which were premised upon assumptions about the universal weakness of the flesh, they would certainly rise above promiscuity and adopt higher and purer standards of sexual restraint than those of their hypocritical parents.

All of this is to say that much of Mao's behavior as a young man conformed with that of the trend setters of his generation of Chinese students. The spirit of the times favored earnestness and slighted romance; body building, physical culture, and the ethos of the YMCA were the preoccupations of student leaders. Yet, within the context of conformity, Mao's conduct was still distinctive, somewhat more extreme than average, and more inwardly guided than mere adherence to popular fashion would require.

He was conspicuous among his peers in being more unkempt and disheveled. Few went as far as he did in his wandering in the countryside, in sleeping under the stars, in being irregular in his eating habits. His essay on physical culture, which we shall have to examine in greater detail when we review his attitude toward power, clearly suggests that he made deeper emotional investments than most Chinese students in the ideals of physical development as the foundation of a new society. Finally, in both abstractly idealizing but actually avoiding women Mao went further than his student subculture required.

The total record of Mao's approach toward women, his capacity to ignore them, to use them, and to abandon them, seems to promise substantial confirmation of our initial suspicion of the nature of Mao's relationship to his mother. Since our interpretation of that relationship colors so much our understanding of how Mao became skilled in the use of affect but remained impervious to the demands of affect on himself, it is necessary to examine in some detail Mao's relations with the women he married and who bore his children. The theme of abandonment is important for confirming that we are near to discovering the core of his personality and the emotions of the private man that have shaped the public man.

The Abandoned Arranged Bride

In Mao's recounting to Snow of his lack of "interest" in women, he mentioned in the midst of his account of his idealistic fervor that when he was fourteen his parents, sensing his coming of age and planning for his future, contracted with another family for his marriage to a girl nearly six years his senior. According to Mao this contracted marriage was never consummated. Yet it existed and he had to repudiate it; thereby in a way he repudiated his parents, and this must have influenced to some degree his early approaches toward other women. We cannot ignore this event as casually as Mao says he did because the institution of arranged marriages profoundly colored the character of the modernizing Chinese youth culture and had far reaching consequences for nearly all who were ever involved with such arrangements.

The Private Man

One of the important reasons why modernizing Chinese youth upheld a puritanical model of sexual abstinence was that the traditional culture against which they were rebelling pressed for early marriage and the ideal of fecundity. Indeed, the root of the traditional Chinese fear of early promiscuity and abhorrence of the idea of "sowing wild oats" was the specter of a son's refusing ever to settle down to the obligation of extending the family line—once this duty was fulfilled the society could be tolerant of a husband who sought additional partners.

The rebellion by socially conscious Chinese youth against arranged marriages thus involved far more than just a desire for greater personal choice and a role for romance; it also was an expression of opposition to the parents' preoccupation with urging their children to assume as early as possible their obligations to maintain the family line. In Mao Tse-tung's case there must have been considerable pressure since his was not the customary arrangement made in early childhood which allowed for flexibility as to the time for the actual marriage. The girl to whom Mao was contracted was twenty years old; obviously it was expected that she would shortly be married and would bear children. It is not unlikely that Mao's parents calculated, as Chinese often did, that their obstreperous and rebellious son might be less difficult if he had a wife. Indeed, in all probability the issue of when Mao was to become a husband was involved, either explicitly or implicitly, in the clashes over Mao's decision to leave home for school.

Little attention has been given to the manner in which the institution of arranged marriages operated in China to preserve parental authority over sons and inhibit the emergence of more manly ideals. Most attention has been given to the ways in which the practice subjugated women, and unquestionably the arranged marriage helped enforce the tradition of the mistreated daughter-in-law by the aggressive and domineering mother-in-law, a tradition which insured the unjust treatment of Chinese women. (Indeed, the fact that the archetype of mistreatment of women rested upon an older woman's cruelty toward a younger woman—which meant that while every woman might have to suffer greatly she could, if she had a son, have her turn to dominate—shows the inappropriateness of applying to China Western concepts of women's liberation which presume that injustice stems largely from male behavior.) The arranged marriage was debilitating to men because it perpetuated the dependency of the son and prevented the Chinese male from breaking away from parental domination even when he had come of age. In most cultures the act of a man taking a wife implies that he is prepared on the basis of his newly found sense of identity to assume all the responsibilities of manhood, for to have and protect a wife is the most basic expression of individual autonomy. In traditional China the arranged marriage denied to the male his chance to realize psychic autonomy. Not only could he not assert himself in the quest for and conquest of a mate, he could not even defend the woman he was given. Indeed, the very act of marriage was a reaffirmation of the son's dependence upon his parents and not the achievement of a new state of independence. His inability to intervene in any way in the manifestly cruel treatment of his bride, his complete helplessness in defending her, meant that he was still seen by his parents, in a strange sense, as impotent.

For all these reasons it is likely that Mao's decision not to comply with the arrangement must have complicated his relations with his parents. On the other hand, Mao's feelings about marriage thereafter would be linked more strongly than ever to his feelings about his parents.

The Private Man

Mao's problem with breaking his arranged marriage could not have ended with his difficulties with his parents. There was also the question of his responsibilities toward the girl. He could not escape some awareness that his actions might have hurt a girl toward whom he had obligations according to tradition. Thus, just as he had abandoned the responsibilities inherent in the traditional Chinese role of oldest brother he now ignored the responsibilities his parents had arranged for him. In both cases he was attacking his parents' authority; in both he ignored what happened to others.

Many Chinese of Mao Tse-tung's generation sought to escape arranged marriages, and most had complicated psychological reactions of one kind or another. Some developed deep antipathies toward all customs associated with marriage and sought to go to the extreme of being "modern" and secular, rejecting any formal marriage ceremony and all personal pledges of obligations. Some took upon themselves responsibilities that far exceeded the traditional commitments of husbands, and endowed their self-chosen wives with ceaseless care and attention. Others found it easy thereafter to treat lightly subsequent marriage obligations.

A common method of dealing with the problem was to go along with the parents' plans, marry a designated girl, and then, while proceeding with school and career, marry somebody else of one's own choice. Sometimes the "city" or "modern" wife did not know of the existence of the "country" wife, but more often she did and accepted the situation as the inevitable curse of custom that would end with her generation. (At times there could be legal complications with respect to the division of inheritances and demands of the children by the different wives, especially if the children of the "country" wife got ideas about their father's obligation to give them an urban education and a modern life equal to that of their half brothers and sisters.)

To ignore completely the parents' arrangements, as Mao Tse-tung did, was a bold act, and also, to a degree, an inconsiderate one, for the girl, still living in her rural environment, may not necessarily have felt that she was "set free," but more that she was abandoned. Indeed, the girl must have suffered, for at that time in rural China an abandoned bride of her age would have little prospects for a new arrangement, and certainly not for a family as well off as the Mao family.

The death of Mao's mother at about this time undoubtedly made it easier for him to ignore the contract, and his father apparently accepted Mao's decisions without further protest. We can take greater confidence in our speculation about Mao's abandonment of his arranged-for bride when we examine the known facts about his behavior toward the three women who subsequently became his wives. With these women the themes of idealization and abandonment became pronounced.

The First Wife: Yang K'ai-hui

If the story of Mao's rejection of his arranged-for wife was one of challenging parental wishes, the paradox in Mao's first actual marriage is that his relationship with his wife-to-be began with his accepting her father as his own. Instead of shirking his responsibilities, Mao's marriage to Yang K'ai-hui a year after her father's death had almost the quality of repaying an obligation to a mentor.

There is no evidence to suggest that Mao Tse-tung had

any romantic relationship before his marriage to Yang K'ai-hui. Siao-yu has claimed that Mao was in love with a Tao Szu-yung, and that they had worked together to establish a bookstore in Changsha in 1920, but discovered that their political views were too divergent, and therefore she broke with him and went to Shanghai.[3] Whatever their relationship may have been it is interesting that it was, first, so closely folded into his political and career activities, and, second, the girl was the best female student of Professor Yang Ch'ang-chi, Mao's sponsor and the father of the girl Mao did in fact marry.

It is significant that Mao Tse-tung found his way to his first association with a woman and to love and marriage as a consequence of what is probably the only male relationship Mao has ever had with an older superior to whom he found it possible to show full deference and affection. Professor Yang Ch'ang-chi was able to give purpose and power to Mao's romantic idealism. The language that Mao has used to describe Professor Yang is the most outgoing and positive that he has ever used about a personal acquaintance:

> The teacher who made the strongest impression on me was Yang Ch'ang-chi a returned student from England, with whose life I was later to become intimately related.* He taught ethics, was an idealist, and a man of high moral character. He believed in his ethics very strongly and tried to imbue his students with the desire to become just, moral, virtuous men, useful in society. Under his influence, I read a book on ethics translated by Ts'ai Yuan-p'ei [Chancellor of Peking National University and patron of the introduction of the social sciences and Marxism into China] and was inspired to write an essay which I entitled, "The Energy of the Mind." I was then an idealist and my essay was highly praised by Professor Yang Ch'ang-chi, from his idealistic viewpoint. He gave me a mark of 100 for it.[4]

* Actually Mao married Yang's daughter after he died, yet he speaks of being "intimately related" as though he had known him as a father-in-law.

Although Mao takes care to note that he eventually moved beyond Yang's idealism when he became a Marxist materialist, he is remarkably generous in acknowledging that Yang was critical in advancing both his thinking and his activities. At Changsha Yang helped Mao in founding the Hsin Min Hsüeh Hui (New People's Study Society), which was Mao's greatest accomplishment as a schoolboy. Yang helped him to transform a group of friends into an organization of some sixty to seventy students from many towns. This was the first organizational activity Mao ever undertook and Professor Yang observed him as he earnestly demonstrated his skills and attracted numerous dedicated students from about Hunan, many of whom later gave their lives for Communism. Yang helped establish contacts with the *Hsin Ch'ing Nien (New Youth)*, the influential magazine edited by Ch'en Tu-hsiu, the founder and first leader of the Chinese Communist Party. In the spring of 1918 when Mao graduated, Professor Yang left Changsha Normal School to take a position at Peking National University. He encouraged Mao to follow him to Peking, and there he introduced Mao to Li Ta-chao, another founder of the Communist Party, who as Librarian at the University gave Mao Tse-tung his job as Assistant Librarian. At this stage Mao was dependent upon Professor Yang, and he accepted Yang's support as he had never accepted his dependency upon his father. There was much in his situation that he complained about, as he had when he was home with his father, but there were considerable advantages.

Physically, Mao's life was miserable at that time: He was paid eight dollars per month, only one dollar more than he had been paid as a common soldier eight years before; he shared a small room with seven other men all of whom slept on a single *k'ang*, or brick bed, where they were packed in so tightly that according to Mao's memory, they had to warn each other before turning over.[5] Yet, intellectually this was possibly the most exciting period in Mao's life for with Professor Yang's helping hand, he was moving towards the center of China's awakening intellectual life. He was, of course, still at the outer circle, and, as we have noted, acutely felt his marginal status.

The year 1918–19 Mao spent in Peking, and he discovered the ancient beauties of one of the great cities in the world. He enjoyed wandering through the parks and tree-lined streets.

> . . . . In the parks and the old palace grounds I saw the early northern spring. I saw the white plum blossoms flower while the ice still held solid over the North Sea (in Pei Hai). I saw the willows over Pei Hai with the ice crystals still hanging from them and remembered the descriptions of the scene by the T'ang [sic.] poet Chen Chang, who wrote about Pei Hai's winter-jewelled trees looking like "ten thousand peach-trees blossoming." The innumerable trees of Peking aroused my wonder and admiration.[6]

There would be little mystery in Mao Tse-tung's behavior if the story were merely one of a provincial boy receiving fatherly assistance from a respected teacher and thereby getting to Peking, succumbing not only to the charms of one of the world's most beautiful cities but also to the daughter of the sponsor. The ingredients for a warm but unexceptional story were all there. The mystery arises when it is remembered that the year 1918–19 was one of dramatic significance in the awakening of Chinese nationalism. The frustrations of Peking's student population were finally to break all constraints in May when the Versailles Peace Conference announced that Japan, one of the Allies, and not China, another supposed Ally, was to receive claims to all of the German concessions in China. The outburst of Chinese student feeling, summarized under the standard title of the May Fourth Movement, was one of the great events of the awakening of Asia and Africa. It completely changed the intellectual tone of Chinese student life. Mao Tse-tung was close to the most progressive people of the times when all of this happened, and yet his reflections and memories dwell on his own embarrassments of status, his physical circumstances, and, most unusual of all, his awe of traditional China and the stories of the past, not the drama of the present.

It is not clear how frequently or in what circumstance Mao saw Yang K'ai-hui during this year when they were both in Peking. Certainly, Mao frequently visited Professor Yang. He mentions, however, that during 1918–19 he "met and fell in love with Yang K'ai-hui," [7] who it is said was "very much like Mao's mother in looks." [8] By the spring of 1919 Mao was caught up with the organizational activities leading to the foundation of the Chinese Communist Party. Although extremely busy and active in student life, he seemed also isolated and outside of events, uncertain and indecisive about his own plans. He became involved with the program which sent Chinese students to France for study and work, a program by which France, alone of all the Western Allies, acknowledged some appreciation of China's contribution to the war effort against Germany, which had taken the form of sending to France workers to dig trenches. Mao wavered as to whether he should go abroad: In his autobiography he suggests that he was not tempted to go since he did not yet know his own country, but others suggest that he did seriously consider going. [9]

What is strange is that by late February or early March of 1919, Mao decided to leave Peking, and his new love, Yang K'ai-hui, and to travel alone, at great expense and suffering, to Shanghai to "see off" those friends who were going to France.

He tells of having only enough money to buy a ticket to Tientsin, where he obtained a "fortunate" loan from a fellow student whom he happened by chance to meet at the station. From Tientsin to Shanghai he left the train at various points in order to visit scenes of the old China and of the Confucian tradition which all of his peers were violently denouncing. He stopped at the grave of Confucius in the small town where the sage had spent his childhood, and a temple where Confucius was supposed to have planted a tree. Mao also left the train to visit the birthplace of Mencius and the home of another disciple of Confucius. In Shantung he interrupted his trip to climb T'ai Shan, the sacred mountain of traditional China. In the attitude of an admiring student of Chinese history he walked around the walls of Nanking and Hangchow, both famous in legends, the latter especially significant for Mao as the scene of significant actions in his beloved romantic history, the *San Kuo Chih* (*The Legends of the Three Kingdoms*). Thus at a time when his classmates were absorbed with the present, incensed with China's humiliation by the West, and passionately protesting what should be China's rightful future, Mao started a lonely trip, visiting the sites of the old China, the China that stood alone, before the coming of the West. During the journey Mao spent his last copper and even had his only pair of shoes stolen. But again "fortunately" he met outside a railroad station an "old friend from Hunan" who proved to be "my good angel" and "lent" him enough to finish the trip to Shanghai.

Mao's peculiar behavior and his odd state of mind were dramatized by his sudden return to Changsha, the scene of schoolboy serenity and successes, after his trip to Shanghai. Apparently, the work-study program in France had enough funds to pay for his trip back to his native province.

These events of a spring seem to reveal that Mao Tse-tung at that stage was still uncertain of his own purpose, but adequately self-assured to go his own way, unconcerned about practical matters. His basic sense of security was sufficient so that no matter what he did he believed he would be taken care of and that no great damage would come to him. He assumed his "luck" to be good. Yet the mystery remains: Why did Mao leave Peking and his beloved Yang K'ai-hui at this particular moment to tour the historic sites of China, a trip that he rationalized as going to "see off" some friends? All we know of his inner state of mind is his blunt statement that he was in love. He tells us nothing about Yang K'ai-hui's feelings toward him. Did she reciprocate his sentiments? Did she put him off? Or was he fearful that once again a woman might withhold love from him.

The matter of fact manner of Mao's statement of being in love tells us little because in Chinese culture it is not presumed necessary to elaborate on the development of sentiments. In traditional Chinese novels, for example, sentiments usually appear instantly and full-blown: the hero sees a "beautiful face" and is immediately consumed with love, a mere smile or even a glance is enough to explain profound passion. There seems to be little fascination in Chinese culture in tracing the ways in which one mood can give way to another, how sentiments can mingle and grow or die; and above all there is little tradition for examining how the feelings of one person can play on the emotions of another. Once the hero is declared to be in love then all attention is focused on the objective conditions—how can he socially arrange a meeting, will her parents agree to marriage—and there is usually no further discussion of the subjective realm.

In Mao's case we do know that his indigent circumstances in contrast to the well-to-do Yang family might have given him little expectation of marriage. Yet, on the other hand,

The Private Man

Professor Yang had been remarkably helpful and he obviously liked the bright young man from Hunan, and therefore it is unlikely that he would have stood in the way of marriage if his daughter and Mao wished it. Mao's behavior suggests an element of timidity in his first approach to love. Seemingly he could not be sure of her feelings, either because she actually had some reservations about him, or, more likely, because he found it exceedingly hard to overcome his fear of being damaged again by committing to another his emotions. We do not know whether he and Yang K'ai-hui even corresponded while he was away.

Back in Changsha, Mao threw himself into highly purposeful organizational activities. The governor was particularly brutal and actively sought to counter the wave of nationalistic sentiment that the May Fourth events triggered in Peking where thousands of students demonstrated against the decision at Versailles. Soon students from the capital scattered to all the provincial centers, and Mao was again absorbed mobilizing friends and students. The closing of the universities throughout the country provided large numbers of young people with both the enthusiasm and the time to engage in political demonstrations and discussions.

It was at this time that Mao struck the balance between writing and active organizational work that characterized much of the period of his rise to power in the Communist movement. He was equally successful in writing articles that attracted the attention of intellectuals and in assigning subordinates to organizational tasks. The warlord governor, Chang Ching-yao, became increasingly aware of Mao's activities, closing down in succession two journals Mao edited and banning the United Students Association which he had helped to form. General Chang called a meeting of student representatives in the fall of 1919 which Mao attended, and lectured to them to stay out of politics, screaming, "If you don't listen to me, I'll cut off your heads." When one of the girl students began to cry, Mao told her to "pay no more attention to Chang than to a dog barking." [10]

Continuing to believe in his charmed existence, Mao stepped up his clandestine organizational work during the rest of the year. Although at this time Mao's attentions were supposedly primarily focused on national political developments, it is significant that the subject into which he put his greatest passion was that of equal rights for women. When a young girl in Changsha committed suicide because her parents forced her into a marriage she opposed, Mao Tse-tung in an extraordinary outburst of energy wrote nine articles in thirteen days denouncing the old marriage customs and hailing the "great wave of freedom to love." [11]

One cannot but wonder to what extent Mao's apparent passion for justice was driven by a sense of guilt over the abandonment of his own arranged marriage. At a time when so many other issues called for the passionate attention of young Chinese, it is striking that Mao's focus was on the need for reforms in marriage. (It is also noteworthy that one of the first major areas of social reform Mao's regime implemented on coming to power was to reform marriage practice.) In any case, Mao's activities at this time succeeded in making him something of a romantic hero in the eyes of both activist boys and girls.

The winter of 1919–20 was a critical period in the emotional development of Mao Tse-tung. He had emerged from the drift of his "moratorium" into activism; he was less the solitary traveler of the previous summer who searched out the old while others were frantically looking for a new China. He was now in the center of action, directing others and focusing not only his own energies but also the emotions of others.

Above all there was boldness in his acts as he became a conspicuous risk taker. It seems evident that his feelings of narcissism were intense and provided him with tremendous energy.

All of Mao's frantic activities were being conducted in the name of politics; yet his one major creative performance of the period dealt with feelings toward women. The boy who had claimed to be "too serious" to have any "interest in women" had, at the moment when he first actually engaged in serious political activities, rather than just talking earnestly about them, suddenly started to "talk" about women. Behind this paradox lay Mao's mysterious behavior of the previous summer when he claimed that he had "fallen in love" but then promptly left the place of his beloved for an aimless trip. Then, instead of writing love letters to her, he poured his energies into writing a public proclamation of the importance and legitimacy of love.

Seemingly, the boy who had learned from his mother both the gratification of narcissism and the dangers of committing one's feelings to another was a man about to risk the attachment of his emotions toward another. Yet he could not proceed directly, so in a sense he tested out the consequences for his own emotions by writing in general terms about love. Again as with his mother he relied upon idealization of women. The result of his commitment on paper to the idea of love was a positive general response—his narcissism was gratified. From this time on, Mao Tse-tung was prepared to be more open in manipulating emotions, for he had learned that he could benefit in the public realm by writing about intensely private feelings.

In January 1920, when Mao was in the midst of these discoveries, Professor Yang died. In February Mao left Hunan and returned to Peking. The man who had provided the structure, the contacts, and the enthusiastic backing which had made it possible for him to find himself had suddenly abandoned him. In a sense he was again alone and unsure as to whether he could rely upon anyone without risking damage to his own feelings. At the same time, there were physical risks in staying in Hunan, for the governor was expressing increasing hostility toward Mao's activities. Mao's decision to go to Peking was thus a combination of a pull to see Professor Yang's bereaved family and the push of an increasingly threatening political situation.

Yet, what is extraordinary is that Mao only stayed in Peking until April. Most of Mao Tse-tung's biographies identify this brief, less than three months, period as a critical time in Mao's development as a dedicated Communist.* It was then that he first read in translation the *Communist Manifesto*, Kautsky's *Karl Marx's ökonomische Lehren* and a history of socialism by Kirkupp. Mao himself said that these three books ". . . deeply carved my mind, and built up in me a faith in Marxism, from which, once I had accepted it as the correct interpretation of history, I did not afterward waver. . . . By the summer of 1920 I had become, in theory and to some extent in action, a Marxist, and from this time on I considered myself a Marxist." [12] Mao had found a new authority figure to replace Professor Yang, the only authority he ever accepted. During that brief period in Peking Mao was also busily reading everything available about developments in Russia, contacting radical students and professors, and serving as the "head of a news agency" that promoted radical views. To have done all of these activities in only three months required extraordinary focusing of energies. Yet, his life at the time highlighted one of

* There is some confusion as to the precise dates of Mao's first and second visits to Peking. In Mao's account of his life to Edgar Snow he says that he made his second visit to Shanghai in 1919 when in fact it must have been in 1920 after his second visit to Peking. Schram and other biographers have identified this slip up on dates, and we are following their reconstruction of the sequence and dates of Mao's movements.

his most basic ambivalences: A tendency to escape into the loneliness and isolation of reading and a craving for action and the attention of younger students.

In this hectic period when Mao was already torn between withdrawal and action, he began seeing Yang K'ai-hui again, and for the first time there may have been the beginnings of a mutual understanding about the future. Professor Yang, having studied for some ten years in Japan, England, and Germany, had been an advocate of changes in Chinese sexual mores and especially of the rights of widows to remarry, and thus his family did not feel bound by the traditional Chinese prohibitions of contemplations of marriage during the period of mourning for a deceased father. Yet, the gap in economic circumstances remained, and clearly Mao Tse-tung was in no position to support anyone who did not share his casual view of risks.

For reasons that have never been satisfactorily advanced, in April 1920, at the very moment when he was intensely involved in finding a full professional and political identity, and when he was also concerned about a protector for the daughter of his deceased mentor, Mao Tse-tung suddenly decided to leave Peking again and to travel once more to Shanghai. On this occasion he also had severe problems financing the trip. He had to sell his only warm winter coat to buy a railroad ticket.[13] The conventional explanation has been that he wished to see Ch'en Tu-hsiu who had been at Peking National University, but because of his involvement in Marxist affairs had gone to Shanghai to seek the relative intellectual and political freedom of the International Settlement where Chinese authority did not reach. Mao has claimed that he discussed with Ch'en his "plan for a League for Reconstruction of Hunan," but why he felt he needed Ch'en's blessings for such plans when the personal costs were so high is not clear. If he had stayed longer in Peking, he would have continued learning more about Communism in a most exciting intellectual and political atmosphere. And, of course, he could have seen more of Yang K'ai-hui.

In bolting a second time from Peking and from his professed love, Mao appeared to have been responding more to psychological impulses than to political calculation. The suggestion that he might have gone to Shanghai on some mission for the Comintern is not convincing. He was not as yet identified by the Comintern agents as a trusted Communist, and furthermore if he were on official business he would have received financial backing. Edward Rice has shrewdly observed that it is utterly implausible that Mao would have accepted any such help because of his deep dislike of Chinese who allowed themselves to become subservient to foreigners.[14] When he arrived in Shanghai he was penniless and at no other time in his life did he live in such poverty. He finally found a job working in a laundry.[15] His situation was truly miserable; he had no friends; and he did not establish a close relationship with Ch'en Tu-hsiu.

Clearly, Mao was psychologically resisting both his career as a revolutionary and his first involvement with a woman. Objectively, he did have a problem in that the gap between her station in life and his was still unbridgeable as long as he was no more than a "radical student." Subjectively, however, he seemed unable to work out an arrangement that would even allow him to be in the same city with Yang K'ai-hui.

Significantly, it was not Mao who took the initiative to solve his problem but rather it was again a former teacher who became his benefactor, extracting him from his miseries in Shanghai and arranging for him to get a job, so that finally he could support Yang K'ai-hui in middle-class respectability.

Mao's fortune began to turn when his nemesis, General Chang Ching-yao, was driven out as warlord governor of his home province of Hunan. The new warlord, T'an Yen-k'ai, selected Mao's old teacher at the Changsha Normal School, I P'ei-chi, as his director of education, and he in turn appointed Mao Tse-tung to be the principal of the primary school attached to the First Normal School in Changsha. This was to be the highest and most substantial position Mao ever achieved outside of politics. By August of 1920 Mao had returned to Changsha and to a position that enabled him to support a wife.

Once again during that fall Mao was caught up in a flurry of activities. Picking up old friendships in Changsha from the previous year, Mao began busily organizing various groups. One was a Russian Affairs Study Group, which had the goal of sending students to the Soviet Union. Another was a Marxist study group, which in time became the key Communist cell in Hunan and sent Mao to Shanghai for the founding of the Chinese Communist Party. Again, as in the period from February to April, Mao combined reading, organizational work, and romance.

It is a commentary on the degree to which Mao's biographers have seen him more in terms of his intellectual and political development than as a full person that there is no agreement on exactly when he and Yang K'ai-hui were married. And no one seems astonished that historians have not resolved such basic matters in the vital statistics of one of the most written about men of modern China as the dates of his marriages and those of the birth of his children.

In speaking to Edgar Snow, Mao said that in "the summer of 1920 I had become, in theory and to some extent in action, a Marxist, and from this time on I considered myself a Marxist. In the same year I married Yang K'ai-hui." [16] Presumably this should resolve the matter for it is reasonable to assume that a man would know the year in which he was married. But even with this account there is the question of when in 1920. If it was when Mao was in Peking from February to April, then his behavior in going to Shanghai and working as a laundryman would be even more inexplicable. Furthermore, this would have meant that Yang K'ai-hui had married only two or three months after her father died when even the most modern of Chinese would still have been in some degree of mourning. It therefore seems, on the basis of Snow's account, much more likely that they were married in the fall or early winter of 1920, but this raises an awkward problem because Edgar Snow also says that their first child, Mao An-ying, was born in 1920.[17]

Most of Mao's biographers suggest that they were married in late 1920. Stuart Schram says that it was Mao's appointment to the post of principal which made " marriage possible in the following winter."[18] Donald Klein and Anne Clark follow this line of reasoning and say, "He won a post as head of the primary school attached to his alma mater and not long afterwards married Yang K'ai-hui."[19] Boorman says that "Yang K'ai-hui had returned to Changsha, and she and Mao were married in the autumn of 1920."[20] Han Suyin says that they were engaged early in 1920 when Mao returned to Peking, and married "that winter," (with Yang K'ai-hui and her mother returning to Changsha that spring even before Mao had left Peking for Shanghai). But then she says that the son An-ying was not born until 1929, only a year before K'ai-hui was executed.[21] Possibly to cope with the problem raised by the wide belief that An-ying was born in 1920 Robert Payne makes the most unlikely proposition that they were married in Shanghai when Mao was working in the laundry.[22] (Frequently Westerners do have difficulties trying to relate age to dates for Chinese because of their practice of counting their age as one *sui* at birth, and therefore when ages are given there is often uncertainty as to whether the counting is by the Chinese or Western method.)

To the extent that Edgar Snow tried to resolve the matter of the time of the marriage he says that: "Their marriage was celebrated as an 'ideal romance' among radical youths in Hunan. It seems to have begun as a trial marriage. . . ." [23] Possibly the most careful chronologer of Mao's life, Jerome Ch'en, solves the entire problem by ignoring Mao's statement of being married in 1920 and asserting that they were not married until October, 1921, and An-ying was born in 1922. [24] A personal and professional acquaintance of the time dates Mao's marriage as 1922 and the son's birth the next year, since he remembers that Mao was two hours late for an appointment for which he apologized, saying "I am late because I had to send my wife to the hospital." [24a]

The problem of the historian has been complicated by the practice of Mao and the Chinese Communists of following the Bolshevik tradition of denying the significance of private matters. In Mao's case, however, the problem is further complicated by the psychologically significant fact that the rhythm of Mao's vacillations between intense political and organizational activities and phases of withdrawal coincided with, and was not an alternative to, stepped up activities in his private sphere. All of the dates suggested by historians as to when Mao and K'ai-hui married were closely related to milestone developments in Mao's political life. Thus, although there is great disagreement among the historians, *all* of them place Mao's engagement or marriage at times when Mao was at a critical stage of increased political activity: when he was becoming a Marxist, or committing himself to secret, underground work and establishing cell groups, or had just participated in the founding of the Chinese Communist Party and was appointed Secretary of the Hunan Committee. No doubt one of the reasons why historians have tended to ignore dimensions of Mao's private life is precisely because of this extraordinary pattern in which the volume of his public activities always overshadowed any increase in his private activities.

The sum of it all is that we do not know when Mao was married. Nobody is aware that any ceremony ever took place. Legend supports the view that there was a romantic quality to Mao's marriage with K'ai-hui. For many young Chinese in the emerging circles of Communism the marriage was seen as a model of radical behavior since it blended free choice with mutual dedication to the larger political cause.

The view that there was something special and romantic in the relationship was also greatly strengthened when in 1957, twenty-seven years after her execution, Mao wrote a poem to a widow commemorating the death of her husband, who was surnamed "willow," and that of Yang K'ai-hui— Yang means "poplar." Entitled the "Immortals," the poem begins with the lines:

> I lost my proud poplar,
> And you your willow.
> Poplar and willow soar lightly
> To heaven of heavens.

One feature in the deification of Mao Tse-tung in the 1960s was the image of Yang K'ai-hui as a revolutionary worker at Mao's side. According to some of these accounts K'ai-hui accompanied Mao during the decade of the 1920s when he was busily traveling about to Shanghai, Wuhan, and Canton.[25] On the other hand, the evidence of the time shows Mao to have been alone on these trips and that this was when the children were probably born and K'ai-hui had to be at home. It seems more likely that Mao and K'ai-hui were together for only a little over two years during the entire period from 1921 to her execution in 1930. The conventional histories all suggest that Mao was not accompanied by his wife as he increasingly moved among the centers of Party activism. Immediately after participating in the founding of the Chinese Communist Party in Shanghai in the summer of 1921, Mao returned to his work as secretary of the Hunan branch of the Party. He enlisted his two brothers to help him organize the workers in the Anyuan Mining Company. His time was also taken up working with Li Li-san who had just returned from France and Liu Sh'ao-ch'i who was now back from the Soviet Union, men who were to become prominent in the development of Chinese Communism and with whom he was later to break all relations. By April of 1923 Mao had to leave Hunan for fear of being arrested and seek the security of the International Settlement of Shanghai. Yang K'ai-hui was then pregnant with their second son and did not accompany him. In Shanghai he succeeded Chang Kuo-t'ao (another comrade he was later to break with) as head of the Organizational Department of the Chinese Communist Party. Although he was rising in Party ranks and had become a member of the Central Committee and held a responsible administrative post, Mao Tse-tung was not happy in Shanghai.[26] The members with whom he dealt were either better educated or had had experience abroad. He did not enjoy the responsibilities of administrative work, and so, near the end of 1924, he pleaded illness and returned to his home in Hunan.

He had been away from his wife for nearly a year and a half. Leaving Shanghai just in time to miss the Fourth Party Congress, Mao returned to what seemed to have been his first love in Party work, direct organizational work among peasants, but he was nonetheless depressed about his political future. Back in Shanghai in January, 1925, Mao was voted out of the Politburo. This was the one time in his life when he was not intensely involved and was also close to his wife. It was, as Mao has called it, a "period of rest." But in four months Mao was restless again. He stayed with his wife only until the end of May, 1925, when he again left home to engage in extensive rural investigation in Hunan. His activities again attracted the attention of the authorities and by July he once more had to flee, but this time it was to Canton where he served as *de facto* head of the propaganda department of the Kuomintang and as director of the Peasant Movement Training Institute. The latter organization was devoted to instructing rural cadres in political and military skills. Mao was appointed the secretary of the Propaganda Department of the Kuomintang and later he became the deputy head of the Department. Although still a dedicated Marxist, he was recouping his political fortunes by advancing himself in the Kuomintang organization with which the Communists were at that time joined in a United Front.

In December, 1925, Mao returned to Shanghai, ostensibly to agitate against the governor of his home province of Hunan, but also to strengthen his Communist Party ties. Although he briefly returned to Canton from February to March, he went back to Shanghai in March to head the Peasant Department of the Party. He remained in Shanghai until August of 1926 when he returned to Hunan, not to live at home but rather to rove about the countryside, as he had done as a schoolboy, investigating rural conditions. In January of 1927, Mao published his famous report on the peasant movement in Hunan.

There is some uncertainty as to whether Mao ever saw Yang K'ai-hui again after he left for Canton in July of 1925. According to Red Guard materials they did see each other in 1926 after Mao returned to Hunan from Shanghai, and indeed

K'ai-hui gave birth to a third son, Mao An-lung, in 1926. Most accounts of Mao's life, however, stress how busy he was traveling about the countryside during 1926 and 1927, serving as chairman of the All-China Peasants' Union, leading the disastrous Autumn Harvest Uprising and finally in October, 1927, escaping into a mountain guerrilla base at Chingkangshan. Even while becoming deeply involved in Party life and fierce political conflicts with the authorities, he continued to assume that his ancestral home was a safe haven where he could leave his family in peace and security. While learning that public affairs and revolutionary success called for deception, the use of force, intense dedication and unrelenting opposition to the foe, he continued to assume that peace would prevail in his childhood village. Even when he had to flee the province, he did not feel any need to take his wife and children with him. Mao's sense of his own ultimate invulnerability caused him to slight any possible threats to his family. Although in his propaganda Mao portrayed the governor as vicious, he apparently never imagined that he would hurt the wives and children of his enemies. In some respects his feeling of responsibility toward his wife and children was similar to his treatment of his brothers and sister. He rejected the conventional Chinese rules of responsibility, seemed impervious to the fact that his activities might endanger them, and when they finally did suffer because of him, he saw it as proof of his own destiny.

In contrast to the stern abstinence of the youthful, pre-marriage Mao, after marriage he did become more interested in women and sexual activities. Edward Rice notes that while Mao undoubtedly loved Yang K'ai-hui, "It should not be assumed, however, that his love for her had caused him to lead a monogamous existence or that Communism was for him a religion which enabled him to sublimate his sexual drives." [27] As Party work more and more took the form of military activities, there seems to have been an increasing tendency for the close associations of men and women to lead to sexual relations. A former officer talks of how Mao showed great interest in the girls in his command, made suggestive remarks about them, and asked what the officers' relations were with them; and then when the officer tried to explain that they were all busy people and that feelings of love between males and females did not arise, Mao remarked that the officer was of course a younger man and that he, Mao, was old enough so that feminine beauty always produced "voluptuous feelings" in him.[28] Mao then smiled mysteriously. Although the Communist code of conduct stressed the modern Chinese youth culture's ideal of purity in boy-girl relations, many of the post-adolescent comrades did take "revolutionary sweethearts" when separated from their wives.

It was therefore not exceptional that Mao Tse-tung, two years before Yang K'ai-hui was to be executed, started sharing his bed with another girl who became his second wife.

Before continuing with the story of Mao's second marriage and his role as father, it is well to summarize certain factual matters about his first marriage to Yang K'ai-hui.

Mao did not have any serious romantic relationship with a woman until he was twenty-seven or twenty-eight.

His initial involvement with a woman required the legitimization of intense political activities. He married a girl who was considerably above him socially. (Yang K'ai-hui not only came from a wealthy and cultured family, but she received a substantial inheritance when her father died.)

When all was going well for Mao he had prolonged periods away from his wife; but when he was depressed he did return to her.

His wife was beautiful, popular, and supposedly looked much like his mother.

He took high risks with the security of his wife and sons, and in the end there was a quality of abandonment in his behavior toward them.

The Second Wife: Ho Tzu-chen

In 1927 Chinese Communist fortunes rose to the point that the leaders believed that national power might shortly be theirs, particularly after the government in Canton was moved to Wuhan on the Yangtze. But then suddenly all was shattered as the alliance with the Kuomintang was destroyed, and Chiang Kai-shek turned against them. Their armies tried to conduct further campaigns, the Autumn Harvest Uprisings, but they failed. Mao Tse-tung was assigned the duty of directing some of these operations in Hunan and Kiangsi. He promptly informed the Party Center that he was going to violate their political line by confiscating and redistributing land, dispensing with the Kuomintang flag, and promulgating the need to establish worker-peasant-soldier soviets—all of which ran directly contrary to the Comintern's policy of trying to continue cooperation with the Kuomintang and not frightening off moderate elements with revolutionary proposals. Mao also in a strange way chose to violate Party instructions by relying mainly upon military forces and not focusing on peasant mobilization—strange in the sense that most of his political career had been given to organizing peasants and not to military affairs.

When Mao both disobeyed orders and failed in his operations, he was censured by the Party and removed from all his Party posts, including membership on the Central Committee and alternate membership on the Politburo. Taking his remnant forces of approximately one thousand men he sought out the security of a mountain base along the border between Hunan and Kiangsi near a mountain named Chingkangshan.

Demoralized by this retreat and struggling to rebuild his forces, Mao Tse-tung met a high school girl whose father owned a bookstore that sold radical publications in a nearby town. Ho Tzu-chen was the branch secretary of the local Communist Youth Corps which Mao himself had helped to organize. They met in June, 1928. Kung Ch'u was told the following story by one of Mao's aides who was present:

> The Chairman convened a conference of Party and league members in Yunhsin to discuss the expansion of the Party and the Soviet movement. This female comrade did most of the talking and had many ideas. After the meeting disbanded at 11 P.M., Chairman Mao invited Comrade Ho to stay behind for a few minutes, saying that he had important matters to discuss with her. That night Comrade Ho and Chairman Mao talked alone for a long time. The next day, Comrade Ho came again and assisted Chairman Mao in his work for the whole day and did not go home that night. They got up at nine o'clock the next morning. After washing, Chairman Mao said to us with delight: "Comrade Ho and I have fallen in love. Our comradely love now has become the love between husband and wife. This is the starting point of our common life." . . .[29]

This brisk and open beginning of Mao's relationship with Ho Tzu-chen, who was also called at times Ho Shih-chen, dramatizes the differences in his approach to the two women. He had been very tentative in courting Yang K'ai-hui; he was awed by her father, anxious to prove himself in his eyes, but also competitive in seeking to be his superior in their involvement with modern currents; he was unwilling to suggest marriage until he was either able to support her or had become a reasonable success in his career as a revolutionary; and while his pursuit of her corresponded to the rhythm of his political activism he made a clear division between his public and his private life as long as the latter involved Yang K'ai-hui. His relationship with Yang K'ai-hui was in some way or other deeply affected by his relations with her father: Either his positive feelings for the father made him sense an obligation for the daughter—which turned out not to be deep enough to insure her security—or he needed to assert himself against the socially and intellectually more respectable Professor Yang by claiming his daughter and then leaving her.

With Ho Tzu-chen the relationship was direct, and her role was entirely functional to his work. Mao saw her as directly linked to his professional activities, a woman with whom he could share his career concerns, but also a person without a clear identity of her own. Her work and her concerns were entirely his. During the six years that Mao sought his political and military fortunes in the Kiangsi mountains, Ho Tzu-chen was always near him physically, and the situation did not call for the periods of prolonged separation as with Yang K'ai-hui.

Among the comrades in the Kiangsi base area Ho Tzu-chen was thought of as Mao's only wife, for few Party people had ever known Yang K'ai-hui. When Mao began living with Ho Tzu-chen he was thirty-five and a leader; and she was only eighteen, yet she was still a revolutionary in her own right. She was entirely committed to being constantly at his side, throwing her insights and ideas into the advancement of his position. In fact, she was to him the completely selfless revolutionary helpmate that the Red Guard materials of the 1960's claimed that Yang K'ai-hui had been. That idolatrous propaganda not only completely ignored the existence of Ho Tzu-chen because Mao was later to divorce her, but also it transferred to Yang K'ai-hui Ho's highly politicized and supportive manner of working with Mao Tse-tung.

Ho Tzu-chen gave much support to Mao as he emerged as the leader of the Kiangsi soviets. Yet as she began to bear Mao's children she became less the radical activist and more a conventional wife. While still in Kiangsi she had three daughters by Mao.* Kung Ch'u tells of seeing Ho Tzu-chen shortly before the Long March began, holding an infant child in her arms, and remarked that she "had changed from an idealistic and dynamic girl to a quiet housewife." [30] The first two baby girls had already been given to peasant families to raise because at the time of their births Ho was too busy working with Mao to take care of them. The third infant was also given away because it was felt that she could not be taken on the Long March. When the Long March began, it was natural that Ho Tzu-chen should have been one of the thirty-five women to accompany the nearly one hundred thousand men, even though she was again pregnant. From a picture of her taken at about the time of their marriage Edward Rice describes her as "a girl of lively but delicate beauty whose appearance suggests

---

* Mao's biographers are vague and contradictory as to the precise number of children Mao had by Ho Tzu-chen, and official Chinese sources are of little help because Ho had become essentially a nonperson after Mao divorced her. All biographers who make any mention of Mao's children by Ho agree that all except the last were given away in Kiangsi and during the Long March. Snow in his revised 1968 edition of *Red Star Over China* states that Mao and Ho had two daughters in Kiangsi who were left in the care of "Red peasants" and were never found, and that they had a third in Shensi (p. 468). On the other hand, Nym Wales reports that Chu Teh's wife told her that the baby in Yenan was Mao's fifth. (*Yenan Notebooks*, Madison, Conn.: By the author, Mungertown Road, 1961, p. 48.) Since there is no way of judging whether Chu Teh's wife knew about the two or three children Mao had by Yang K'ai-hui, many scholars have assumed that she probably meant that there were five born to Ho Tzu-chen. All that can be firmly said is that there were either two or three daughters left in Kiangsi and one or two born after the Long March began. For the purpose of our narrative I have assumed that there were five daughters since that is the number used by several of the leading Mao biographers. Our psychological interpretation of Mao is in no way affected by whatever number of daughters he had by Ho.

that she had been gently bred." [31] During the Long March Ho was severely wounded, eighteen to twenty pieces of shrapnel having pierced her body.[32] By the end of the Long March she had become, according to another photograph, "a woman whose clothes hung on a frame that was scarecrow thin." [33] Their fourth daughter was born during the march, and was immediately given to a peasant family. Finally, shortly after arriving in Yenan Ho Tzu-chen had her fifth daughter. Her health never recovered nor did she ever regain her beauty. Mao began to show interest in other women, and in 1937 he took Chiang Ch'ing as his third wife. Ho Tzu-chen was sent to Moscow for "prolonged treatment for what was described as a nervous disorder." [34] Reportedly after the Communists came to power, Ho Tzu-chen was brought to Peking, given modest quarters and a routine and undemanding position. Other reports say she never returned from Russia.

There is evidence that during the Long March Mao and Ho had grown apart. Mao's orderly, a boy by the name of Chen Ch'ang-feng, has described his daily routines with Mao throughout the Long March, and he does not make any mention of Ho Tzu-chen's presence. The boy claims he did all the cooking and washing for Mao, and that Mao would work late into the night, a lonely figure with pen and books.[35]

The breakup of Mao's marriage to Ho Tzu-chen was acrimonious, and the cause of some scandal in Yenan. The Party leaders were nearly unanimous in opposing his divorce. There have been reports that Chou En-lai was one leader who took a tolerant view of Mao's preferences, and it was out of this sympathetic support that the close relationship between Mao and Chou originated. Another was K'ang Sheng, head of the Party's Central Intelligence Department, who introduced Chiang Ch'ing to Party membership.

Evidence of the bitterness of Ho Tzu-chen on being

abandoned is to be found in an account by Yang Tzu-lieh (Madame Chang Kuo-t'ao) who tells in her recent memoir about meeting Ho Tzu-ch'en in the office of the Eighth Route Army in Sian, just before Ho went to Moscow in September–October, 1937. Yang was on her way to Yenan to reunite with Chang Kuo-t'ao after almost ten years of separation:

> A female comrade was lying in bed. When she saw me enter, she quickly got up. She was thin, worn out and pale. She was of medium height and looked weak and shy. Ying-ch'ao (Chou En-lai's wife) introduced her to me:
> "This is Comrade Ho Tzu-chen, Chairman Mao's loved one." . . .
> I got up the next morning together with Ho Tzu-chen and we began to talk. . . . (I asked),
> "Why do you stay here and not return to Yenan?"
> "My health is poor and I hope to go to Moscow to cure it."
> "Since you can not depart for some time, you do not have to stay here. Let us go to Yenan together."
> "I am not going back to Yenan. Tse-tung is not good to me. We quarrelled and fought. He picked up a bench and I picked up a chair. Aye! He and I are finished!" she sighed.
> Sometime later Liu Chung-hsien told me secretly: "Lan-ping made herself up very pretty and Old Mao was very attracted to her. Tzu-chen was jealous and so they quarrelled often. . . ." [36]

According to Edgar Snow's former wife Nym Wales, who was present in Yenan at the time, Ho Tzu-chen charged that the "star actress of Yenan, Wu Kuang-wei or Lily Wu had 'alienated her husband's affections.' " [37] Nym Wales reports an occasion in Agnes Smedley's cave in Yenan when Lily Wu, professing to have drunk too much sat by Mao and held his hand, thereby proposing a degree of intimacy inconsistent with the morality of Party leaders. Later Lily Wu and also Agnes Smedley were asked to leave Yenan at the insistence of

Ho Tzu-chen. In Nym Wales' words, "Mao was the type of man (and in the prime of life—age forty-four in 1937) who especially liked women, but not ordinary women. He liked a feminine woman who could make a home for him (as Ho Tzu-chen did well), and he appreciated beauty, intelligence and wit, as well as loyalty to himself and his ideas." [38]

According to a onetime senior official in the "Democratic Alliance," Chow Ching-wen, who left China in 1959:

> Mao Tse-tung himself perhaps set the example for others to follow [marrying girls of non-proletarian background]. He married four times. [Presumably he was counting the arranged marriage.] His fourth wife is Lan-ping. When Mao first saw her in Yenan, he was so infatuated with her that he used to carry a small lantern and visit the leaders of the CCP in the middle of the night and say, "without Lan-ping, I cannot go on with the revolution." . . .[39]

Mao was to have his way: The Party leadership had no alternative to accepting his divorce of Ho Tzu-chen and his marriage to Chiang Ch'ing when Mao told them that his new love was pregnant. At this point, as so often in the past, Mao's peers had to yield to his will because he had demonstrated a willingness to carry an issue beyond the point of their resolve. According to accounts a stern session was held at which there was blunt talk and a deal was struck. His colleagues agreed that Mao might divorce Ho Tzu-chen and send her off to Moscow, as was his wish, but he was not to bring Chiang Ch'ing into any public roles or to allow her to be a force in Party affairs. After the regime was established in 1949 it was decided that Liu Shao-ch'i's wife, Wang Kuang-mei, would occupy the public role of ranking hostess of the Communist movement; and it all came out into the open in the mid-1960s during the Cultural Revolution that Chiang Ch'ing was deeply embittered by her enforced seclusion and angrily resented Wang Kuang-mei's monopolizing the limelight among the wives of the senior Chinese officials.

The Third Wife: Chiang Ch'ing

Unquestionably, Chiang Ch'ing was brighter, more sophisticated, and more ambitious than any of the other women in Mao's life. She came from an exceedingly poor rural family named Luan in Shantung province and tragedy occurred early in her life when her father died. Her mother took her back to her own family where she assumed the maternal grandfather's surname of Li. Accounts differ as to how Li Yun-ho left her home while still in her early teens, but they all agree that she had an early commitment to the theater, and that she adopted the stage name of Lan P'ing. In time she was accepted at the Provincial Experimental Drama Academy and attracted the attention of one of the leading teachers. Then, in almost identically the same sequence as in Mao Tse-tung's story, her teacher left the school to accept a university appointment, but he arranged for her to follow along and got her a job as assistant in the university library.[40] She thereafter had repeated love affairs, and moved on to Shanghai where she had some minor parts in several movies. Late in 1934 or early in 1935 she married another actor named T'ang Na. Reports are that as she became professionally prominent he became depressed, once attempting suicide.[41] In 1937 when the war with Japan broke out and fighting erupted in Shanghai, Lan P'ing fled first to Hankow, then to Chungking, and finally to Sian and Yenan. In Yenan she changed her name to Chiang Ch'ing and aggressively sought the attentions of Mao Tse-tung in competition with another actress, Lily Wu, and some of the leading female intellectuals. Li Ang describes Mao with his long hair and unkempt appearance as having a strong physical appeal for actresses and intellectuals, including such writers as Ting Ling.[42]

Mao is generally believed to have had two daughters by Chiang Ch'ing. The first was known in childhood as Li Na, a name some people believe to be a combination of Chiang Ch'ing's adopted name and her first husband's name, but now she is said to go by the name of Hsiao Li. The second daughter's milk name was Mao Mao, but at school age she took the name of Li Min.*

The relationship between Mao and Chiang Ch'ing remained highly private for nearly thirty years in accord with Mao's agreement with his Politburo colleagues. The Party officially ignored Mao's marriage. She did not appear in public with him and she was not present when the wives of the other leaders gathered. Then, in the explosive drama of the Cultural Revolution, she became a central figure in both the ideological and power struggles.

Thus while Chiang Ch'ing's marriage with Mao began entirely as a private matter, as was his marriage to Yang K'ai-hui, it was to become an open political arrangement of far greater significance to the Party than his collaboration with

---

* Roxane Witke has told me that Chiang Ch'ing informed her that she had only one daughter by Mao and that the other girl was the daughter Ho Tzu-chen took to Moscow with her. According to this account Chiang Ch'ing brought up Ho's last daughter by Mao when her mother was no longer fit to look after her. If this is true it makes Chiang Ch'ing's relations with Mao even more puzzling. Jerome Ch'en, a principal biographer of Mao, has identified Mao as having two daughters by Chiang Ch'ing; so has Mao's former bodyguard, Chai Tso-chun; and Donald Klein and Anne Clark say, "Chiang had two daughters by Mao, both of whom were living at home in 1957. According to a former classmate, one of the girls was a third year student in the history department of Peking University in 1959 but left school the same year." (*Biographical Dictionary of Chinese Communism*, p. 678).

the Party worker, Ho Tzu-chen. It is a strange paradox that while Mao rejected his first marriage, which conformed to the pattern of the traditional peasant's planned arrangement, his last marriage was eventually molded into the stereotype of the traditional Chinese ruler's, in which the consort wielded inordinate power from behind the throne and created great crises of state because of her willfulness and her envious rivalries. During the years of her obscurity Chiang Ch'ing apparently developed a gnawing animosity toward Wang Kuang-mei, the charming, well-educated wife of Liu Shao-ch'i who served in public as China's first lady. During the Cultural Revolution Chiang Ch'ing viciously denounced Wang Kuang-mei and asserted: "When Liu Shao-ch'i was opposed to me in Yenan, he actually pointed the spearhead at Chairman Mao." [43] Thus, in time, Chiang Ch'ing reversed the relationship between public and private motivations, suggesting that instead of her private feud with the Party leaders affecting public events, it had been their political opposition to Mao that had forced her into a demeaning position. She passionately sought for a public role, and Mao was ready to collaborate fully in giving his wife a base of political power and to accept that his relationship with her had become essentially political.

Yet, even during the Cultural Revolution, and more conspicuously since, Mao has shown that he was not an unqualified political backer of his wife. In post-Cultural Revolution politics, especially since the fall of Lin Piao as Mao's chosen successor, Mao's support has gone more to the policies of his elderly colleague Chou En-lai and in several instances he has directly opposed both the policies and the political interests of Chiang Ch'ing.

There is considerable evidence that the aged Mao's relationship with Chiang Ch'ing is not that of intimate companionship and that at the personal level he has in fact abandoned her as a wife: In recent years they have not appeared in public together; they do not appear to share the same domicile; available samples of their correspondence suggest that Mao feels a need to instruct her in much the same manner as he would guide the behavior of a considerably subordinate official. On April 12, 1967, during the Cultural Revolution, in a speech to the enlarged meeting of the Central Military Affairs Committee Chiang Ch'ing described Mao's relationship with her in terms which hardly seemed to be those of husband and wife:

> The Chairman has always been strict with me. He treats me first and foremost as my strict teacher. To be sure, he does not coach me literally by holding my arms as some others do. But he is very strict with me. Many things are unknown to me. The Chairman as a person, I think, you comrades know more than I do. We live together but he is a man with few words. Sometimes he talked and would comment on politics, economics, culture, international and national affairs, almost anything under the sun.[44]

Mao for his part has been conspicuously silent about Chiang Ch'ing's political emergence, and has not particularly championed her interests. Indeed, he has cooperated with her political enemies. In one of his few references to her he told a Party gathering which was hostile to her views that they "could take Chiang Ch'ing" and he would go back into the mountains and raise a new Red Army and fight back to power. The statement was a direct threat, but the suggestion also brought to mind the fact that Mao could speak of abandoning Chiang Ch'ing in the same breath as he mentioned living in a mountain retreat—as he had done with Ho Tzu-chen.

Mao Tse-tung as Father

Mao Tse-tung's relations with his third wife are consistent with his manner of dealing with his comrades, a matter we shall come to in discussing Mao the public man. Instead of pursuing further the details of his relations with Chiang Ch'ing, it is appropriate now to return to the question of Mao's behavior as a father. Just as Mao's approach toward women reveals much that confirms the hypotheses about the nature of his relationship with his mother, so his conduct as a father helps to clarify the real character of his relationship to his own father. And the combination of these relationships tells much about the manifestations of affect in Mao's personality.

By the women he has lived with Mao Tse-tung has fathered seven to ten children: two and probably three sons by Yang K'ai-hui; three or five daughters by Ho Tzu-chen, two or four who were left with peasant families and one who was taken to Moscow with her mother; and probably, but not certainly, two daughters by Chiang Ch'ing.

The lack of precise information about the number of Mao's children reflects in part the Chinese Communist style of down playing the importance of the children of all high officials. This practice is more exaggerated in China than among the Russian Communists, who started it, in some measure precisely because Mao himself wanted it that way. Mao has on several occasions described the misfortunes of his own children not as tragedies but rather as providing him with the right to demand that others also sacrifice their children for the revolution.

The sad events began with the fate of his only sons after

Yang K'ai-hui's execution in 1930. At that time the oldest boy, Mao An-ying, was either eight or nine, the second, Mao An-ch'ing, was a little over a year younger; and if there was a third son by the name of Mao An-lung, he would have been only four. Whether this youngest boy ever existed or not— and it seems unlikely that his existence would have been purely imagined by the Red Guards—it is certain that he was completely lost to his family and history as soon as his mother was arrested. Presumably whoever took care of him decided to maintain forever the secrecy of the adoption.

There is considerable uncertainty as to what happened to the two older boys. According to one report An-ying and An-ch'ing were imprisoned with their mother, but a relative arranged their release and took them to Shanghai to the Party Headquarters.[45] According to another Red Guard publication it was the Party which devised ways and means to secure release of the boys.[46] The boys were taken to Shanghai, but then either because Mao was out of favor with the Party officials at the Center or because the "underground organ of the Party had been destroyed at the time" [47] the children were left on the streets to make out as best they could. Living in alleys and doorways, and "picking garbage" they somehow survived for nearly seven years.

A third Red Guard version by Tung Lin says that the three boys were with their grandmother after K'ai-hui's execution, and Mao sent a letter by an underground Party worker instructing that they should be sent to Shanghai. They were escorted on the trip by an uncle named Li Chung-te.[48] They were taken to a wine shop which was an underground office of the Party. Possibly sensitive to the apparent unconcern of Mao for his sons, Tung Lin claims that "although Chairman Mao was very busy" he went to see them for a morning and then asked his brother Mao Tse-min to take care of them. This could not have been the case because Mao was not in Shanghai in the period after K'ai-hui's execution and neither was his brother. They were both in Kiangsi with the emerging Red Army. The rest of Tung Lin's account, however, is credible as it tells of how the boys were "scattered," and the oldest one was briefly taken into a home as a "servant" before they ended up as street urchins, able to earn a bit selling papers. They also used false names during this period: An-ying was called Yang Yun-fu and An-ch'ing was called Yang Yun-shou. *That is to say they took their mother's maiden name.*

After the establishment of the Second United Front following the kidnapping of Chiang K'ai-shek in Sian, the Shanghai authorities helped to locate the two boys and they were taken by the Party to Yenan. They arrived at just the time when Mao was divorcing Ho Tzu-chen and marrying Chiang Ch'ing. Mao immediately placed them in separate peasant households. Then at about the time Ho Tzu-chen left for Moscow, the two boys were also sent there for their education and for security, as the war with Japan had just commenced.

In the Soviet Union the brothers were assigned to a special school in Ivanovo run by the Comintern for children, often orphans, of revolutionary martyrs and leaders of foreign parties. At this time the older son was given the Russian name of Sergei and the younger was called Nikolai, with the nickname of Kolai. Sergei roomed for a while with the son of Luigi Longo, later the head of the Italian Communist Party.[49] They both became proficient in Russian, but in time it became awkwardly apparent that neither could read or write Chinese. They were therefore transferred to the institute where Russians were being trained in the Chinese language. Consequently, a high proportion of Russian specialists on China personally knew the two boys. Sergei is remembered as a modest, likeable, somewhat spoiled boy who never spoke of his father. Nikolai was intense, given to all-consuming interests of limited duration, and somewhat odd in his behavior. Later it developed that Nikolai had serious mental problems. Mao Tse-tung in 1958 told a Party gathering that his second son was "insane." [50] It is not clear what his problems were, whether they went back to birth or to the shock of his separation from his mother and his years of insecure wandering as a street urchin. One Soviet scholar claims that he heard that the problem was schizophrenia, another Soviet professor says that Nikolai once explained to him that when he was being sent from home to home after his mother's execution, he was taken in by a Western missionary who hit him on the head with a stick and that was the cause of his problems. Now the official line in China is that during his year of wandering An-ch'ing was beaten by "ruffians" and became mentally abnormal.

In any case, while the boys were at school Sergei developed some friendships while Nikolai went through phases of playing chess, falling in love with a blond Russian girl, and even being fascinated by the philosophical polemics that were raised in 1947 over Professor G. Alexandrov's book, *History of Western European Philosophy*. Clearly, the boys received special treatment from the Soviet government, but none of their fellow students knew who they were at the time.

It is not clear when the two boys returned to China. Mao's relations to the two remained quite distant. Edgar Snow on the basis of a rumor he had heard once asked Mao if it were true that the younger son had been trained as an engineer, and Mao answered evasively that he did not know what "they" had taught him.[51] Some Soviet schoolmates of Nikolai reported that they saw him in Harbin after 1949 where he continued to live a Russian life style. Chinese reports have

suggested that the younger son continued to live in the countryside after his father came to power and in time became an
"accountant" in a commune.[52] This would not be inconsistent
with a Soviet report that he was sent to Russia in 1950 for
treatment and a period of institutionalization. Whatever happened to him is not clear except it is certain that his father did
not take him back into his household.

The oldest son saw his father in Yenan after the Japanese
surrender. His father greeted him by saying, "You have graduated from a foreign university but you are not yet a graduate
from the university of China. China is a labor university." [53]
He then immediately sent his son to live in a peasant household. By 1948, however, An-ying was back in Manchuria
serving as a Russian language interpreter. In the next year
when a Russian Konsomol delegation was traveling in North
China, he accompanied the group and shared interpreting
duties with one of his former Russian schoolmates. One Chinese official, in front of the Russians, asked him, "Have you
learned any Chinese yet?" Subsequently, he was sent to Peking and did have some associations with his father as he continued to serve as a Russian language interpreter. Mao then
sent An-ying to Korea to be attached to the headquarters of
the Chinese "volunteer" forces. He arrived on October 25,
1950, and exactly one month to the day later he was killed—
one report says that it happened during an American air
strike, another says that he died in an air crash. In any case,
"When the news of his death reached Peking, the reaction of
Chairman Mao was calm and serene. It is said that the Chairman, arms at his back, walked around the room for awhile.
Then he declared to those surrounding him: 'In war there
must be sacrifices. Without sacrifices there will not be victory.
To sacrifice my son or other people's sons are just the same.

There are no parents in the world who do not treasure their children. But please do not feel sad on my behalf because this is something entirely unpredictable.' " [54]

We have already provided the outlines of the story of Mao's abandonment of his daughters by Ho Tzu-chen. He presumably never saw any of them after the days of their early infancy. We have no evidence that Mao was ever particularly excited over the experience of being a new father or that he was greatly disturbed about abandoning his daughters. When he has spoken of the sacrifices of his family for the revolution, he has dwelt only upon those who were killed and has never mentioned the children he gave away, never to see again.

It is impossible to know whether Mao and Ho believed they were acting purely in terms of a "revolutionary ethic," whereby they saw themselves making great personal sacrifices, for a larger cause, by giving away each of the first four daughters shortly after birth, or whether they were simply acting under the traditional Chinese cultural style which permitted such treatment of female infants. The test, of course, would have been how they would have treated a son if they had had one. It is not unlikely that a girl who grew up in the society that Ho Tzu-chen did, even though she became a dedicated revolutionary, would have still retained some feeling that she was cursed by having only daughters, and that to some degree her husband had a right to obtain another wife who might bear him sons.

In Mao's case, however, there is no evidence that the sex of his offspring affected his feelings in the slightest. In fact he remained more distant from his sons than from the daughters he has known, that is those by Chiang Ch'ing. Whereas he kept sending his sons to live with peasants and never brought his mentally or emotionally "insane" son home, he kept Hsiao Li and Li Min in his secluded compound near the old Forbidden City. They attended Peking University,[55] and lived at home. There is some speculation that the older one is married to Yao Wen-yuan, one of the leading power contenders for the post-Mao era and a champion of the more radical faction led by Chiang Ch'ing. Edgar Snow mentioned that in 1965 when he met Mao in Peking: "Two or three simply dressed young women had been in and out of the room, sometimes standing in the background, as if orderlies. Could they have been Mao's daughters? One held his arm as he stood up." [56]

The Generation Cycle

In summing up Mao's role as husband and father we find that his behavior provides telling support for our hypotheses about his childhood. The manner in which he treated his wives reinforces the thesis that he was deeply ambivalent about his mother. He wanted women when he felt that they could gratify his narcissism; he was hesitant for fear they would ultimately reject him; in time he overcame his initial hesitancy, but he never overcame his fear of ultimate dependency and hence he was always ready to abandon them.

Mao's relations with his children lends support to our hypotheses about the essential nature of his relations with his father. Basically, Mao seems not to have wanted any sons because he knew how vulnerable a father could be. He acted so that no son could do to him what he had done to his father.

Had Mao's childhood experiences been of such a nature as to make him feel that his father was simply inconsiderate, selfish, avaricious, and unduly harsh, then it would have been reasonable for Mao, when it was his turn to be a father, to have striven to be considerate, generous, and kindly toward

The Private Man

his sons. Instead, Mao avoided as much as possible the responsibilities of parenthood and used his political activities as justification. Any sense of guilt he may have had must have been
eased when others publicly admired his refusal to shield his
kin and saw his readiness to sacrifice their welfare as justifying
his requiring similar sacrifices from others.

Mao also on occasion has justified his ignoring of his children on the grounds that parents should be tolerant of them
and should not seek unduly to control their lives. Chiang
Ch'ing has reported in a speech to high Party officials:

> One should not adopt the feudal attitude of "I am the head" and
> rule in this manner. On this we should learn from the Chair-
> man. Our family is very democratic; the children could refute
> the father. Sometimes we deliberately wanted them to argue
> with us. Now after the argument, of course, we reason with
> them. But often they do not intend to argue with but actually
> pay respect to the parents. Let them argue. This has good
> points. Let them revolt. What is wrong with that? What is so
> good about children conducting themselves with "Yes,
> Mother," or "Yes, father"? . . . .[57]

This posture of permissiveness is consistent with a deep-
seated desire to avoid being trapped into the father's role. Indeed, this is more than likely when permissiveness is combined with moments of explosive rage about the lack of character in children, as Mao has so often done. We have the
report, for example, of how Mao in a conversation with his
nephew, Mao Hsuan-hsin, the son of Mao Tse-min, first
made fun of the boy because even though he was in the army
he had not learned to shoot a gun. It was a cold day and they
had been swimming and the nephew in coming out of the
water and feeling the chilly air said:

"It is more comfortable in the water." Chairman Mao stared at him and said, "All you care for is comfort, and you shun hardships. You only care for yourself and think about your own problems. Your father did not bend or waver when he faced the enemy, because he served the majority of people. If it had been you, you would have knelt on the ground and begged for your life. Many members of our family were murdered by the Kuomintang and imperialisms. You youngsters have grown up on eggs and candy, and don't know what hardship means. I should feel satisfied if you don't become a rightist but a middle roader. You have never suffered. How can you be a leftist?" [58]

Permissiveness thus also becomes a way of letting others reveal their weaknesses so that it is easier to criticize them, a tactic Mao frequently used politically and publicly defended when speaking to a Party conference in 1958: "How can we catch the snake if we don't let it come out? We must let the scoundrels appear. . . . Let them express themselves and feel pleased with themselves." [59]

Thus a key to understanding Mao's historic role is that while he refused to be the father to his own children he has sought to be the father of a revolution. He largely turned his back on the responsibilities of socializing his own offspring, but more than any other leader of China he had been preoccupied with the socializing of China's youth. Ultimately, however, Mao even rejected China's youth in the form of the Red Guards as being inferior and inadequate as "sons and daughters of the revolution."

It is not so rare for a man to have difficulties with his own children and still seek to be an authority on the problems of raising children. What is significant in Mao's case is that his ambivalence is precisely between the poles of permissiveness—one must let youth find its way—and the demand for greater hardships—life has been made too easy and parents should demand more of their children.

Mao's ambivalences about being a father have thus profoundly colored his perspective on the future of the Chinese revolution after he passes from the scene and have left him with constantly vacillating feelings about how Chinese youth should be educated and generally treated. Mao's preoccupation with education policies, and his convictions about the need to send children out to work in the fields, which his father made him do, thus seem to be related to sentiments about his own father and were reinforced by the ways in which he treated his own children. Mao has been able to rejoice in describing his struggles with his father, and he was quite aware of the psychic nature of his victories for he knew his father was weak. He in turn must have emerged from that experience with such a low sense of self-esteem that he wanted thereafter to avoid the role of responsible father while idealizing in general terms the responsibilities of socializing entire generations.

We have reached the point where it is appropriate to go from our analysis of Mao the private man to Mao the public man.

PART THREE

The Public Man

9

Political Creativity: The Skills

IT IS BEYOND our power to measure the precise importance of Mao's personality in permitting him to become more successful than others before him in bringing together all the scattered forces of one hundred years of Chinese revolution and create the phenomenon of the Chinese People's Republic. There is no denying, however, that the public Mao has been in part a great creator. Somehow those qualities of his private life, which we have just observed, proved in the setting of Chinese politics to give him a public potential for creativity.

The secret of his creativity has been his ability to combine miraculously two quite separate powers, that of using words and that of calculating power. In most cultures, but more particularly in modern China, a man of both words and actions is exceedingly rare.

Mao Tse-tung not only combined both skills but also excelled in each. In the realm of words and ideas he was an ideologue and an orator, whose style has been that of agitator and spokesman, and also sloganeer. As a calculator of actions he has been both a military and political strategist. Distinguished students of intellectual history—Benjamin Schwartz, Stuart Schram, and Frederick Wakeman—have found in Mao's works links to the great thinkers of East and West. Those unacquainted with the esoteric structure of intellectual history are less likely to be impressed with the substance of Mao's writings, but all who read his works will recognize their historical importance both as objective analyses of conditions and events and as statements evoking passions. Similarly, in the realm of action Mao Tse-tung has been idealized by some as a creative genius in both military and political calculations, and even those who take a more qualified view of Mao as strategist will still acknowledge his unusual abilities.

Historically, whenever a great leader has manifested this combination of creative skills, for example, Jefferson, Lenin, and Churchill, people have tended to temper their appreciation with a grain of skepticism, precisely because it seems so unnatural to excel in both words and actions. It is somehow more understandable that a Woodrow Wilson, gifted with words, should be flawed in consummating political actions, and that a Roosevelt, in spite of the inspired powers of his voice, should be remembered as the statesman of action and not of words.

There are good psychological reasons for this. Men skilled in the manipulations of words tend to seek the privacy of scribbling on paper or orating from the security of a platform. Such men can dream of changing the world while only risking the possibility of being misunderstood. Freud himself illuminated the ways in which some writers avoid harsh realities and painful confrontations by clinging to the infantile illusion of the "omnipotence of thought" that lies in the magic of words, and which has its origins in the miraculous experience of the baby in commanding his total environment by merely uttering cries and sounds. The close linkage between the mechanisms producing this illusion of the omnipotence of thought and the psychodynamics of narcissism helps to explain why some people find such satisfaction from "putting themselves" so completely into their words, and why authors can be so sensitive to criticism and even to editing.

In some respects the political man who relies upon words is similar to the journalist, as described by Leo Rosten:

> . . . the energies which lead men into newspapers are . . . the desire to startle and expose; the opportunity to project personal hostilities and feelings of injustice on public persons under the aegis of "journalistic duty"; the inner drives for "action" plus inner anxieties about accepting the consequences of action. The last is particularly important. There is a sense of invulnerability attached to newspaper work. . . . Reporters derive a vicarious pleasure in experiencing the excitement of events as observers not participants, without personal risk in the outcome of those events.[1]

The man of action, in contrast, must confront power and bear responsibilities more directly. True, he can experience more directly the drama and the heroics of events, but he also risks total oblivion, while the most mediocre scribbler has a more realistic hope for immortality—for the magic of words is such that herculean efforts are made to preserve nearly all that gets printed. Even the most trivial of Mao's words will be better preserved than the story of most of his acts.

The Public Man

Mao Tse-tung's success lay largely in his ability to bring to his public life the very ambivalences that dominated his private life. The "monkey" in him made him want to use the safe magic of words to startle and shock, to agitate and to play with the emotions of others. The "tiger" in him made him sensitive to the physical realities of power and the sources of people's awe of authority.

Throughout his public life Mao Tse-tung constantly shifted back and forth between being a man of words and one of action. At times, when his role as political strategist was blocked, as when he began to lose power to Liu Shao-ch'i and Teng Hsiao-p'ing after the failure of the Great Leap, he suddenly reversed his fortunes by becoming a man of words, as when he delivered his Lushan speech. At other times, when his role as ideologue had apparently lost life, as it did during the last days of the Cultural Revolution, he could suddenly revert to being the strategist who could shed all the pretentions of the magic of his thoughts and reshape the world order by the act of inviting President Richard Nixon to China.

It is striking that most of Mao's poems were written when his political fortunes were low: in 1929 and 1930 when he was in his mountain retreat, in Yenan (where he also did most of his theoretical writings), and in 1956 and 1969 when in phases of public withdrawal.

In a strange fashion the basic ambivalences in Mao the private man have conspired to give a degree of "integrity" to the various guises that circumstances have forced on the public man. With all political leaders there is some need to be the imposter since there can never be a perfect fit between the private personality and the public role. In Mao's case, however, his need to change his public stance has inevitably coincided with a facet that was "real" in his personality. For his true self has always contained the contradictions of both the "monkey" and the "tiger."

It would be easy to demonstrate by a routine review of history the way in which Mao Tse-tung has protected and advanced his public career by vacillating between the role of articulator and strategist. It is more difficult, but also more important, to appreciate that this was a time when the Chinese people were at a point in their collective history in which their paramount needs were precisely a new vision based on the articulation of ideas and efficacious political action, that is, new words and new actions. It is not an unreasonable case to argue that the essence of the Chinese Revolution has been a dual search, first, to replace the Confucianism of traditional China and, second, to find a new system of action for administering the largest society in the world. But this is not the place to trace in detail the Chinese longings for ideas and actions that could restore them to their rightful place in the world scheme.[2] Rather our purpose here is to show how it was that Mao personally manifested such mastery in providing both the words and actions which could mobilize the Chinese people and provide them with a new emotional base for their national life.

The requirements of exposition force on us a distortion: the need to treat separately what was in fact intimately related. Thus, although the way Mao learned to use words and ideas was part of his discovery of how best to act with respect to power and achieve authority, we shall begin with how he became creative as an ideologue and then turn to his development as a strategist.

The Public Man

Ideology—The Magic of Words

On the face of it there is something improbable about Mao
Tse-tung's discovery that the emotions of a largely illiterate
society could be touched by words and guided by esoteric
ideology. Ever since the Russian Revolution there have been
in all societies, and especially in the colonial and backward
countries, eager students of Marxism-Leninism who have
perused doctrinal texts in search of the formula for power; but
of all these aspirants, Mao Tse-tung alone has been the truly
successful ideologue of revolution.

In part, the miracle of Mao resides in the character of the
Chinese people who, while largely illiterate, have long had a
deep sensitivity to the grandeur of language and the importance of political beliefs. Historically, rule by *literati* was the
most natural form of authority for the Chinese. Consequently,
all Chinese accepted from childhood the idea that their betters
were those who were their superiors at letters. In this Chinese
and Europeans have much in common, for Western civilization has also made much of the sacredness of the Book, the
power of the Word, and the right of respect for those who can
argue knowingly about the words of the Law, be it sacred or
secular. In the case of Chinese civilization the mark of the elite
was the mastery of words, and for over two thousand years
Chinese have stood in awe of the thoughts of one man,
Confucius.

Indeed, the most revolutionary act of Mao Tse-tung was
to suggest that the thoughts of one not certified by the grand
tradition could be sacred. But note that the audacity of his act
also loses its revolutionary claims because in the end his ideological alternative conforms to the tradition that rulers should
be specialists with words. Mao Tse-tung himself has not been

unaware of his dilemma, and he has vigorously extolled the merits of practical experience and the evils of bookishness. Deeper still is Mao's ambivalence about books and learning, which, as we shall see, is a part of the spirit of the impish monkey brought to the domain of ideology.

The hallmark of Mao Tse-tung as a political leader has been his ability to be both the uncompromising champion of Marxist orthodoxy and also the innovator of new doctrines rightfully called Maoist. He has insisted endlessly upon the need for correctness of thought and has required all Chinese to spend unconscionable hours raising their level of political consciousness by discussing his thoughts. Yet he himself has been ready instantly to cast aside doctrines in favor of pragmatic accommodations if this could prove more useful politically.

The public Mao has been so identified with ideological matters that his name has been quite understandably at the center of controversies and conflicting interpretations. No sooner had Mao's forces come to power in Peking than Western students of Chinese Communism were debating whether Mao was a heretic or a true believer because of his emphasis upon peasants.[3] Later there were to be debates over the intellectual qualities of Mao's voluminous essays on warfare, peasant relations, intellectuals, liberalism, and Marxist philosophical matters. Of course, in the greatest conflict of Mao's life, his confrontation with Moscow, ideological issues bulked large.

It is not our purpose to evaluate Mao Tse-tung's ideology nor to trace his intellectual development. Careful students of Marxism have pointed to the unevenness of Mao's theoretical writings and have suggested that they fail to reveal normal growth in sophistication; some may in fact have been ghost-written.[4] Stuart Schram, Mao's principal biographer, has revealed plagiarism from the writings of minor Russian theoreticians in Mao's works.[5] There are also questions as to how personally Mao was involved in penning the Chinese responses in the remarkable ideological polemics between Peking and Moscow during the 1960s. Finally, there is the mystery of Mao's relative silence on theoretical matters since coming to power, and the question of why his "complete" works have not as yet been published. Our focus lies elsewhere, with the psychological dimension of his use of words and ideas. Our approach will be first to make some general observations about Mao's uses of ideas, and then to trace how these were modified according to circumstances at different stages in his political life.

The Agitator and Adversary Relations

Just as there is a difference between a man of words and one of action, so there are differences among men of words depending upon whether they are writers or speakers. Again, Mao seems to have surmounted the differences that separate other men, for he has been both a writer and an orator. In general, orators seek immediate gratification of their narcissistic needs, they strive for style, sometimes at the expense of discipline and rigor, in order to manipulate the affect of their audience and gain instant feedback. Writing, on the other hand, demands greater discipline, more structure, more sustained outpouring of psychic energies, and a delay in narcissistic gratification.

Over his career Mao has tended to blur the distinctions between writer and orator. In his early years he did pour his emotions into his pen, and he was capable of writing rigorous and well-structured reports. Yet to an extraordinary degree

Mao Tse-tung's "writings" originally turn out to have been speeches and lectures later transcribed and edited by others. Some of his most important works on military strategy, philosophy, literature, class struggle and China's place in history were all oral creations.

We know little about the process of editing that altered these works to conform more with the conventions of written communication, but we do know something about Mao's style as an orator and therefore what the gap must have been. As we learned from one of our firsthand reports about Mao the man, he was not an animated or vigorous orator, but rather he achieved dramatic effect by appearing to be almost physically removed from the emotions his words provoke. From unedited transcripts, we also know that he can be rambling, disjointed, long-winded, but above all in his use of words he can be crude, rude, earthy, even obscene. He has enlivened the Chinese political vocabulary with a host of vivid phrases: he speaks of the enemy as "man-harming vermin" (*hai-jen ch'ung*), "monsters and freaks" (*niu-kuei she-shen*, literally, "bull monsters and snake spirits"), "poisonous weeds" (*tu-ts'ao*). The humor of impotence runs through his metaphors: ". . . like lifting a rock to drop it on one's feet"; ". . . like ants trying to shake down a tree"; and ". . . like bedbugs trying to carry off the blankets."

Clearly, the purpose behind Mao's use of words is to shock and provoke the emotions of his audience. In this basic sense he is an agitator. Yet Mao's style does not conform to Harold Lasswell's description of the classic agitator who "externalizes his private rage" and is consumed with "high anxieties." [6] Mao's objective, however, is that of Harold Lasswell's agitator type in that he strives to aggravate the emotions of his audience by relating to their problems without explaining rational solutions or diffusing their sense of anxiety or pain.

Mao's oratory generally has been consistently directed to making his audience sense how bad things are or were; he has rarely told an audience that they should try to forget their misfortunes, except when they might see him as the cause of the difficulties. The key to Mao the speaker is that he strives to legitimize the privately held anguish of his audience by joining their most suppressed feelings to a permissible public outcry. It was Mao who gave to Chinese Communism the practice of public meetings where people could lament their misfortunes and "speak bitterness."

His style is to be close to their emotions and yet he himself remains nonemotional, almost aloof as he plays the role of the startling, provoking, but clever "monkey." He is an orator able, in the words of A. F. Davies, to know ahead of time "the rough shape of his audience's affect" [7] and as a theorist he is able to guard his own emotions so that he only has to "lip read the emotions of others." [8]

Mao as orator does not seek the heroic or grandiose posture, nor is he the moralizing preacher. Rather, as an agitator he has an extraordinary sense of mission for himself and by extension his country. In speaking Mao always acts out the role of being *special*. We have already seen how the deaths of his brother and sister confirmed in his mind his own specialness. In a sense he has acted as though he needed to prove that even if his mother could not continue to make him the special one, then history would.

What was the pain, which Mao the orator sensed, that governed the emotions of his audience, which was China? The answer is relatively simple: At what American politicians would call the "bread and butter level," not enough Chinese were above being consumed by passions of coveting. But they needed legitimization for their suppressed feelings and this could only be found in depicting the entire country as the victim of immoral exploitation.

Mao Tse-tung was better situated than most potential Chinese leaders to speak to these emotions. Even though he came from a better off rural family, it was not a long-established family, but rather one that was still on the way up. Furthermore, as someone from the interior of China he knew the humiliation in coping with the coastal Chinese of the big cities.* Once he had made his way, with the help of his professor, into the circle of Peking intellectuals, he was the ideal marginal man of China. He could speak for rural China because, while not being of the lowest class, he had felt the stings of discrimination; yet to make his own complaints legitimate, he had to shift the issue to the larger matter of the national standing of China.

Mao Tse-tung was able to perform this feat of being the spokesman of Chinese nationalism against all foreign powers because long ago he had discovered that there was exhilaration in being the bold challenger of presumed power and authority. As a rural boy, he had learned that it was not so dangerous to challenge the most austere authority he knew, his father.

This brings us back once more to Mao's confrontations with his father and the issue of books. Mao was quite precise in stating that issue: "I knew the Classics, but disliked them. . . ." I succeeded in continuing my reading, devouring everything I could find except the Classics. This annoyed my father, who wanted me to master the Classics. . . ." [9] Mao further observed that ". . . when I was thirteen I dis-

---

* The author knows from personal experience the deep divide between interior and coastal China, a divide which goes far deeper than that between rural and urban, a sociological distinction known to all societies and therefore nothing special in China. As one who was born in the interior, I can testify to the problems of living down that fact in the society of Peking where I went to school.

covered a powerful argument of my own for debating with my father on his own ground by quoting the Classics (to prove my point)." [10] There are several matters of interest in these words of Mao. First, it is noteworthy that long after Mao was out from under his father's direct control he apparently relished quoting from the Classics and the history books of traditional Chinese scholarship. It has been calculated that in the *Selected Works of Mao Tse-tung* there are more than five quotations from Confucius for every one from Marx.* Second, Mao persisted in using such quotations for precisely his father's reasons, to challenge an adversary in debate. Third, Mao has throughout his public life consistently appreciated the usefulness of employing the expressed values of an opponent to embarrass and defeat him.

From his clashes with his father, which he generally won, Mao learned at an early age the rather sophisticated notion that ideas, in the form of the apt quotation, the *bon mot*, could be used for tactical purposes in adversary relationships. The concept of taking words and ideas normal to one social context and utilizing them in a quite different context is usually a late intellectual development that most people never achieve. It is true that in traditional societies in which the storehouse of wisdom is presumed to be finite and known, it is common to

---

* The percentages of references and quotations in the *Selected Works* are as follows:

Confucian and Neo-Confucian writings	22%
Taoist and Mohist writings	12
Folklore legends, pure belles lettres	13
Other Chinese and foreign writers, unclassified	7
Marx and Engels	4
Lenin	18
Stalin	24
	Total 100%

Source: Vsevolod Holubnychy, "Mao Tse-tung's Materialistic Dialectics" *The China Quarterly*, No. 19 (July–September, 1964), p. 16.

use axioms, proverbs, saws, and quotations from sacred texts in all social contexts. To this extent Mao's use of words had a traditional quality, indeed a quality that always made it easy for him to communicate effectively with Chinese peasant audiences. Yet he turned the method to quite untraditional uses when he sought adversary relationships rather than harmony and consensus.

Then, when Mao went to school he continued to utilize ideas and words from books for combative relationships with both teachers and classmates. It will be remembered that shortly after Mao prevailed upon the headmaster of the Tung-shan school to admit him, he was engaged in sharp disputations with his teachers over the historical correctness of the romantic history, the *San Kuo Chih Yen Yi*.[11] Later after he went to Changsha and was involved in the incident of forcibly cutting the pigtails of more than ten classmates, he had to debate the propriety of his actions with a law school student who sought to quote the "Classics to clinch his argument," but Mao developed a counter-theory with a political basis, and "thoroughly silenced him."[12]

This use of words and ideas to "silence" others has characterized Mao's political style throughout his life. While at times he does use words as weapons to damage the self-esteem of others, more often he attributes an almost innate power to words, in the sense of believing that everyone else can be reduced to impotence if one can confront them with the right word. Mao can shift his commitments from one idea to another as he searches for the right set of words to silence an opponent. All of this is testified to by the ease and skill with which Mao has constantly used his opponents' values against them.

This does not mean that Mao has not been interested in ideas or that he fails to get satisfaction from exploring concepts. His early fascination with romantic histories and his urge to read whatever he could lay his hands on certainly testify to an active, imaginative mind and a sense of curiosity. His reading, however, was also a very private matter; a way he had of escaping from others, of getting away from the requirements of social relations. He tells of hiding behind a knoll in the fields in the day time and of covering up the window of his room late at night in order to read. At school he would cover up a popular novel "with a Classic when the teacher walked past." [13]

During Mao's adolescence he persisted in using books as a means to privacy. Yet at this stage we begin to find contradictions and ambivalences that were to become much more pronounced in middle and old age. The first contradiction was the way Mao combined reading as an escape with a strong faith in the power of written words to affect reality and guide life. It will be remembered that Mao, in Changsha, although he had withdrawn from school, went through a phase of compulsive reading in the public library, a pattern consistent with his use of reading to achieve privacy. But then suddenly when he was seeking to end this "moratorium," he became an eager believer in newspaper advertisements and was prepared to utilize a series of advertisements for educational and career purposes.

The extent to which Mao's reading in the Changsha library was a private experience is suggested by the fact that he never later used quotations from what he read then—Adam Smith, Darwin, Mill, Rousseau, Montesquieu and books on the history of Greece, Rome, Russia and America—as words to silence his adversaries. Throughout his later life, Mao continued to use reading as a private escape, but not entirely passive activity—for there is evidence that Mao constantly interacts with what he is reading: by making marginal notes;

sometimes debating with the authors; sometimes agreeing; and at other times seeking to make historical generalizations or suggesting similar incidents, usually from Chinese history.[14] Furthermore, everyone who has seen Mao in his most private retreats, whether in his Yenan cave or his house next to the Forbidden City in Peking, has commented on the stacks of books on the tables and shelves, from which protrude strips of paper marking passages and suggesting extensive reading and reacting. Certainly, since the Cultural Revolution Mao has been the only person in all of China to live in rooms lined with bookshelves and surrounded by piles of reading material. In modern times few world figures have read so much or revealed so little of what they have read.

The other activist side of Mao's reading began with fascination with newspapers when he first came upon them during his experience as a soldier in the Revolution of 1911. At the time, it will be remembered, he earned the equivalent of seven dollars a week in salary, of which two went for food (and an indeterminate amount had to be spent buying water since as a student he could not "condescend to carrying" it himself) but "The rest of my wages were spent on newspapers, of which I became an avid reader."[15] After his "moratorium" and his return to school at Changsha Normal School, Mao reports that he spent $160 in all, of which ". . . I must have used a third for newspapers, because regular subscriptions cost me about a dollar a month, and I often bought books and journals on the newstands. My father cursed me for this extravagance. He called it wasted money on wasted paper. But I had acquired a newspaper-reading habit, and from 1911 to 1927, when I climbed up Chingkangshan [that is, withdrew to the isolation of his guerrilla base area] I never stopped reading the daily papers of Peiping, Shanghai, and Hunan."[16]

For Mao saw the media, unlike books which provided

privacy, were very much related to action. We have already noted how shortly after arriving in Changsha Mao was moved to make his first act of expressing political opinion: "I was so agitated that I wrote an article, which I posted on the school wall." [17] From the time of that first wall poster, Mao increasingly linked the media to action and to the expectation that words could change the world. Even before he was out of school he published an article in a national journal, and he was, of course, to found the *Hsiang-chiang P'ing-lun* himself the year after he graduated from Normal School. The journal did not last and its significance was limited to Mao's contributions.

Yet the distinction in Mao's mind between written words as providing privacy and as a vehicle for action is a bit too neat and does not capture the full ambivalence Mao has for books, ideas, intellectuals, and "battles of the pen." Over the years in speeches only months apart Mao has vacillated between praising and denouncing books and intellectuals. In a speech in March, 1964, for example, he would declare "Intellectuals are really the most ignorant" of people,[18] but then in May of the same year he would admit, "Intellectuals are quite important; we cannot do without them." [19] With respect to books Mao has frequently warned against reading too much: "We also do not want to read too many books . . . The more you read, the more unclear things become." [20] On the other hand, he will also stress: "One cannot do without reading books. But one must not read too much." [21]

Similarly, in spite of Mao's exceptional skill in using words to achieve his objectives in action, he also has at times dismissed the power of the media, as when he remarked, "In 1959 I put out thirty or forty thousand words of material, but it is clear that a mere 'battle on paper' is useless." [22]

Some of this ambivalence about the power of ideas can be

explained by his sensitivity toward different kinds of intellectuals, for he has noted, "There are several types of Chinese intellectuals. Engineering and technical personnel have accepted socialism more satisfactorily. Next came those who study science, while those who study liberal arts are the worst." [23] Yet as we have already observed, Mao has, over the years, repeatedly expressed views about the uselessness of books and education that seem to be precisely the same as his father's views which he once opposed. A couple of vivid examples should suffice: "It is counterproductive to study too much. Emperor Wu of the Liang Dynasty (6th century) did all right while he was young, but later, after he had studied to excess, he faired quite poorly, and ended up starving to death in T'ai-cheng." [24] And, "Today, too much schooling is harmful. There are too many courses at the present time and the work load is too heavy . . . Myopia has increased many fold among primary and middle school students." [25]

Exploiting Ambivalences

As with his other basic ambivalences, Mao's contradictory feelings about words, books, and knowledge have made it possible for him to respond to different circumstances in radically different ways. Over his career he has combined in a variety of ways the aggressive use of ideas and different blends of privacy and action in employing the language of ideology. As a youthful radical he turned to Marxism in search of a key to change Chinese society; but he also tempered his enthusiasm for the new faith by both traveling to the historic sites of traditional China and by seeking love for the first time. Then, from 1921 to 1927, Mao treated Marxism as a highly practical guide to help him identify political friends and foes and locate the sources of exploitable tensions and conflicts in his society. Although the rhetoric of Mao and other young Chinese of the day was devoted mainly to the polar vision of revolution and repression, what they were discovering in practice was not apocalyptic drama but rather the routine clashes of interests that make up the stuff of day-to-day politics in all open societies but that had been completely stifled in the traditional Confucian order of China in which only a bureaucratic elite was supposed to concern itself with public affairs. In China the initiation of even a modest degree of social conflict was conceived of as revolutionary. During the years of Mao's marriage to Yang K'ai-hui, when he was busy seeking a role in the organizational activities of the new Party, he accepted Marxism as little more than a partisan political label and the vague intellectual authority of his profession. Mao wrote about class conflicts in rural Hunan in much the same way as any bright political strategist might have analyzed potential friends and foes, classes, and interests in preparing for a campaign. Ideology was not as yet a guide to tactics but only a general orientation in searching out tender spots for political exploitation.

From 1922 to 1935, when Mao was out of favor with the Party leadership and expanding his forces in guerrilla isolation in Kiangsi, Marxism provided him with the rhetoric for asserting his self-esteem and his political legitimacy. By identifying with an international ideology in his period of travail, Mao could defy his political opponents without slipping into the obscurity of the innumerable bandit gangs, which have historically roamed the Chinese countryside. He not only refused to accept rejection by those in charge of the Party in Shanghai; he had to prove to them that it was they who had failed him.

After the Long March and during the Yenan years, Mao discovered that ideas were invaluable not just in fighting a foe but in organizing one's side. In his lectures during the *cheng-feng* movement Mao sought now to raise the standards of ortho- doxy and to Bolshevize the Chinese Communist movement. This was the time when Mao discovered that ideas could re- make the man, and that the revolution demanded the making of new men. After the hard-won objective successes of the Long March, Mao was compelled subjectively to prove his su- periority by being more knowledgeable about Marxism than any of his associates—just as the young Mao had learned early that he could propel himself ahead of his peers and even his teachers by claiming to understand better than they what was written in books.

After victory in 1949, Mao's first concern was to achieve legitimacy. In his need for respectability, he also displayed a curious degree of dependency upon his ideological master, Stalin. Mao felt he had to publicly extol Stalin precisely be- cause he could not accept the possibility that someone he wanted to impress might not have undivided admiration for him. Victory and dependency, the same pair of feelings of omnipotence and dependency, have been central in Mao's psy- chic life since his idealized mother gave him the gratification of her undivided attention.

Then, of course, after the death of Stalin, Mao expected that at last he would be universally recognized as being supe- rior to all his peers. When Khrushchev sullied the tradition by attacking the memory of Stalin and refusing to recognize that Mao was something special, he again used words in an effort to silence his enemy.

Shortly before Mao's great political and military victory of 1949, just when he had won all of China and gained supremacy among his colleagues, his health forced him to give up writing and rely entirely upon dictation. Years later in 1964 Mao explained:

> "On the Current Situation and Our Tasks" was spoken by me in 1947. Someone transcribed it and it was revised by me. At that time I had contracted a disease whereby I could not write. Now when I want something written, it is all done by a secretary, not by my hand. Of course, some things may be written for me by other people. For instance, the speeches delivered by the premier when he leaves the country are done by Huang Chen and Ch'iao Kuan-hua. When you are ill, you may have someone write down what you say. But if you never take the initiative and rely on a secretary, it is just like having a secretary assume your responsibility for leadership work.[26]

This health problem, which at the time was suspected as being Parkinson's disease, may account for the decline in Mao's writings after he gained power. But it is probably not the whole explanation. For as Mao became more confident in his historic role, he also found it less necessary to use words aggressively since he could now also command physical power. Thereafter, he only had to revert to the written word when he felt weak and mistreated, as he did during the period of his polemics with the Russians.

Yet as he saw himself the legitimate heir to the Marxist intellectual tradition, he not only wrote less but also allowed his writings to become increasingly sanctified. Ultimately, during the Cultural Revolution, Mao permitted his written words to become the obsession of the entire Chinese people. Indeed, in 1967 the Chinese publishing industry was almost totally absorbed in printing only Mao Tse-tung's works: In that year alone China published 76,400,000 copies of his *Selected Works*; 350,000,000 copies of the Little Red Book of Mao's Quotations; 47,500,000 copies of *Selected Readings from*

Mao Tse-tung; and 57,000,000 copies of his poems—in all, nearly 540,000,000 of Mao's books, a total in excess of the number of literate Chinese. And, moreover, his works were translated into 23 foreign languages for distribution abroad.

From Charisma to Power

Psychologically, Mao the reader seeking privacy was linked to Mao the highly revered author who no longer wrote. As Mao himself has explained, his early practice of escaping into the privacy of reading involved the experience of fantasies of heroic adventure and his identification with misunderstood but recklessly brave men. Mao's early reading of romantic historical novels was also, as we have observed, associated with his struggles with, and easy mastery of, his pretentiously authoritarian but actually weak father.

Therefore, it is not surprising that his ambivalence toward his father was in time mirrored in his feelings about words and ideology. More specifically, he has vacillated between strict adherence to doctrine and outright scorn for what can be found in the written word. At times Mao Tse-tung has been identified with the virtue of rigid orthodoxy and the careful study of near sacred texts. During other times Mao has debased orthodoxy, attacked blind faith in formal doctrines, and called for learning through experience as against book learning. He has thus appeared as both the true believer and the detached critic, a combination certifying that he was above being a prisoner of his beliefs, and hence was a natural born leader. The ideological leader, like the high priest, must tread a narrow path between appearing to be enough of a believer to tap the power presumed to inhere in an enduring doctrine while yet seeming detached enough to manipulate the doctrine as necessary.

But the successful ideological leader must also convey authenticity as he alternates between appeals for disciplined adherence to doctrines and pragmatic innovations that ignore such strictures. He must avoid the dual pitfalls of appearing to be either a timid slave to doctrine or a cynic who immorally uses words for his changing purposes. Mao's genuine ambivalence about books and formal learning has insured that in his public vacillations he would understand the clear limits of legitimacy in making his swings while achieving the maximum effect from surprises.

A second and deeper psychological link between Mao's private relationship to words and his public appeal helps to explain his extraordinary charismatic powers. From what we have observed about his fascination with romantic heroes and his strong tendencies to narcissism, it seems apparent that Mao had no problem with the "suspension of disbelief," or the capacity to find reality in the make believe worlds of fiction and poetry. Both as a reader and as a theater goer, Mao was easily and enthusiastically swept up into the world of the imagination. But Mao was also able to act, and in his acts he has tended to set few limits upon the possible. Thus, he has tended to blur the distinctions between wishing and wish fulfillment, between his own desires and the responses of others, between his sense of his own goodness and the capacity of others to respond to his wishes to control and change his universe. All of these feelings could have been limited to the domain of the private man if Mao had not also felt the need to use words to communicate his visions to others.

The Chinese public has clearly appreciated that Mao has tapped forces within his personality for the collective benefit of the entire country. Indeed, most Chinese sensed that there need be no clear distinction between Mao's personal greatness and the restoration of national greatness: Therefore, by merely empathizing with and revering his personal sense of romantic vision, they could also experience greatness. If it were not for what we know about the psychological dynamics of omnipotence and dependency, we might not realize that apparently contradictory feelings are closely associated. The connection goes back to the universal human experience of complete dependency in infancy and yet of being able to make one's wishes control entirely one's environment. Chinese culture, more than many others, has rewarded dependency and encouraged the view that to be completely in command is indistinguishable from being completely cared for. The Chinese male child is not only nurtured and treated as a precious object but also in his early years he is a center of family attention and indulgence. Childhood is seen as the golden period of life when one has no cares and one's wishes can command one's environment. It is expected that in old age the Chinese male will revert to this state of simultaneous dependency and authority, of receiving nurturing care and of having his every wish respected.

Thus the distinctions between omnipotence and dependency, between being great and manifesting helplessness is easily fused. Just as Mao has blurred the difference between his own aspirations and actions, so the Chinese people have psychologically dismissed the distinction between respectful conformity and self-assertion. Mao's own sense of Marxism, which he has kept alive and revitalized by his practice of reading and of public communication, seems to have stimulated in the Chinese people an awareness that they too could recapture the exhilaration of omnipotence by being so good, in their words and acts, as to revive their memories of a time when they could have all they wanted because they were seen as deserving by their parents. This is the psychology frequently found in the "raising of political consciousness."

Mao Tse-tung's charismatic tie to the Chinese people thus seems to lie in his ability through his own sense of narcissism to spark in the Chinese public a feeling that they too can find greatness if they can only submit to demanding moral standards that will help them recapture this infant sensation of being so good as to deserve having their wishes respected.[27] Mao the leader and the Chinese people as followers have thus been bound together by the same psychological mechanism that join together, in different degrees, feelings about the virtue of the self, omnipotence, and dependency.

This relationship began with, and has been largely maintained through Mao's use of words and the Chinese people's responses to those words. Over the years the character of those words has changed first as Mao became less the writer and more the orator, and later as he gave up oratory for the cryptic remark and the guiding slogan. But the power of Mao's words has consistently rested upon their ability to mobilize affect and to reassure the Chinese people that they represent revealed truth. It is this latter need to make his words meaningful to the Chinese people which has sometimes made it difficult for foreigners to appreciate the power of their appeal.

The secret of the orator and the sloganeer is precisely his ability to elucidate the obvious with such a coating of affect that the audience ignores its obviousness and comes to see the trite as the truth. For those caught up in the relationship of leader and follower, there is magic in this act; for the nonparticipant, it may seem only ludicrous. Thus, Americans thrilled to John F. Kennedy's excited declaration that "From the youth of today will come the leaders of tomorrow"—no one seemed to ask from where else could they possibly come.

Cultures do differ in their responsiveness to different styles. In the American political culture humor still loses out to moralism, and television has failed to make the ponderous, rolling intonations of the convention speaker the mark of a pompous fool. In Chinese culture the power of slogans is greatly enhanced by a tradition of confusing symbols and reality. In most cultures there is usually some feeling that to manipulate symbols and to change the words is in fact to change reality, but this seems to be particularly strong in China with its long history of rule by scholars. Mao himself was subscribing to this tradition when he once said, "A single word can rejuvenate a country, a single word may bring disaster to a country. This is the mental changing the material." [28]

To a remarkable degree, therefore, Mao has been able to rule by using cryptic slogans rather than having to explain in detail policy alternatives. He has, for example, chosen to characterize his policy of using both old and new, primitive and advanced technologies to develop China—an eminently reasonable policy since there is no practicable alternative—as "walking on two legs." For the rest of the world the slogan may have little meaning for how else can walking be done. But for the Chinese, there is a sense of illuminating the truth in recognizing that two legs make walking possible.

Mao's use of aphorisms and the Chinese people's use of quotations from the Chairman brings us finally to the way in which Mao has given an essentially religious dimension to his words and ideas. So much has been made of this that we need not pause to cite all the miracles that have been attributed to the power of Mao Tse-tung's thoughts. [29] What is important to note is that Mao's ambivalence about the value of books and formal education coincides with a deep ambivalence within Chinese culture between the scholarly, formal, ethical spirit of Confucianism and the intuitive, mystical, spontaneous spirit of Taoism. Historically, Chinese culture was always divided against itself: neither Confucianism nor Taoism was completely adequate to provide the religious sanctions of legitimacy for both state and society; furthermore, it was impossible to fully blend ethics and mysticism to create a single religious basis for the polity. The extraordinary paradox of Mao Tse-tung is that, while denouncing the need for any religion, he has succeeded in giving the Chinese a single, coherent set of ideas in which the value of correct moral and ethical behavior (Confucian principles) are directly linked to achievements which go beyond the limits of mere human reasoning (Taoist principles). Traditionally, the Chinese always had a curious ambivalence about the relationship between religious thought and public affairs. Communism has provided the Chinese with a new set of ethics to replace Confucianism and a new understanding of the non-rational to replace Taoism and traditional counter-Confucian mysticism. Possibly more important, Mao's thoughts have fused what was hitherto inadequately joined. Mao's very personal ambivalence about ideas and feelings has forced him to treat doctrine as more than just reason. Thus, he has made his political thoughts into an ideology that encompasses both reasoned explanations and the powers of faith and belief.

Action: Power as Willpower

Mao's revolutionary effectiveness involved more than mobilizing the sentiments of the Chinese people; he also taught the Chinese that there should be no limits to what they could accomplish if they were prepared to act purposefully.

Although we have stressed the fantasy element of Mao's

early escape into reading, we must recognize that Mao also found control and mastery in reading. As we saw earlier, Mao was able to control his father in his use of words and reading. As he entered school he found that by trying to know more than anyone else he could gain superiority and be the master among his peers. His phase of compulsive reading in the Changsha library must also have been inspired by a desperate search for mastery and effectiveness. Power lay in words and ideas.

But if Mao had been an unequivocal believer in the omnipotence of the human spirit, there would be little more to say about the psychological dimensions of his approach to power. What is significant, however, is that although Mao has strongly upheld the importance of willpower and hence of voluntarism in human affairs, he has also struggled against his own tendencies to value wishfulness and extolled a much more physical notion of power.

As we have already noted, in his adolescence Mao passed through a period when he was absorbed with the need for physical toughening: "In the winter holidays we tromped through the fields, up and down mountains . . . If it rained we took off our shirts and called it a rain bath . . . We slept in the open when frost was already falling and even in November swam in the cold river." [30] All of these activities seem to have been directed against his own feminine characteristics, especially his identification with his mother that was so much a part of his faith in willpower and his association of goodness with omnipotence.

In April 1917, Mao Tse-tung published his first article that prophetically praised physical exertion while in part giving sovereignty to the subjective realm. The article was entitled "A Study of Physical Education," signed with the pseudonym "Twenty-eight-stroke student" (the number of strokes necessary for writing the three characters in Mao Tse-tung's name) and appeared in *Hsin Ch'ing-nien*, a new journal edited by Ch'en Tu-hsin, the man who was to be the first leader of the Chinese Communist Party. The theme of the article was that physical fitness was a direct cause of national greatness and that national strength and military ability were synonymous: "Our nation is wanting in strength. The military spirit has not been encouraged . . . The principle aim of physical education is military heroism." [31] In part of the article Mao explicitly gives a primary role to physical strength. "When the body is strong, then one can advance speedily in knowledge and morality, and reap far-reaching advantages," or: "In order to civilize the mind, one must first make savage the body. If the body is made savage, then the civilized mind will follow." Contrasting the civilized and the savage, Mao feels a curious need to praise the latter and to make physical exercise into an almost elemental activity: "Exercise should be savage and rude. To be able to leap on horseback and to shoot at the same time; to go from battle to battle; to shake the mountains by one's cries . . .—all this is savage and rude and has nothing to do with delicacy. In order to progress in exercise one must be savage."

Yet throughout the essay Mao still gives sovereignty to the subjective and to willpower: "If we wish to make physical education effective, we must influence people's subjective attitudes. . . ." "The will is the antecedent of a man's career." "We should have perseverance in all things," etc.

Periodically in the years after this adolescent essay, Mao Tse-tung would, apparently quite out of character, suddenly assert aggressive views in the praise of violence. From time to time Mao apparently felt a need to rise above subjective will and prove himself in terms of physical toughness. As an extreme example, Mao has, on several occasions, shocked the world by dismissing nuclear weapons as "paper tigers": "Yes, we must have missiles, atomic bombs, hydrogen bombs—no matter what the country we must surpass them. I have said before, when the atomic bomb is exploded, even if one-half of mankind perishes, there will still be one-half left. When Snow was talking with me, he asked me why I did not deny the rumor, and I said I did not want to. I simply said that if war breaks out and one-half of mankind dies, the other half will still be left." [32]

This need at times to make the aggressive, "savage" statement has apparently tripped Mao up on occasion and compelled him to assume political positions he may not have carefully thought out. For example, the way in which Mao identified himself with the first tyrant of China, Ch'in Shih Huang-ti, during a speech at the Second Session of the Eighth Party Congress in May, 1958, which was cited earlier, has this somewhat flippant, aggressive quality.

> I was happy to read a recent article by Comrade Fan Wen-lan. It was straight talk. Many facts in the article prove that respecting the modern and belittling the ancient is a Chinese tradition . . . but it is regrettable that he did not quote Ch'in Shih Huang-ti. He was an expert in respecting the modern and belittling the ancient . . . (Lin Piao interrupts: "Ch'in Shih Huang burned the books and buried the scholars alive.") (Mao continues:) What did he amount to? He only buried alive 460 scholars, while we buried 46,000 . . . I once debated with the democratic people: You accuse me of acting like Ch'in Shih Huang, but you are wrong; we surpass him 100 times. [33]

As we have already noted, Mao had complex feelings about violence because while he has ceaselessly praised struggle and disorder, in his poems he has also consistently used his favorite defense mechanism of idealization in writing about battles. And there has been a curious tentativeness whenever he has had to talk about the need for severe repression: "This year we will not prohibit killing, but next year we will discuss it more. When the crime is exceedingly great, proceed slowly. Handle counter-revolutionaries according to regulations. If the masses demand nothing less than death, and it is reasonable, your leadership can wait a bit." [34]

On several occasions, Mao has taken a very functional view about violence and war. "We should be wary of killing people and should not repeat our past mistakes. The Soviet Union killed too many people . . . there are a few people who should be killed because otherwise the people's indignation cannot be relieved." [35] Also he declared that China had benefited from the Japanese invasion: "Once some Japanese in Peking apologized to me for attacking us. I said: 'You did us a good deed. Precisely because of your invasion and occupation of more than half of China, we were able to unite . . .' " [36]

Whereas most modern Chinese political leaders have accepted the reality of war and strife, Mao's approach to violence has always had a somewhat compulsive note to it. Oddly, this has given him a great advantage as a strategist, for while others have moved naturally to the employment of violence, he has done so more unexpectedly, more as a result of an inner feeling that he must not be weak in responding to objective considerations suggesting that violence is inescapable. Consequently, Mao's entire style with force has been to build upon surprise.

Although there is thus an important element of spontaneity in Mao's use of force, he has never apparently turned to violence because of his own anger. Instead, he has recognized that the potential for anger in others makes it easier to mobilize them for conflicts. He has since childhood been much too guarded about his own sentiments to allow them to carry him into the risks of conflicts.

These personal characteristics of Mao have given him the further strategic advantage of always appearing to be out of rhythm with others: When others are expecting harmony and peace, Mao has startled with the suggestion that the time is ripe for conflict; when others are agitated and demanding action, Mao can call for reason and calm calculation.

Ultimately, Mao's secret—in appearing out of step and managing to compel others to change their step—is that he has been able to redefine the possible by insisting that the proper application of willpower can change the entire definition of what is realistic. If Mao's powerful subjective sense of omnipotence was only obscuring reality, then of course he would have consistently met with failure because reality is not so adaptable to wish fulfillment. The key to Mao's political success is that, out of his need to guard his feelings, stemming from his fears of abandonment, he has developed an acute appreciation of the importance of adapting instantly to situations and thus, paradoxically, to be more sensitive than most people to reality. Skill in acting "as if" requires that one be able to penetrate to the essence of any particular situation so as to exploit it.

Precisely because Mao was faced from earliest childhood with his own shock of abandonment he learned early that in human affairs power rests ultimately upon the insecurities people feel and their need to cling to whatever advantages they perceive they may have. In dealing with the masses, therefore, it was necessary to remind them of whatever benefits they had gained from his actions. Furthermore, even with his closest associates, it was imperative never to let them forget what they owed him.

Yet with both the masses and colleagues there was always the danger that they would come to take for granted what he had done for them—"forget their time of suffering when they had to eat bitterness." Or even worse: they might turn the tables, and instead of being dependent upon him, they might take advantage of him.

Bringing together all the complex dimensions of Mao's extraordinary feelings about words and power, the most economical explanation of the psychological basis for his creative genius is that, first, he tempered his basic appreciation of the tie between willpower and narcissism with unexpected recourse to the physical dimensions of power; and second, he could appreciate the insecurities of others because in spite of his apparent self-assurance, he knew the full meaning of anxiety.

This brings us to the opposite side of Mao's success: his fear of others taking advantage of him, and hence his need to abandon before he was again abandoned.

CHAPTER

10

Political Abandonment: The Fears

POLITICS involves more than ideas and power, programs and actions; it depends upon people working together. Although decision-making can be a lonely art, leadership generally begins with comradeship. The great actor needs the trust of his supporting cast. Mao Tse-tung's remarkable success with words and power was at the expense of personal ties with his friends and colleagues.

Out of his style of ruling and reigning, of standing above the scene in lonely isolation and then intervening in specific decisions, Mao preserved the advantage of flexibility and the element of surprise that is inherent in adaptability. The zigs and zags of China's revolutionary progress reflect largely Mao's style with ideas and actions; they also have created great problems for his lieutenants.

Great leaders can capture dramatic effects and appeal to a fascinated public by advocating surprising or novel policies, but it is always difficult for subordinates who have supported enthusiastically certain programs to accept unexpected change. Understandably, responsible officials invest an element of their ego into the programs they champion. The pride of the subordinate blends readily with his sense of the rightness of what he has been doing. Those experienced with governments know that the inertia of bureaucracies lies not just in the complexities of communication and the limits of control, but also that change is far more than just an intellectual matter when people believe in what they are doing. It requires the redirection of emotions, and given the inherent difference between wit and sentiment, changes in affect are always more traumatic than recalculations.

The great leader with strong narcissistic feelings, such as we have seen in Mao Tse-tung, tends to focus his psychic energies inward into his own ego, and he thus has fewer emotional attachments to external realities, even when these are seen as his own creations. Mao's confidence in himself and his faith in his unlimited capacity for creativity have apparently made it easy for him to accept emotionally changes in policy, so long as he has felt that the changes were his and had not been forced on him.

Well beneath the top leader, the officials who make up the bureaucracies have their own ways of protecting themselves emotionally from the consequences of policy changes. The secret of the bureaucrat is, of course, that he has learned to invest his emotions, not in the substance of policies that can be changed, but in the means of policies. That is why routinization is not mere habit, but is reinforced by strong emotional commitments. In China this has meant that the rank and file of party cadres can busy themselves with the rituals of activity and spontaneity in support of whatever the current policies may be.

The group most vulnerable to change is always among those officials immediately surrounding the great leader whose visibility is associated with particular policies. They cannot escape into the realm of procedures the way lesser officials can, and if they try to commit themselves only to gratify the ego of the leader, they become impotent sycophants. And if the leader's narcissistic cravings were compromised by the withdrawal of affections of the nurturing figure, as apparently occurred with Mao Tse-tung, there is certain to be ambivalence toward admiring followers. Gratification can suddenly become suspicion and distrust.

In most political systems there is an instinctive understanding of the unbridgeable gap between intellectual understanding and emotional acceptance of major policy changes: hence, the near universal expectation that new policies call for new men, and the customary comings and goings associated with changes in administration and governments. In Communist systems, however, the relationship between personnel and policy is supposed to be different. In theory, supreme loyalty is to the Party and to the cause of revolution, and the dedicated cadre accepts the needs for changes in the "line" and does not allow his emotions to become attached to particular programs. In practice, of course, the human problem exists, and changes in Party line are frequently accompanied by internal struggles and purges.

Therefore, to some degree, the politics of China and the history of tensions between Mao Tse-tung and his associates is not surprising. Also, given the normal relationship between strategic choices and policy commitments, it is entirely understandable that these tensions should have been less when everyone accepted the need for tactical flexibility during the struggle for power and greater when power had to be directed to the innumerable and often conflicting goals of administering a huge and varied country. Several studies in recent years have examined in careful detail the various objective bases for policy disagreements among China's rulers, and particularly between Mao and his immediate followers.[1]

Beyond the conflicts inherent in the logic of different administrative perspectives and commitments, another objective structural basis for conflicts between Mao and his associates lies in his institutional relationship with them. We have already noted that Mao's style of rule has not been that of a chief executive in constant command but has vacillated between aloof withdrawal and intense interventions, between reigning and ruling. This manner of using power is not entirely peculiar to Mao; it can be found in many contemporary organizations as well as in the traditional ways of Chinese emperors.

For example, Mao's relationship to those of his followers responsible for administering substantive programs resembles the not uncommon, but often highly complex, relationship between the chairman of the board of directors and the chief administrative officers responsible for on-going operations. This is a relationship that can be extremely delicate, particularly if the chairman has a strong personality, an activist's instincts, and is old enough to doubt the abilities of the next generation to match his accomplishments. But this relationship, which has strangely enough at times profoundly affected the fortunes of corporations, has rarely been systematically studied, and therefore, we have little guidance for understanding the relationship between Chairman Mao and the administrative officers under him. [2]

Probably a much more useful analogy for appreciating the objective basis for tensions between Mao Tse-tung and his immediate associates is the traditional Chinese clash between Emperor and ministers. Descriptions of the Chinese Imperial system tend to exaggerate the monolithic character of Emperor and bureaucracy or stress only the conflicts among ministers and officials. In practice the most persistent conflict in most dynasties was between the Emperor himself and his immediate ministers. [3] Much of Chinese writing on statecraft has stressed the need for emperors to constantly distrust their ministers and for ministers to be cautious about arousing the wrath of the ruler. The spirit of this relationship is well revealed in the writings of Han Fei-tzu, the most articulate writer of the Legalist School of political philosophy which Mao Tse-tung has extolled when he set the stage for his anti-Confucian attacks of the early 1970s. Typical of the spirit of this approach to government is Han Fei-tzu's remarks about *Wielding the Sceptre*, which Mao must have read:

> The Yellow Emperor made the saying: "superior and inferior wage one hundred battles a day." The inferior conceals his tricks which he uses in testing the superior; the superior manipulates (policies) in splitting the influences of the inferior. Therefore, the institution of rules and measures is the sovereign's treasure, the possession of partisan and adherents is the minister's treasure. Such being the situation, if the minister does not murder the ruler, it is because his partisans and adherents are not yet sufficient. Therefore, if the superior loses one or two inches, the inferior will gain eight or sixteen feet . . . . The ruler following the right way never empowers any minister. Because once empowered and enriched, the inferior will attempt to supplant the superior. [4]

The objective situations in which Mao has found himself, especially since coming to power in 1949, have frequently demanded that he worry about such Byzantine calculations as were suggested by this early philosopher. Mao himself has repeatedly told of how he has had to fight to maintain his revolutionary influence and how in the innermost circles of the leadership there has been a profound life and death struggle "between the two lines," between him and his misguided associates. Indeed, it is significant that the concept of a struggle between "two lines" has both a structural and an ideological basis. The term "two lines" first came into the vocabulary of the Chinese elite after Mao's partial withdrawal in 1958. At the time it was arranged that there would be "two lines" of leadership: a "first or higher line" consisting of Mao who would be concerned only with grand issues of policy and a "second line" led by Liu Shao-ch'i consisting of those officials responsible for the day-to-day operations of the government. During the Cultural Revolution, this structural division became the basis for the ideological clash between the "two lines" of the true revolutionaries under Mao and the "revisionists" associated with Liu Shao-ch'i.

The story of the inner Party tensions, which have dominated Chinese Communism since the onset of the Cultural Revolution and more particularly since the question of succession has become more acute, has involved certain rational and objective issues: differences between the historic perspective of Mao and the more limited visions of those with administrative responsibilities; the natural clashes between an elder statesman and day-to-day executives, between a man who must play out the role of ultimate ruler and those who would replace his authority. In varying degrees all of the accounts of contemporary China, whether written by critics or apologists of the regime, revolve about such themes and issues. Yet, the full story of the dynamics of contemporary Chinese politics cannot be mastered by the "objective" analysis of these issues alone, genuine though they are. This is so because the principal actor, Mao Tse-tung, is a man so sensitive to emotions and so inclined to respond to his own deep inner contradictions. It is precisely because of Mao's personality—especially his idealization of conflict, combined with his hypersensitivity to criticism, his idealization of fraternal ties combined with an inability to maintain reciprocity, his ambivalences about using others and being used, his belief in the power of the collective wills of the people but also his need to insure the supremacy of his own will—that the psychological dimension of these clashes is so important.

All the substantive issues that have divided the Chinese leaders have taken place in an emotional context which is heavily colored by the personality of Mao because central to Mao's being are problems about intimacy and fears that others may exploit his feelings, a fear that throughout his life has made it necessary for him to abandon others before they are able to abandon him.

Although the screen of secrecy around Chinese elite politics makes it difficult to identify all concrete issues, there can be no mistaking the dominant emotional tone of elite relations, which is a pervasive sense of suspicion about the genuineness of fraternal sentiments. Mao's own idealization of a pure form of brotherhood began, as we saw, as a reaction formation to his feelings toward his own brother. It was further strengthened and given solid content by his adolescent readings of romantic accounts of friendships in brigand bands. Thus, he once told his intimate associates, Ch'en Po-ta, his personal secretary and sometime ghost writer, and K'ang Sheng, head of internal security and defender of his decision to marry Chiang Ch'ing, that he had learned nothing from formal education, "I only learned something from brigands." [5] For, as Mao went on to suggest, brigands share a pureness of heart that is the essence of comradeship. Yet, Mao's idealization of comradeship notwithstanding, there is no record that he ever succeeded in maintaining any truly fraternal relationship.

In the early stages of his political career, when he was making a name for himself by building a power base among peasants and establishing the Kiangsi Soviet, Mao did not have any particularly close friendships. At that time his name was closely associated with that of Chu Teh, but their relationship was one of complementary skills and a common alliance in marshalling guerrilla bands.

The story of how Mao Tse-tung emerged as a commanding figure in the Communist movement is still shrouded in an unusual degree of mystery. Numerous attempts have been made to fathom what transpired at the Juichin Conference of November 7,1931, when Mao was elected Chairman of the Chinese Soviet Republic, and what happened at the Maoerhkai Conference of August, 1935, when his authority was confirmed in competition with Chang Kuo-t'ao. In spite of research revealing the probable issues and the respective interests and ambitions of the principal participants, the mystery persists largely because it is impossible to put one's finger on precisely what it was that made those involved turn to Mao as the most appropriate leader.

Much of the mystery recedes when due attention is given to Mao's personal quality of being able to make his viewers see in him expressions of their own personalities and ambitions. This fundamental quality of Mao's personality, which made it possible for him to fulfill so many roles so readily, came as we have seen from his remarkable combination of sensitivity to affect in others while striving always to deny affect in his own behavior. Mao did not have to give much of himself for others to see in his persona exactly what they wanted to find.

This quality in Mao's personality, when combined with his outstanding intelligence and the logic of the circumstances in which all the Chinese Communist leaders found themselves, made it entirely natural that he would be singled out for public recognition as the appropriate leader when the time arrived near the end of the Japanese war for the Chinese Communists to "personalize," to make more human and understandable, their political movement. The very quality in Mao's personality that made it possible for him to inspire confidence in a variety of quite different personalities within the inner circle of the Party also made him the logical choice to become the symbol of the Party when it was ready to drop its more impersonal image of "guerrillas" and the "Eighth Route Army" and seek general popular support.

After victory Mao continued to exert this hold on his colleagues. Each of his associates from time to time felt utterly convinced that Mao personally supported, sympathized with, or at least understood what he sought. As he became an increasingly aloof and oracular figure it became progressively easier for subordinates to read their intentions into any clues about Mao's wishes. All the evidence we have about Mao's conduct in personal meetings suggests that his style was often relatively passive. He encouraged others to speak out, and as a "listener" he allowed them to inflate their trust in him by not directly challenging their basic views. Mao's manner, with a few notable exceptions, has been not to use power or criticism in face-to-face relationships; instead, attacks are made, often cryptically and indirectly, in larger or more public meetings, or by delegation.

This style of minimizing direct commands or signals

while allowing others to assume that they know his will has been Mao's characteristic way of relating changes of policy to appropriate personnel. Grasping at mere hints as to Mao's intentions, colleagues have always stepped forward to champion a new policy or a new campaign, declaring it to be the will of the Chairman and thereby elevating themselves. Mao's aloof manner does allow others to implement their interpretations of his wishes; and, of course, it also insures that failure will be at the risk of the implementor rather than a threat to the charismatic mystique of Mao.

This pattern can be detected even in those dramatic policy initiatives most generally acknowledged as manifestations of Mao's revolutionary spirit. For example, during both the Great Leap and the Cultural Revolution when China was caught up in revolutionary turmoil, it was universally assumed that his hand was behind all developments. Yet after the events, retrospective reviews revealed that it had been others who had been most vigorous in carrying out the will of Mao, while Mao himself could pretend he had remained remarkably aloof. With respect to the introduction of the communes during the Great Leap, Mao made only the public remark that "the communes are good"; and, even more amazing, during the entire time of the Cultural Revolution Mao did not make a single nationally publicized statement defending or advocating any particular program. At most he spoke to limited groups or sent letters to one or another Red Guard unit. The final signal that favor had been withdrawn from the Red Guards took the cryptic form of Mao presenting a "gift" of mangoes to one of the first "Worker-Peasant-Soldier Mao Tsetung Thought Propaganda teams."

It would be wrong to infer from this tendency of Mao's to evoke initiatives from colleagues while standing aloof from implementation that his personal feelings do not become engaged in actions. On the contrary, the very essence of Mao's method of not stating publicly what he wishes policy to be, but of forcing others to evoke his persona to legitimize what they feel needs to be done, is that they have to make a claim to intimacy with him and thus they have to "use" him. And as we have seen, the basis of Mao's ability to be aloof and control his emotions while remaining sensitive to the feelings of others is his even more fundamental fear of ever having his emotions "used" again. Thus, those who would be bold enough to make claims on him run the inevitable risk that he will feel compelled to pull back and "abandon" them before they, like his mother once did, "abandon" him.

Throughout Mao's career the most persistent pattern has been one of building and then breaking personal ties with associates, first with superiors and then with subordinates, and especially potential successors. In the early years of the Communist movement, the durability of his personal relations with the leading figures of the Party was completely out of Mao's hands since he had only a very marginal role in the struggles that toppled the first leaders of the Chinese Party. On the other hand, Mao's response to these purges foreshadowed his capacity later to suddenly break his bonds with colleagues. For example, even though Mao had once idealized the first leader of the Party, Ch'en Tu-hsiu, to the point of leaving the excitement of Peking and the comradeship of his first love, Yang K'ai-hui, on the excuse that he had to see Ch'en, who he said had influenced him "perhaps more than anyone else," [6] he calmly accepted Ch'en's downfall on the technical ground of his "right opportunism" and subsequently felt justified in dismissing his former hero because "after defeat Ch'en was no longer lively" [7] and had become an "insignificant personality."

Mao had no reason for holding any special feeling for the

next leader of the Party, Ch'ü Ch'iu-pai; yet significantly he never expressed any feeling over his fate even though Mao's brother's death was linked to Ch'ü's execution. When Mao moved off on the Long March, Ch'ü was abandoned with the group that was left behind including Mao's youngest brother. Ch'ü was, along with Mao Tse-t'an, executed by the Nationalists.

Mao has claimed that he was never a friend of the next leader of the Party, Li Li-san, even though the two had first known each other as school boys. He told Edgar Snow that when he was in the Changsha Normal School, he had felt "the need for a few intimate companions," and therefore he did what was not odd for him, given what we know about his psychological approach to words and communication: he placed an advertisement in the paper. He says that he got "three and a half replies . . . . The 'half' reply came from a non-committal youth named Li Li-san. Li listened to all I had to say, and then went away without making any definite proposals himself, and our friendship never developed." [8] Although Li was soon deeply committed in the politics of China's radical youth, neither he nor Mao ever overcame the mutual antipathy resulting from this first meeting. It seems likely that both were far too ambitious to be able to accept the other in friendship.

The subsequent story of Mao's falling out with colleagues is in fact the history of the Chinese Communist movement. For once Mao achieved some position of authority in the Party, he began a remarkable pattern of intimacy followed by abandonment. The only exceptions are a few cases of instantaneous distrust and the two significant cases of marginal abandonment, his wife and Chou En-lai, which in their turn, as we shall see, tell much about Mao's nature.

Mao's original rise to power in the Party revolved around

his intense conflict with the "Return Student" leadership of the Party; they were safe in the International Settlement in Shanghai while he was building his guerrilla retreat. At a conference during the Long March he asserted his claims to being the "older brother" and the leader of his peers. The tribulation of the Long March was marked by his break with Chang Kuo-t'ao, the commander of forces which were then probably greater than his. Once he was accepted as symbolic leader of the Party, his relations with Chu Teh declined, an older military commander whose name had been so closely linked with his that the Red Army was once generally known as the "Chu-Mao forces."

After the victory of 1949 there was a brief period of stability, but then came the increasingly frequent and ever more dramatic purges. First to be purged was Kao Kang, the principal leader in Manchuria, and his associate, Jao Shu-shih, to be followed by the respected and commanding military figures of P'eng Teh-huai and Lo Jui-ch'ing. But these purges only set the stage for the abandonments of his "closest comrades in arms" and designated successors. First to go in the turmoil of the Cultural Revolution were Liu Shao-ch'i and Teng Hsiao-p'ing who were denounced as "monsters and freaks." They were to be followed by the fall from grace of Ch'en Po-ta and a host of others. And, of course, as soon as order was restored after that traumatic upheaval there was the elimination of the next chosen successor, Lin Piao. At the time of writing the world remains puzzled over Mao's refusal to give unqualified support to either the moderate elements of Chou En-lai or the radical forces associated with his wife, Chiang Ch'ing. Presumably each feels in some degree that Mao is close to abandoning their causes.

Clearly substantive issues and objective considerations contributed to this long record of intense clashes. So did the

Communist traditions of intra-Party struggle, self-criticism, and mutual criticism which legitimized the practice of exposing deviations and seeking out wavering loyalties. Yet a closer examination of the record of these many conflicts reveals that Mao's personality, especially his personal enthusiasm for conflicts, played a central role, and he has repeatedly acknowledged this.

From the time of his youth when Mao wrote in a poem, "One draws endless pleasures from struggling against the soil, and against other people," [9] he has held that only good can come from even the most personal of conflicts. Mao's spirit of rejoicing in contradictions and seeing something positive in death has given him apparent enthusiasm for his divisive conflicts with associates:

> Our party also has two possibilities: consolidation and split. In Shanghai, one Central Committee split into two Central Committees; in the Long March, we split with Chang Kao-t'ao; the Kao-Jao Incident was a partial split. Partial splits are normal. Since last year, splits occurred within the leadership group in half of the provinces of the nation. Take the human body for instance. Every day hair and skin are coming off. It is a death of a part of the cells. From infancy on, a part of the cells will die. It benefits growth. Without such destruction, man cannot exist. It would have been impossible if men did not die since the time of Confucius. Death has benefits; fertilizer is created. You say you don't want to become fertilizer, but actually you will. You must be mentally prepared. Partial splits occur everyday. There will always be splits and destruction. [10]

Mao is aware that others do not share his enjoyment of controversy and indeed that most Chinese tend to avoid overt personal conflict. After the purge of Kao Kang, for example, Mao detected a spirit of timidity, if not outright silence, permeating the Party. Therefore he admonished a meeting of the

Politburo in April 1956: "There are those who show no vigor and vitality in their expression of opinion. The relationship of the lower echelon and the higher echelon is like that of a mouse when it sees a cat. It is as if their souls have been eaten away." [11] While others must have been shocked that Kao Kang's humiliation had driven him to suicide, Mao dismissed the matter by distinguishing between what he called "destructive" activities, such as those of Kao Kang and Jao Shu-shih, and "constructive" clashes. He called for a policy of "Let a hundred flowers bloom" and "Let a hundred schools of thought contend." History, of course, reveals that Mao's appeal for contending views produced a result that proved too much even for him. [12]

Hostility and Comradeship

Within the circle of his immediate associates Mao's ceaseless desire for fraternal relations combined with his higher zest for combative argument has made enduring relations difficult. Mao's ability to shift from light humor and tolerant acceptance of others' faults, to acerbic comments, insensitive humiliations, and even outright insults and denunciations suggests an inability to control aggression. Yet, as we have seen, Mao has not been given to aggressive impulses. Rather he generally controls his emotions and manages to startle others by phasing his emotions and behavior so as to be out of rhythm with others. Mao's capacity to exhibit feelings different from what the context seems to call for—being relaxed while others are tense, and appealing for tension when others are inclined to relax—has been, as we have seen, a critical element in his charismatic appeal. But for those who had to have direct rela-

In the triangle of Mao, Chou, and Chiang Ch'ing the attraction between the two men was less that of shared values than of the way they complemented each other's strengths and weaknesses. Within the Communist movement they represented two distinct traditions, and in time each found that he needed the other. Whereas Mao came from an aspiring peasant family, Chou was a product of the declining mandarin tradition. Chou's own father died early but he was brought up in the household of an uncle who was a petty official, part magistrate, part police officer. He was, however, given a good education, sent to a university, and qualified to go to France on the work-study project for which Mao only "saw off" some friends during that first trip to Shanghai. Chou became a Marxist in France and returned to China with appropriate connections with the most influential leaders in the newly founded Chinese Communist Party.

Chou's personal manner was that of an urbane, cosmopolitan, at home in the world of treaty port radicals; while Mao was from the interior of China, never a peasant but a man of the village. When Mao sought recognition among the coastal city people, his only logical role was that of the bright radical who could speak of the agonies of the rural masses of China. Chou, on the other hand, has always appeared so sophisticated that nearly everyone has found it hard to believe that he was a revolutionary. When he was a university student at Nankai Chou was arrested on charges of radical activities, but his university president, vociferously denouncing the authorities for being ignoramuses who could not tell the difference between a patriotic liberal and a Communist revolutionary, secured his release from the shamed-faced police who only later learned that his involvements ran far deeper than they had ever suspected.

tions with him it had a decidedly threatening quality. The masses perceive strength in a distant leader whose emotions are not governed by the drift of the moment; immediate associates, however, can only feel unease in not knowing where they stand in relation to an ambivalent and powerful superior.

Even on those occasions when Mao may have sought to reassure his colleagues, this fascination with contradictions and propensity for surprise, so important an element in making him such a masterful strategist, must have unnerved his colleagues. Take, for example, his address to the Central Committee in 1961 shortly after the purge of Marshal P'eng Teh-huai: "We should beware of killing people and we should not repeat our past mistakes. The Soviet Union killed too many people. At Yenan we declared that no cadre was to be killed . . . there are a few people who should be killed because otherwise the people's indignation cannot be relieved. In case members of the Central Committee make mistakes, then killing is out of the question. We will not make Stalin's mistake; we will not make Khrushchev's mistake either. He was more civilized, merely dismissing them from the Central Committee." [13] How could his listeners have failed to note his ambivalence about the too harsh Stalin and the too soft Khrushchev?

This element of threat that inevitably crept into Mao's relations with his associates can best be understood by recognizing that, although Mao has always rejected the requirements of fraternal bonds, he has been tentatively willing to play the father role with colleagues (while refusing to be one for his sons). As the ultimate authority figure in the Party, it would have been plausible for Mao to adopt the role of the elder brother toward his associates, but, as we know, for personal reasons Mao had been unable to treat anyone as a brother.

Therefore, at times Mao understandably used the traditional methods of the father in Chinese culture, such as shaming, humiliating, and upholding "negative examples" to improve the conduct of his subordinates. (Apparently he found it easier to play the "father's" role in the relative security of a public setting than in his own family context.) Mao's style in administering punishments has been distinctly paternalistic. For example, in deciding in 1957 what should be done with troublesome writers, something he had once been himself, Mao said, "Regarding people like Hsiao Chun and Ting Ling, execution, imprisonment or control would be ineffective. What we should do is to find their faults and disgrace them in society." [14] In the same talk Mao revealed his ambivalence over the father's role by wavering between tolerance and punishment. He insisted that within the Party diverse views should be tolerated and "grievances should be aired," but then he added, "Party members who make trouble in schools should be subject to thorough criticism, and then expelled from the Party," and finally he must have left his listeners uncertain as to whether he was the sympathetic or the malicious "father" when he exclaimed, "we should not hurriedly expel them." [15]

In general over the years Mao has sought to convey to his associates a rather tolerant attitude, counseling against excessive punishments and suggesting that reform or rehabilitation is always possible. Shortly after he initiated the purge of Kao Kang and Jao Shu-shih he spoke to the Politburo about "punishment within the Party" and said, "In regard to some cadres in the counties, districts and townships, (punishments) have been too much and too severe. In regard to high level cadres (including bureau chiefs and above) who commit errors and on whom it is difficult to reach a conclusion, punishment should be carried out. . . . It is not right for punishment to be too severe or too heavy. With the exception of counter revolutionaries, they should be given the chance to reform." [16]

Mao's associates have had trouble deciding where he draws the line between behavior that is reformable and behavior that is beyond redemption. They can never be sure how Mao decides that some errors but not others can be exorcised by proper self-criticism. The one clear thing, however, is that in Mao's thinking the higher the official—that is, the nearer he is to Mao and the closer the relationship is to a potentially fraternal one—the more Mao feels it appropriate to demand severe punishment. Speaking about the "Ten Great Splits" in the history of the Party, Mao once declared that in his view reform was no longer possible once a comrade achieved the status of leadership: ". . . it is difficult for leaders to change their ways. Take a look at history, did Ch'en Tu-hsiu change? Did Ch'ü Ch'iu-pai, Li Li-san, Lo Chang-lung, Wang Ming, Chang Kao-t'ao, Kao Kang, Jao Shu-shih, P'eng Teh-huai or Liu Shao-ch'i change? No they didn't." [17]

This ambivalence about performing the father's disciplining role, when combined with Mao's ambivalence about fraternal relations, has made it hard to determine whether certain Chinese Communist practices constitute punishment or thought reform, or are merely routine attempts to revive revolutionary commitment. Since the Cultural Revolution, for example, officials have been sent down to "May 7th Schools" in rural areas from six months to six years to "learn from labor," but it is not clear whether such assignments constitute punishment, reform, or merely a chance to revitalize one's revolutionary fervor. Some who have gone through the "schools" deny that they were being punished, while others have no doubts that they were being punished. A hint as to Mao's purpose may lie in the name "May 7th" which refers to both a letter Mao wrote to Lin Piao on May 7, 1966, and to something Mao Tse-tung did in 1915. At that time the politically conscious youth of China were shocked to learn about President Yuan Shih-k'ai's secret dealings with Japan. The young Mao in Changsha is supposed to have written on the cover of a book entitled *Know Shame* that "May 7 is a great shame for the Republic, and it is up to us students to decide when to wreak vengeance." [18]

This linkage of shame and vengeance, of humiliation and hate, is common to Chinese culture with its widespread use of shame to repress aggression.[19] But for Mao shame and repressed aggression are specifically linked to his problems with fraternal sentiments.

It is generally a reasonable presumption that individuals who intuitively understand that shaming others may provoke them into desirable, but also aggressive actions probably have problems themselves in suppressing aggression, and therefore need to idealize manifestations of aggression. Mao's belief that some people can be provoked into redeeming themselves through humiliation and shame is not based on a benign view of human nature. Rather it seems to be related to his own feelings of aggression, which are strongest toward those who have most damaged him. Probably Mao has a reaction formation against his feelings of aggression because his use of idealization often takes the form of exaggerated generosity toward those who have once hurt him. Indeed, he seems at times to enjoy shocking people by saying that his enemies have many good qualities. Thus in most unlikely situations he has spoken well of American policy, Chiang K'ai-shek, and the Japanese invaders of China. Near the beginning of the Cultural Revolution in a speech to the Politburo Mao Tse-tung must have startled his old comrades by insisting that he held no bitterness toward the "Return Students" who in the 1930s had dropped him from the Politburo and pushed him off the Central Committee.[20]

The relationship between Mao's manner of turning his hostile feelings into generous acts of rehabilitating subordinates and his early emotional development is well illustrated in the case of Teng Hsiao-p'ing, a vilified target of the Cultural Revolution who, after experiencing six years of a form of house arrest, was dramatically rehabilitated, restored to the Politburo, and made vice premier, and chief of staff of the army. It will be remembered that in attacking Teng as a "monster and a freak," Mao had complained that he had "ignored me," "was deaf to me," "stayed on the other side of the room." [21] Mao's exceptional bitterness at being ignored is reminiscent of how he must have felt when his brother was born and he was no longer the sole object of his mother's affections. The suggestion of such a linkage is reinforced by Mao's further descriptions of Teng Hsiao-p'ing's behavior as being like the treatment of "parents" at "funerals"—as will be remembered the birth of a sibling is often associated with the first vivid sense of nonexistence, of death—and while there is a reversal of roles as to who is dead and who alive, there is still consistency in that in both cases it was Mao who fantasized himself dead, and who expected that others should feel pain for that fact. Teng by acting "deaf" treated him as though he were dead, just as his mother must have been "deaf" to him when he was just learning to speak, making him want to hurt her back to the point of fantasizing himself dead. In both situations the rage Mao must have felt could be suppressed with the thought that: I am innocent, I deserved my mother's love, I deserved my subordinates' attentions; it is they who have turned on me, while I had no malice. Therefore, my way of hurting them back will be to deny that I hold any malice—I shall idealize my mother, idealize brotherhood, and show such charity toward a wayward subordinate that he will always be helplessly indebted.

While this may seem like extreme speculation, we do have evidence in Mao's own words that he has been inclined to picture himself as a mistreated man of pure heart when he was forced to engage in Party struggles. In July 1964 Mao described to a visiting group of Japanese socialists his feelings about having been ousted from the top ranks of the Party by the "Return Students":

> When the rightists emerged in our Party, I became a leftist. When the leftists appeared, I was then branded a rightist opportunist. No one wanted to have anything to do with me. There was only one lonely me. [Again we have Mao's imagery of the humble, ignored, isolated, mistreated, impotent individual.] So I say, there once was a Buddha who was quite efficacious at the beginning. But then he was thrown into the cesspit and became quite stinking. Afterwards, during the Long March, we held a conference, it was called the Tsunyi Conference. I, the stinking Buddha, then became fragrant again.[22]

In his relations with associates in power the flow of Mao's feelings between amity and enmity is quite unmistakable. Indeed, the shifts in the emotional atmosphere surrounding his breaks with all the colleagues who have been purged can be readily charted. Here again it is possible to see the same emotional reactions that we discovered in the private Mao's relations with parents and in his role as father and husband. Even brief summaries of his breaks with Kao Kang, P'eng Teh-huai, Liu Shao-ch'i, and Lin Piao can reveal that seemingly unexpected or exaggerated emotional reactions fall into patterns corresponding with our understanding of Mao's psychic development.

The Public Man

The relationship with Kao Kang, for example, was typical of a pattern that would begin with intense positive feelings and high trust and then become marred by suspicion based on jealousy and finally deep distrust. Mao first met Kao Kang when his troops entered Shensi near the end of the Long March and released Kao Kang from a jail where he was being held by the local Communists for his pragmatic, "anti-Left" line. Mao immediately accepted Kao Kang as a worthy leader and publicly acknowledged him as indispensable because he "knows more about local conditions in the Northwest than I do." [23] Throughout the Japanese war Mao gave increasing responsibilities to Kao Kang and by the time of the Japanese surrender, he sent his vigorous and articulate subordinate into the Soviet occupied Northeast. When Lin Piao's forces moved south of the Great Wall in 1946 to press on with the civil war, Mao placed Kao in charge of Manchuria, the largest liberated area at the time.

Shortly thereafter, however, Mao gradually became distrustful of Kao's increasingly independent style, which consisted largely of not reporting any details about his administration. Serious problems began when Mao went through Manchuria on his way to Moscow in November 1949, and discovered everywhere pictures of Stalin but almost none of himself. Then according to Khrushchev, when Mao got to Moscow he was told point-blank by Stalin that Kao Kang, by-passing Peking, routinely communicated with him as would the head of any independent Communist Party.[24] Furthermore, each year thereafter on the anniversary of Japan's defeat, Stalin would send Kao a gift of a new limousine. No doubt Stalin wanted to establish the notion that Manchuria should have some special relationship with the U.S.S.R., possibly even in time becoming a buffer state much like Outer Mongolia. He must also, however, have been aware that he was spreading distrust within the top ranks of the Chinese Party.

Mao had every right to be seriously concerned with Kao Kang's behavior, and a straightforward dismissal was certainly in order. Yet, the problem involved relations with Stalin, the one man with whom, as we shall shortly note, the adult Mao ever publicly accepted a dependency relationship. Just as Mao never publicly criticized his mother, so he never publicly offended Stalin. But when, as in the analogous situation in his childhood he found he had competition for the undivided attention of the one person with whom he felt he had a special relationship, Mao responded by completely guarding his feelings and accusing Kao of "ignoring" him and of building his private "kingdom." What is surprising is only that it took until 1954 for Mao to complete his abandonment of Kao, who was finally driven to suicide.

Whereas the purge of Kao Kang occurred at a time of ostensibly close relations among Mao, the Chinese leadership, and the Russians, the dismissal of P'eng Teh-huai happened when deep divisions were emerging within the Party. The trouble began when Mao Tse-tung, over strong opposition within the leadership, insisted upon the bold measures of the Hundred Flowers campaign in 1956 when he self-assuredly called upon all, but especially the intellectuals, to criticize the regime, and the Great Leap in 1958, which brought the communes and frantic policies to speed up industrial development. By 1959 the economic problems resulting from centrally directed communization had caused most of the Party leaders to back away from Mao's programs, and the Chairman was clearly on the defensive. The year before, Liu Shao-ch'i and Teng Hsiao-p'ing had worked to get him to step down from his post as Chairman of State and now they seemed to want to retire him further. The state and Party bureaucracies could see chaos ahead, and indeed by 1961 and 1962 there were widespread food shortages and economic stagnation. As China's leading military figure and a long trusted member of the Party's leadership P'eng Teh-huai took the initiative to challenge Mao's policies. He did this after returning from a visit to Moscow. P'eng thus made the first move against Mao.

In this atmosphere, Mao struck back, determined to fight on against all who would challenge his role. On the evening of July 23, 1959, he confronted a gathering of the entire Party leadership: "You have spoken so much; permit me to talk some now, won't you." [25] By way of introduction Mao said that he had just taken three sleeping pills but that they had not worked. Now he was aroused. "When I was young and in the prime of life, I would also be irritated when I heard some bad remarks. My attitude was that if others do not provoke me I won't provoke them; if they provoke me, I will also provoke them; whoever provokes me first, I will provoke him later. I have not abandoned this principle even now."

Mao's counterattack was successful to a degree. The leadership persisted on the need to modify the more extreme policies of the Great Leap. But they agreed to Mao's demand that Marshal P'eng Teh-huai, his most open critic, be dismissed. Worried about the morale of the army and the state of the economy as a consequence of the Great Leap, P'eng had, indeed, criticized Mao's management of affairs. In his "confession" he recalled the words of another dismissed leader, Chang Wen-t'ien to the effect that "Comrade Mao Tse-tung was very brilliant but also very strong-handed in rectifying people . . . like Stalin in his late years." Furthermore, P'eng observed, "the first emperor of any dynasty in the past was always strong-handed and brilliant." [26]

Mao's impassioned and startlingly bold response to P'eng's first "confession" probably forced the hands of all the others because Mao, in the spirit of the monkey, audaciously spelled out what he knew others were saying about him:

> So I am supposed to have reached "the declining years of Stalin" and to have been "arbitrary and dictatorial," not granting "freedom" and "democracy"; I am supposed to be "vain" and "pompous" and one-sided in accepting and trusting some of you; also I am supposed to "let followers go to extremes," also I "will not turn around until the wrong has reached its end," and "once I change, I make a complete turnabout," having "deceived you," "drowning you like fishes" and "resembling Tito." No one was supposed to be able to talk before me except you leaders. The situation is so bad that only you people can rescue it.[27]

Mao's style in seeking to win over his associates by focusing on his principal critic and by depicting himself as being grossly misunderstood and mistreated is reminiscent of his youthful method of seeking to elicit the support of his classmates by viciously attacking the Headmaster and by complaining of injustice and mistreatment. Actually, of course, it goes back even further—to his childhood belief that by denouncing his father he could effectively mobilize the rest of his family behind him. The way he told Edgar Snow that he had formed a "united front" against his father, leaves no doubt that he believed that, by recounting how he was mistreated by his father all who heard would instinctively have to agree with the merits of his case. Clearly, Mao never imagined that anyone would conclude that it might be his father and not he who deserved the sympathy. Mao's narcissism was so great that during the P'eng Teh-huai case, as in other comparable situations, both earlier and later, he dismissed the risks in publicizing the views and arguments of his enemies; he has always been sure of his ultimate ability to command the affections of all who heard him. In Mao's polemics with the Soviets during the 1960s he constantly challenged them to publicize his side of the debates and boldly released the Russian arguments in China.

This striking combination of craving praise while publicizing the criticisms of others confirms our belief that Mao's strongly developed feelings of narcissism must have been severely shocked by a sense of unjust abandonment: having been deeply and in his eyes unjustly hurt by the one person he valued most, his mother, it was easy for him to dismiss the less threatening criticisms of his father. And so in later life Mao found that he could assert his own inherent goodness by giving voice to the criticism of others. Mao's manner of defending himself against the pains of abandonment and his awareness of criticisms was to shield himself with idealization and to manifest apparent understanding and generosity toward his apparent critics.

Just as in childhood Mao had been able to turn his father's criticism into a way of confirming his own sense of moral superiority over his father, so P'eng Teh-huai's ultimate abject "confession" made it possible for Mao to appear serenely gracious. P'eng wrote Mao: "I sincerely thank you and other comrades for your patience in educating and helping me . . . I have been unworthy of your teaching and patience with me for the past 30 years. . . . I therefore petition the Central Committee . . . to go to a people's commune in Peking where I may learn and labor. . . ." [28] Mao instantly ordered that P'eng's letter be distributed throughout the Party together with his own comments: "If he thoroughly changes and makes no more major vacillations (minor vacillations are inevitable), he will 'instantly become a Buddha' or rather a Marxist. . . . Let us severely criticize the mistakes he has made and at the same time welcome every improvement he has made. . . . It is a good idea to study for a few years. However, a man advanced in age is not fit for physical labor. It is all right for him to go to factories and rural areas to observe and investigate. . . . The Central Committee will discuss this matter with comrade P'eng Teh-huai and make a proper decision." [29] P'eng has never been heard from again.

The next example of political abandonment comes with Mao's break with Liu Shao-ch'i, the man who was widely proclaimed as his "closest comrade in arms" and who was his first officially designated successor. This rift, of course, involved all the drama of the Great Proletarian Cultural Revolution that nearly shattered the structures of Party and government. Here our aim is not to add to all that has already been written about this monumental event in the history of Chinese Communism, but rather to explore some of the emotional dimensions of this upheaval.

Although all standard accounts of the Cultural Revolution acknowledge the importance of Mao's personality in what transpired, few have sought to treat explicitly the emotional dynamics of Mao's relationship with Liu. There were, of course, solid policy grounds for disagreements and there were also well recognized differences in the political styles of the two men. But what is psychologically significant is not only the differences in character but also the emotional intensity of the enmity, which ultimately would reach such an extreme as to involve the basic elements of personality.

Mao's relationship with Liu began in 1923 when Mao was first finding himself as an effective organizer in Hunan.[30] The death of his mother and father had just relieved him of any lingering overt pressures to uphold the Chinese obligations toward his family. He had, in fact, just recruited his brothers and sister for the exciting but dangerous tasks of rebellion. Although he had a wife and one son at home, his energies were concentrated on his quest for new forms of fraternity and leadership. The relationship between Mao and Liu, however, only became really close during the "Round Table" at Yenan when the younger man took the lead in helping to Bolshevize the Party and transform what had been political cliques and military columns into a Leninist party. During the first years of the regime there emerged a division of labor, if not a divergence of views, with Liu concentrating on matters of discipline, organization, private norms, and generally the work ethic and a vision of progress through savings and sacrifice; while Mao held to the magic of revolution, the idealism, risk taking, and above all the importance of willpower, spontaneity and enthusiasm.

Much has been written about these two different approaches. Lowell Dittmer, in particular, has acutely observed that Liu conformed to Harold D. Lasswell's model of the "compulsive" character, and Mao to the "dramatic" character. Ultimately, these differences apparently proved to be too much. But this did not have to happen; such differences might have produced a complementary relationship. Indeed, while strains may have threatened earlier, both Mao and Liu continually needed each other. They were, for example, clearly on different tracks by 1955, but then the decline in the economy in 1957 threw them back into each other's arms so that by 1958 and the start of the Great Leap they were possibly closer to each other than their opinions would have suggested.[31] By the end of the Great Leap they were still able, at least on the surface, to patch up their differences. But, of course, after the Cultural Revolution was ignited in 1966, these differences all emerged with explosive force.

Psychologically, Mao's ultimately intense antagonism toward Liu Shao-ch'i is reminiscent of his hostility toward his father. Both Liu and Mao's father symbolized the power of routinized behavior, persistent dedication to economic progress, and the Chinese version of the work ethic. Mao was to accuse Liu of being the advocate of bourgeois values in "high places." And, absurd as the charges may have been in terms of objective standards for measuring the "restoration of capitalism" in China, in a deeper sense. Mao was correct because Liu, like his father, was committed to the middle-class ethic of improving one's economic lot and material well-being.

Throughout his childhood Mao had believed that he could win the sympathy of his mother and of his brothers and sister by attacking his father's overriding commitment to sacrificing everything to the economic advancement of the family; similarly, Mao believed that he could demolish Liu and his allies by striking at their commitment to economic growth and the powers of compound interest. For Mao it is not just revolutionaries, but all right-thinking people who should despise bourgeois attitudes. Mao's contempt for the humdrum routines of middle-class life provides the psychological linkage between his attack on Liu and his feuds with his father. And, of course, throughout the world there was widespread recognition that the Cultural Revolution involved precisely these psychic issues and not just substantive policy matters. People who did not have the slightest interest in public policies for a developing country but who shared a broad distrust of the values of their parents and of other spokesmen for middle-class values saw Mao as their champion.

The clash with Liu Shao-ch'i thus involved differences in style, temperament, policy judgments, all of which came together in a direct confrontation in which Mao needed to prove, as he had in his fights with his father, that his inner feelings, his "monkey spirit," provided a surer guide to action than conventional reasoning. Liu's, like his father's, total lack of appreciation whatsoever for the powers that go with the spirit of the "monkey" made Mao supremely confident and

ready to take extraordinary risks precisely because they provoked in him a need to test the magic of omnipotence that his
feelings of narcissism gave him.

After the drama of the Cultural Revolution there would
seem to be little that could be added concerning the ways in
which the private Mao affected the colleagial relations of the
public Mao. Yet Mao's break with Lin Piao is possibly the
most stark example both of Mao's need for adoration and his
disbelief and distrust of any protestations of affection. None
of Mao's associates went further in proclaiming his greatness
than Lin Piao, and toward none of them did Mao become
more profoundly distrustful.

Mao and Lin Piao first met in 1928 when Mao was withdrawing into his mountainous guerrilla retreat in Chingkangshan and Lin was a young officer with Chu Teh's army. As
commander of the First Army Column in the Kiangsi Soviet,
Lin apparently became pessimistic about ultimate victory, and
in 1930 Mao sent his friend a letter which was later publicly
released as "A Single Spark Can Start a Prairie Fire." During
the Long March Lin's health began to fail and when they arrived in Yenan Mao gave him a rest from active command of
troops and made him the head of the Red Army Academy. At
the outbreak of the war with Japan, Mao began "to set Lin and
P'eng Teh-huai against one another . . . [and] deliberately
slighted Lin by giving P'eng command of the First Front
Army." [32] From then until 1959, Lin Piao, in spite of impressive achievements in the face of continuing illnesses, remained
second to P'eng Teh-huai. For example, even though it was
Lin Paio's Fourth Field Army, which had fought throughout
the country to liberate ultimately Hainan Island, and which
had been returned to the Northeast once victory in the civil
war was achieved, it was P'eng and not Lin who commanded
the Chinese "volunteers," who were mainly from the Fourth

Army, when they crossed the Yalu to join the Korean War. It was only at the Eighth Plenum of the Eighth Central Committee in August 1959, in which P'eng was finally purged, that Lin was made Minister of Defense and thus achieved leadership of the People's Liberation Army.

Lin now seemed on his way to becoming Mao's ever closer associate. And on the surface it did appear as though Mao was increasingly placing his confidence in Lin Piao, especially after he called upon the entire nation to "Learn From The People's Liberation Army," seemingly implying that the civilian leadership of Liu Shao-ch'i and Teng Hsiao-p'ing should emulate Lin Piao's policies. Mao had to depend upon Lin's army during the Cultural Revolution and finally to restore order at the end of the Cultural Revolution. Yet by September 1970 Mao claims he was in direct conflict with Lin and his generals. Specifically, he claims that at the plenum of the Ninth Central Committee, seven military commanders, including Lin Piao, launched a "surprise attack" on him by reversing Mao's orders that the new state constitution should not include the office of Head of State or State Chairman. Mao called the incident "a struggle between two headquarters." The circumstances are still obscure, but apparently the more Lin and the officers pushed for a head of state role for Mao (and of course ultimately his successor), the more suspicious Mao became of their motives: "First they concealed things, then they launched a surprise attack. . . . They certainly had a purpose in doing all that." [33] According to him he had urged them, "Do not establish a State Chairman, and I will not be State Chairman—I said this six times—and each time it was just a simple sentence, wasn't it. Even if it had been six thousand sentences they wouldn't have listened. My words aren't even worth a sentence; they aren't worth anything." [34] From our knowledge of Mao it is not at all strange that he should sound so bitter over feeling that he had been ignored.

What is even more significant psychologically is that Mao felt he was being ignored by a person who had done so much to flatter him and to exploit his narcissism. During the years of the Cultural Revolution Lin Piao directed the mass idealization of Mao; it was he who wrote the preface to Mao's "Little Red Book," and who ceaselessly praised the powers of Mao Tse-tung Thought. Whatever Lin Piao's ultimate intentions, it is revealing that Mao soon became suspicious of the very person who was doing the most to feed his narcissism. He wrote to his wife, Chiang Ch'ing, that he had been "quite uneasy at some of Lin's thinking. I have never believed that some of the booklets I wrote could have so much supernatural power. Now, after he exaggerated them, the whole notion was exaggerated. . . . It seems that I have had to concur with them. This is the first time in my life that I unwillingly concurred with others on major questions." [35] Later when Mao made public his attack upon Lin Piao he charged that throughout the Cultural Revolution and in all of his championing of Mao Tse-tung Thought, Lin had been "Left in form but Right in essence." That is, he appeared to be sympathetic and supportive of Mao, when in fact his motives were quite different.

Mao's ambivalence about Lin's flattery, his need to concur with it while becoming ever more distrustful of any attempt to influence his feelings, is reminiscent of his experience with his mother who gave him both his sense of worth and his fear of abandonment. Lin clearly understood that Mao's psychic energies were focused inward onto the drama of his ego and not outward toward any specific objects or concrete goals. But he misjudged his man when he assumed that this meant that Mao would settle for an appropriately honorific role and not demand control of substantive matters, a position which would normally entail the commitment of responsibility. Lin correctly understood that Mao shied away from responsibilities, but what he misunderstood completely about the character of Mao was that the source of Mao's apparently unquenchable thirst for flattery also triggered his potential for suspicion and unrelieved distrust. Viewed from Mao's perspective, it is clear that his hypersensitivity to the possibility of differences between the "appearances" of Lin's behavior and the "essence" is related to a lifelong awareness of this contradiction in himself, a contradiction which must have been rooted in his earliest need to use idealization to control his reaction to his mother's need to be pragmatic in her attention and affections.

The only way Mao could have denied that his break with Lin Piao was not heavily influenced by such deep psychological considerations was to prove that on objective grounds Lin Piao's perfidy exceeded the bounds of imagination. The lengths Mao felt he had to go in providing "objective" grounds for discrediting Lin Piao suggests that he was unconsciously aware that others would not be able to accept his subjective reasons for abandoning his designated successor.

Throughout the country cadres were told that on three occasions Lin had sought to assassinate Mao Tse-tung; yet the fact that there was not an instant and spontaneous outcry of indignation suggests that many Chinese had difficulties with the "objective" account of the split between Mao and Lin. It became necessary to provide details about a purported plot by Lin which had the crude code name of "571 Plan"—a number which, when pronounced in Chinese, with slight changes in tones and emphasis, does sound like the words for "military uprising" or "coup." In order to further establish the credibility of Lin's plot, Party cadres were given a document that allegedly outlined the plotters' scheme and that referred to

Mao as "Old B–52"—an allusion to the Chairman's propensity to "fly" high above and out of sight of the world, dropping his bombs, and staying "out of reach" of everyone. The document described Mao in terms that should have aroused the anger of the Party cadres but that also came precariously close to the truth: "Today he woos A and strikes at B; tomorrow he will woo B and strike at A. . . . Viewed from several scores of years of history, has there been anyone promoted by him and who escaped a political death sentence later? . . . Has there been any political force which can cooperate with him from beginning to end?" [36] It has thus been necessary to go to extraordinary lengths and risk great embarrassment in describing Mao's behavior in order to make plausible the "objective" basis for the break between Mao and Lin. Finally, Lin Piao was purportedly killed in a bizarre air plane crash in Outer Mongolia when he was presumably seeking to escape to the Soviet Union.

Thus, the Lin Piao case, as with all the other examples of Mao's breaks with his associates, reveals that Mao, when confronted with substantive controversies over policies, has consistently had emotional responses which have made it impossible for him to continue any personal association with his perceived opponent. Although the patterns differed, they all fit one or another of the various primary reaction formations which we have discovered to be basic in the emotional character of Mao the private man.

The Three Exceptions

In Mao Tse-tung's public life there have, however, been three relationships that seem to defy in some degree these general patterns: his relations with Stalin, Chou En-lai and to a considerably lesser degree his last wife, Chiang Ch'ing.

On objective grounds Mao Tse-tung had more reasons for breaking with Stalin than with most of the people he abandoned, yet Mao has never publicly denounced Stalin and to the end of Stalin's life he deferred to him as a revered figure. It is true that in private conversations and in secret Party meetings Mao has criticized many of Stalin's specific acts, but he has never attacked the full character of the Russian dictator or showed strong hostility toward him. Mao's personal formula about Stalin, which has become dogma in the Chinese Party, is that "Stalin was 7 parts right and 3 parts wrong."

It is noteworthy that Mao's judgment of Stalin is divorced of any affect and involves remarkably objective and even technical evaluations of his policies and practices. Whereas strong overtones of affect characterize Mao's descriptions of most people, his characterizations of Stalin have been coldly objective, even when Mao has commented on the policies of Stalin calling for strong emotional reactions, as Stalin's purges. "Stalin taught the wrong thing to many people. They became metaphysical and stagnated in thought and consequently they committed political blunders. . . . But actually, Stalin could not enforce severe penalties. He did not execute or imprison all renegades. He put to death more people in 1936 and 1937 but fewer in 1938 and still fewer in 1939. This shows that we cannot kill all dissenters." [37]

Unquestionably, Stalin was the one man of whom Mao stood most in awe in his whole life, and toward whom he seemed most prepared to acknowledge a degree of dependency. We have already commented upon Mao's extraordinary act of going to Moscow less than two months after he established his regime and staying for three months. This was his first experience in a foreign land, and when he was in the presence of Stalin he seemed not only awed but also conscious that he was participating in the flow of world history and not just the events of China. His stay was prolonged not only by his insistence on dealing only with Stalin but also by his illnesses and by the difficulties of negotiation. Yet he never showed overt resentment about the need for hard bargaining with Stalin for aid in developing China, but rather in his later description of what happened he was pleased with his ability to match wits with Stalin. In 1957 he told a group of high-level provincial officials: "Even we ourselves had differences with Stalin. We wanted to sign a Sino-Soviet treaty of amity but he didn't want to. We asked for the return of the Chinese Eastern Railway but he was reluctant to give it up. However, there is still a way to get a piece of meat from the mouth of the tiger." [38]

Stalin was clearly for Mao the "tiger," and he had to be at his best as a "monkey." Mao's position was that he had to work to get the attention and the respect of Stalin. Years later Mao was to tell another group of Party leaders that Stalin did not think highly of the Chinese Communists and it was only after China's involvement in the Korean War that Stalin saw them as worthy of attention. Mao was aware, however, that even when Stalin seemed to belittle the Chinese before the Korean War he still appreciated China's potential for greatness. In his speech at the Eighth Party Congress when Mao was in the euphoria of the beginning of the Great Leap and his boasts of China's entering the phase of true Communism ahead of the Soviet Union, he told of how in June 1949, he had sent a Party delegation to Russia, and at the banquet Stalin proposed a toast to the future when China would be surpassing the Soviet Union. The Chinese leader said he could not drink to the toast because, "You are the teacher and we the pupil." Stalin replied: "Incorrect. If the pupil cannot surpass the teacher, he is not a good pupil." [39]

Mao thus was driven by a need to prove himself in the eyes of Stalin, he was sensitive to Stalin's ignoring of the Chinese, but he was also aware that Stalin was predisposed to think well of China's future. Of all the relationships in Mao's private life the one most reminiscent of his manner with Stalin was his relations with the teacher "who influenced me the most," Professor Yang, the man who gave him his great opportunity to go to Peking and meet radical intellectual leaders and who also provided the daughter who became his first sex partner. Stalin was also someone who could help him advance, whom he felt he could impress by his intellectual, and especially philosophical, knowledge. Both before and after Stalin died, Mao on numerous occasions has gone to great lengths to evaluate, praise, and above all criticize the philosophical writing of Stalin. Whereas Professor Yang was an idealist, Mao's most explicit criticism of Stalin was that he minimized the importance of human will; Mao's notes on Stalin's *Economic Problems of Socialism in the Soviet Union* begin: "This book by Stalin has not a word on the superstructure from beginning to end. It never touches upon man. We read of things but not of man." [40] Mao further faults Stalin for not knowing that, "Man's ability to know and change Nature is unlimited. . . . What cannot be done now may be done in the future." [41]

The obvious basis of Mao's continued acceptance of Stalin, with marginal criticisms, was the Chairman's vision that he was the most worthy one to follow Stalin in the apostolic succession of Marxism-Leninism. And, of course, the intensity of his emotional break with Stalin's Soviet successor was in part fueled by his conviction that he had been denied his rightful spot in the history of world Communism. There is no need for us to document here the intensity of Mao's hatred for Khrushchev except to point out that it reflected the essential structure of Mao's emotions in that he felt no need to reconcile contradictions, and could denounce the Russian in the same speech for contradictory qualities: "Khrushchev is too cautious, too unbalanced. He is lame in one leg. He does not walk with both legs," and "Khrushchev also knows how to create a tense situation" and to engage in adventurist acts.[42]

Quite conceivably, had Stalin lived longer, Mao's relations with him would have also come to a personal breaking point. Yet it is significant that, in spite of all the bitter feelings Mao has expressed about Soviet behavior, he has conspicuously limited his criticisms of Stalin. Conceivably, this is in part owing to his loyalty to an ideal that once might have made him the acknowledged leader of all Communists, and therefore to denounce Stalin now would be to discredit his own one-time ambitions.

Mao's unlikely persistence in apparently respecting Stalin's role in history may also stem from an awareness that they both shared to a degree a similar impostor's pretensions in their claims to historical greatness: Both Stalin and Mao were caught up in a tradition in which their claims to legitimacy required that they pretend to be philosophers and not just political leaders. And certainly Mao, from his experiences with Professor Yang, knew that as much as he might enjoy philosophical discussion he did not belong to world class philosophy; and of course he knew that Stalin did not either. Therefore, Mao has been prepared to expose Stalin's weaknesses as a philosopher only to the point of strengthening his own claims as a dialectical thinker. Beyond these modest criticisms, Mao has gone along with the pretension that they are both philosophical thinkers.

It is true that since the death of Stalin and subsequent developments Mao can never expect to be acknowledged as the supreme leader of all Communists, and he has become less interested in philosophical discussions. He agreed with Lin Piao's thesis that his "thoughts" had power, but he has been less inclined to pretend to philosophical sophistication. Yet he was not prepared to negate what might have been, and therefore he has felt an enduring need to remain loyal to the pretensions he shared with Stalin. On the other hand, the explosive bitterness of Mao's criticisms of the Soviet Union after Stalin's death in part may be attributed to the resentment that must have steadily built up within him because he had to defer for so long to an inconsiderate superior. Whereas he had never been passive toward his equally crude and inconsiderate father, Mao had practiced self-control toward Stalin, again suggesting that Mao was always confident that he could ultimately win out over his father's mistreatment of him. At the same time, Mao unquestionably concluded from his experience of humiliation by Stalin that he would never thereafter publicly defer to anyone.

Mao's uncharacteristic acceptance of a subordinate position to Stalin is matched by his equally uncharacteristic stable relations with Chou En-lai. The standard interpretation of Chinese Communist politics is that the durability of Chou stems less from Mao's personality and more from Chou's ability to trim his political sails to the prevailing winds of the moment and to content himself with the security of ranking no higher than third in the hierarchy. While there is considerable truth in this view, their relationship appears to be somewhat more complex.

Indeed, Mao's relationship to Chou has always been a part of a complex of relations involving another major figure. At first there were the various purged leaders and then Chiang Ch'ing.

In the first year that Mao and Chou worked within the Communist movement the cultivated cosmopolitan and the rural provincial were consistently on different sides in inter-Party matters. Chou identified with the Moscow oriented leadership in Shanghai while Mao was out of favor in his mountainous base in Kiangsi. When Chou first ventured into the rural and military parts of the movement he gravitated to some of Mao's competitors. It was only during the Long March, when Chou was severely ill, that the two men joined their fortunes. From that time Chou En-lai seemingly recognized that the vitality of the Communist movement would have to come from a leader who understood the rural masses of China, and almost simultaneously Mao recognized that he needed a "Mr. Outside" who could represent his movement to the world at large.

Over the years, this division of functions has created a form of mutual dependency. Chou has been able to understand Mao's purposes without having to indulge in flattery, and Mao has accepted the necessity of Chou's skills without making them a part of his own public image. Thus as public figures the two men are generally seen as separate and distinct actors, often playing somewhat contradictory roles. At the personal level, however, there are signs of genuine affection and understanding. One of the legends of the Party holds that when the leadership was forced to withdraw from Yenan at the outset of the civil war, Chou was ill and Mao thoughtfully insisted that he ride on the mule-borne litter reserved for the Chairman. Outsiders who have seen the two men together are impressed with the lack of ceremony between them. A Frenchman, for example, reports that when he was given an audience with Mao, Chou En-lai sat beside the great man, idly turning over the pages of a newspaper and apparently paying no attention to the words of the Chairman—a scene which amazed the Frenchman—"Imagine anyone reading a newspaper next to de Gaulle." [43]

In spite of the contrasting styles of Mao and Chou, people at both ends of the political spectrum have generally assumed that Chou has reflected accurately Mao's purposes. During the Cultural Revolution, when the Red Guards were at the height of their campaign of destroying all vestiges of the "old," Chou En-lai was able through a telephone call to prevent rampaging students from destroying the most valued art objects in ancient Hangchow because even the most radical "Maoists" knew that the sober, unemotional Prime Minister could speak for their revered Chairman. At the other extreme, Secretary Henry Kissinger and President Richard Nixon never doubted that in negotiating with Chou they were in fact dealing with Mao, a conviction which was reinforced by Chou's practice of frequently excusing himself from sessions apparently in order to check his instructions from Mao.[44]

Yet in the strange triangular set of relations between the Chairman, Chou En-lai, and Chiang Ch'ing, which have governed Chinese politics since the fall of Lin Piao, Mao has conspicuously refused to give full public support to either his minister or his wife in their political struggles with each other. Behind the scenes he has given backing particularly to Chou's foreign policy but also his domestic policies; yet he allowed the anti-Confucius, anti-Lin Piao campaign of 1974 to have anti-Chou overtones. Mao's reluctance to publicly champion Chou was most telling at the Fourth National People's Congress in early 1975 when Mao conspicuously failed to give his blessings to what otherwise was a clear triumph for Chou En-lai and his more moderate elements.

On the other hand, neither in public nor behind the scenes has Mao given effective support to Chiang Ch'ing. Mao clearly found it useful to allow her a public role at about the time their private relationship declined. Politically, each has found the other useful—Mao had need for a radical spokesman, particularly in the cultural realm, who would have no threatening administrative powers; and Chiang Ch'ing has needed the authority of being Mao's wife. Yet Mao has been extremely sensitive, as always, to the question of who might be using whom. The complexity of the relationship is revealed in remarks between the two during a meeting with Red Guard leaders in July, 1968, when Mao was beginning to apply brakes to the Cultural Revolution. Between comments with the young leaders Mao and Chiang Ch'ing exchanged pointed words with each other. She, for example, observed, "We have political responsibilities toward you. But to help you politically is not enough. You also have to help yourself." (Clearly he would have interpreted this as a confession of the limits of her abilities to "nurture" him and therefore of his need to look after himself.) Mao allowed the remark to pass, but then later, and almost out of the blue, he was sharp with her: "You always blame others; you never blame yourself." (A view he seems to have had about other women as well which, again, seems to go as far back as when his mother made him "look after himself.") Chiang Ch'ing could only later respond by saying, "Don't put me in a position where I cannot do anything to help you although it is my wish." [45]

Mao's fascination with contradictions, which has given him opportunities to express his ambivalences, seems to be the key to the triangular relations with Chou and Chiang Ch'ing. He has not been moved to completely abandon either, as he has all of his other close associates, because the tensions between the two are enough to prevent either from being a threat to him. By allowing the contradictions between his "minister" and his "wife," between "moderates" and "radicals" to dominate the political scene of his old age, Mao has been able once again to shield himself from the need to make emotional commitments and to be free to act out the role of the "monkey" as he pleases.

Thus, Mao's relations with Chou En-lai and Chang Ch'ing, which first appeared to be exceptions to his pattern of abandoning close associations, prove to be abandonment in another, and possible historically, more telling form. In abandoning Lin Piao, Liu Shao-Ch'i and the other earlier associates, Mao was in part reacting to their threat to dominate his emotions. By refusing to side openly with either Chou or Chiang Ch'ing Mao has gone beyond withholding commitment to any particular colleague who might aspire to succeed him—he has withheld commitment to any unequivocal definition of what he wishes for the future of China after he can no longer be the ruling "monkey." Is China to proceed according to policies consistent with Chou En-lai's moderate style or is it to be governed by Chiang Ch'ing's more radical views? Mao's personality makes it as difficult for him to answer this question as for him to accept the need for a successor.

CHAPTER

11

The Problem Revisited

BY JUXTAPOSING Mao the private man and Mao the public figure and identifying common patterns in the flow of emotions, we have sought to understand better what has made possible this great man of history. At the outset we suggested that all people, including great men, have rights to privacy, and that we should only penetrate the private life behind the public figure if by doing so we can add to our understanding of his public behavior.

This we believe we have accomplished. Up until now all conventional interpretations of contemporary China recognize that Mao's personality has been a major determining force in the politics of Chinese Communism. Yet these interpretations generally stop at the point of observing that Mao is a "revolu-

tionary romantic," "distrustful of routinization and bureaucracy," a believer in "human will" rather than "technology
and rationality." Some interpretations have gone further and
identified Mao as having a most un-Chinese fearlessness about
disorder, an enjoyment of conflict and controversy, and little
of the usual Chinese craving for order. He has been seen as the
"dramatizing" or charismatic leader whose political style
requires ceaseless upheavals, endless calls for enthusiasm, and
profound dissatisfaction whenever tranquillity and orderly
progress prevail.

We are now able not only to see the sources of these and
others of Mao's characteristics but also to recognize how they
seemingly fit together to provide the mold for recurring patterns of thought and behavior. The strong nurturing support
of his mother gave him an enduring craving to recapture the
bliss of omnipotence and thus turned his psychic forces inward onto his ego, thereby providing him with his sense of
narcissism that became the basis of his charismatic appeal. Yet
she also "abandoned" him, and thus taught him thereafter to
constantly guard his commitment of feelings, and never to
direct his affect toward persons or objects close at hand, but
rather to use idealization as a defense mechanism and to reserve his feelings for abstract and distant objects, such as utopian revolution, world political forces, and the movement of history. His mother's "abandonment" of him also fed his deep
ambivalence about fraternal relations: his persisting inability
to be a true brother but his profound understanding of the at-
tractiveness of the ideal of brotherhood. From his experiences
with his father Mao learned the vulnerabilities of authority; he
became contemptuous of those who pretended to power, and
yet he sought their attention; and ultimately he determined to
avoid at all costs being put in the position of "father." He
avoided the role with his own children, and in time became

obsessively opposed to the idea that China should have even a symbolic head of state, clashing with Lin Piao about the need for a Chairman of State and finally eliminating the post in the new constitution of January 1975.

The key to understanding Mao as a revolutionary spirit is that he was not a man whose life had been stifled by oppressive authority and who needed to rebel against excessive controls. Although he used the rhetoric of those who have been brought up in excessively puritanical and tyrannical family environments—for that is, after all, the only conventional rhetoric of rebellion—his father ignored him more than he restrained him, and he was always able in the end to have his way against his father's wishes.

The sources of Mao's rebelliousness came from another quarter. His sense of rage with the world came from having once experienced such security and supporting reassurance, which when it could not be sustained made him feel that he was forever after being cheated. In his own mind his right to rebellion lay in his sense of moral goodness, his feelings that he should always be "heard" and never "ignored," and conviction that those with power were thinking only of themselves (as his father did) and were not responsive to his "needs."

Historically we can distinguish two general types of rebels, those who need to destroy authority because they were once excessively repressed, and those who need to change the world because of their profound dissatisfaction at no longer having the security they once knew. We know that Mao belongs to the second category not only from the evidence of his childhood experiences but also because he has combined his need to rebel with a profound understanding of people's craving for security, a sense of community, and a degree of recognition—common goals of those who rage because their world cannot sustain the levels of reassurance they once experienced.

The Public Man

Although Mao spent his critical childhood years in the nineteenth century, his spirit of rebellion was not analogous to that of Westerners of his generation who felt the need to rebel against a confining Victorian or puritan order. Instead Mao can better be understood as having many of the qualities of the contemporary generation of Western radicals whose parents went to inordinate lengths to ensure that their infancy was free of all insecurities and frustrations, whose fathers were never effectively severe, but whose world could never live up to these implanted expectations and who therefore in time came to constantly feel that they were being mistrusted, ignored, not allowed to participate in the discussions that affected them—people whose ambivalent goal in rebellion has been to attract attention yet also find anonymity in a "family" that can provide the intimate sense of security which their own families once provided them but could not realistically sustain.

The style of Mao the public man is that of both the rebel and the provider of security. Mao's genius in understanding the emotions of others made him appreciate the linkage between leadership and dependency. Out of his own narcissistic needs he understood that everyone must have their own lingering cravings for the security and joys of infancy when the "omnipotence of the wish" has not been differentiated from dependency. The universal power of this memory of how wonderful existence can really be is attested to by the rareness of suicide and persistence of fear of death among those for whom life would seem to hold little or no promise.*

Mao's ability to mix the character of the "monkey" and

---

* This point was made by Harold D. Lasswell in a private communication. He further observed that it would be no exaggeration to say that "everyone" must be influenced by latent memories of infantile bliss in which dependency and omnipotence are blended because any infant who did not experience such treatment would not survive infancy.

the "tiger" and to play out in public his various ambivalences and contradictions also depended upon his refusal to allow his own emotions to become involved so as to become "committed" to any immediate, concrete objects or persons. The fact that his greatest emotional shock came from his mother's actions, and the appearance of a brother he knew he should have loved, encouraged him to use idealization as a principal defense mechanism while holding back his real emotions. Thus his ability to deal in high abstractions and worthy causes, while keeping at the tactical level his affect so completely detached that any change or maneuver was possible.

The plausibility of our interpretation of Mao's emotional development is supported by a critical fact which the careful reader may have noted as it has appeared implicitly in our account, but which we have not felt it necessary to comment explicitly on until now. This psychologically important fact is that from the time of Mao's childhood confrontations with his father he has, at every stage in his life, always acted so as to maneuver someone else into a conflictional, adversary relationship with himself. He has not been given to diffuse hostilities or to taking on the whole world. On the contrary, his practice has been to engage one person, a single main "foe," with whom he would lock himself in the embrace of conflict. Regardless of predispositions of the other one Mao seemingly could draw the person into conflict with himself, and then he would focus his psychic energies on elaborating that single conflict of the moment.

This pattern began with his relations with his father; it became more pronounced when he chose, apparently gratuitously, to clash with his teachers and headmasters. After adolescence and throughout his career in the Party he has invariably found someone with whom he has felt it necessary to clash, and these conflicts have tended to give structure to his life. Nearly every conflict has required a dramatizing or acting out of roles that seem to be more vividly perceived in Mao's mind than in the "opponents." His conflicts have generally involved personal relationships, but at times he has built his bonds of conflict with a larger opponent: America at one time, Japan at another, and most intensely, the Soviet Union.

In carrying on these struggles he has been able to adopt numerous postures and roles, appealing to a variety of audiences. He has always acted as if his personality was secure. At close range this quality of adaptability has made him the master of his other colleagues. Within the ring of the Politburo and the wider one of the Central Committee he has always found at any moment a majority who could identify with whatever persona he might happen to be presenting. At the more distant range Mao has always presented himself as a figure capable of meeting the public demands of the moment. In all contexts, Mao's personality and the role he is performing at the time seem to fit "as if" they belonged together naturally.

The psychological considerations illuminating the mysteries of Mao's extraordinary charismatic powers in mobilizing the emotions of the Chinese people may also, however, account for his problems in stabilizing the gains of his great revolution. For as we have just seen, Mao's basic fear of again being hurt by someone else commanding his emotions, a fear which has run so deep as to make him "abandon" all of his wives and children, has also made it impossible for him to give permanent support to any of his associates.

This theme of abandonment has made it impossible for him to devolve his charismatic authority upon his lieutenants so that they can carry on what he has accomplished with his authority. The problem is not just that his successors cannot possibly rule by charisma and thus they will have to fall back upon routine practices and bureaucratic institutions—forms that Mao deeply distrusts. Mao's deeper difficulty seems to be his profound inability to maintain positive feelings for anyone, so that he cannot accept anyone as his worthy successor.

The unthinkable thought must thus be raised: Mao's remarkable personality, which made it possible for him to reshape the oldest and largest society, may also make it impossible to preserve his accomplishments. By having to "abandon" his immediate associates he may in effect be "abandoning" what he has idealized most, his revolution. From Mao's personal perspective there must be a tremendous gap between immediate associates, who are so close that he cannot allow his affect to be directed toward them, and his revolution which is distant, abstract, and hence a safe object for attaching his emotions. Yet the historical process rests upon particular people carrying out specific tasks even in the search for the most abstract ideals.

The succession to Mao Tse-tung will in time be worked out, and China will have new leaders. Regardless of whatever private feelings they may have about Mao, they will have to acknowledge his greatness in the making of modern China. As all great men in history he will be honored, especially by those who will seek the magic of his greatness to insure the legitimacy of their authority. Thus it is likely that as time goes by the public Mao will become increasingly shrouded in myth, and it will become even more difficult to penetrate to the domain of the private man where must lie the secrets of his greatness. Just possibly, however, history may take a slightly different turn, and, as unlikely as it may seem now, there may be revelations of more facts about the life of Mao Tse-tung making it possible to evaluate better our interpretation of his greatness.

Mao Tse-tung's place in Chinese history is, however, secure, and his successors, whoever they may be, will be of quite different character. Mao's belonged to the era of China's response to the modern world: He wanted China to change, to become strong and powerful in the eyes of all the world; yet he also wanted China to be true to itself. He was a leader out of rural China, educated in a provincial setting, and unacquainted with any foreign language. His distrust of cities reflected in part that he was not at home with the more cosmopolitan generation of Chinese who went further in exploring foreign ways than he was ever ready to do.

Although the underlying issue of how far Chinese society will go in breaking with the essentials of its Confucian traditions is still unresolved, Mao has certainly applied his political and charismatic genius to remake China in a new form. Yet, Mao cannot escape his own life history, and therefore his version of a new China still manifests in innumerable ways qualities that have always been associated with Chinese greatness: stress on the group rather than the individual; emphasis upon correctness in behavior; faith in the importance of ideology and morality; concern with the proper ways of socializing children; sensitivity to the opinions of others and to humiliation; and all the other qualities associated with Sinic civilization. Mao has been able to bring about amazing changes in China precisely because he understands the compulsive forces that still impel the products of this civilization to strive for correctness and greatness.

The lenses of psychology can give vividness only to life histories; they cannot serve as a telescope to foresee the future. Mao's ultimate place in history will be determined by not just the persisting grip of his childhood on all the phases of his life but also by considerations that will only appear tomorrow. Today there are two views of Mao contending for historical acceptance. (That is if we properly exclude the voices at the fringes that would make him either a demon or a demigod.)

The one depicts Mao as largely an emotional phenomenon, a romantic revolutionary, always ready to upset the consensus, create disorder, and, while adding spice to life, on balance deterring progress and increasingly preventing China from realizing her full potential. The other view of Mao rejoices in his destabilizing acts, applauds his unconventional vision, and prays that he prefer egalitarian intimacy to material progress.

Our psychological interpretation of Mao Tse-tung provides no answer as to which perspective history will hold as "right" or "wrong." Instead we have been seeking to discover the ambivalences that lie at the heart of the personality of Mao and which give authenticity to both perspectives.

The aged Mao has continually worried over whether the next generation of Chinese will sustain the revolutionary spirit that he felt had guided his life. The certainty, of course, is that there will always be some rebellious spirits in China, for the inescapable character of the process by which humans emerge from their prolonged periods of dependency insures that there will always be some who become restless rebels. Mao's legitimate worry, however, is that in the future there will be few who respond to the same historic forces that shaped his early life.

Thus there is a strange contradiction in the significance of Mao's life. Viewed in historic terms he belongs to a past era when rural China was at home in its old traditions and only its most restless citizens sought change in modern terms. Viewed psychologically, however, Mao's life takes on a timeless and universal significance. With respect to the emergence of modern China the public Mao's relevance was to a phase of the Chinese Revolution that is now nearly completed; with respect to the psychological development of charismatic, revolutionary leadership the story of the private Mao has enduring relevance.

The Public Man

As insightful as Mao has been about his own character, he seems in his old age to be unable to distinguish between the moment in history when he was the appropriate revolutionary leader and the need for a different role for future revolutionary spirits in China. In his anxiety over whether the youth of China will manifest commitment to the "revolution," he seems to picture the goal to be the achievement of a static state that conforms to the utopian ideals of his generation, and he overlooks the reality that the goal of any succeeding generation of revolutionaries will be to bring about changes beyond the imagination of his generation. Thus we find that Mao is ambivalent even about his presumed cherished value of rebelliousness and revolution: He worries whether the next generation of Chinese will be adequately "revolutionary," whether they will adequately "conform" to his concept of the proper revolutionary. As the "father" of the Chinese revolution his problems are now like those of parents. Mao's dilemma, of course, is whether he truly wants China's youth to be inspired by his own "monkey spirit" and in their spontaneity possibly alter all that he has sought to give to China, or does he want them only to "play at" spontaneity in lock-step conformity?

The climax of Mao as Public Man and as Private Man is perfectly captured by his words in a poem written to Chou En-lai early in 1975 shortly before the meeting of the Second Plenum of the Tenth Party Congress. As we have so frequently found, starting with his poem of mourning for his mother, Mao's use of words reveals both his conscious concerns and his deeper inner anxieties. The title of the poem is, appropriately, "To Reveal One's True Feelings" and reads as follows:

> Loyal parents who sacrificed so much for the nation
> Never feared the ultimate fate.

The Problem Revisited

Now that the country has become red, who will be its
  guardian?

Our mission unfinished may take a thousand years.
The struggle tires us, and our hair is grey.
You and I, old friends, can we just watch our efforts be washed
  away?

The first two lines sound a note of solid confidence as
they uphold the idea that parents who make sacrifices can be
absolutely sure of what will follow for their children. In the
next line doubt emerges and Mao reveals his uncertainty and
anxiety about what might happen when there is no strong
"guardian" or real "father." Then in the last lines despair takes
over as Mao acknowledges the limits of his own capacity as
"parent." The contrast between the first and the last lines
gives emphasis to Mao's view that while others can be firm and
confident parents, he knows that he himself, who was so successful as a rebellious son, lacks the capacity to be an influencing "father." Behind the surface appearances of self-assurance,
there lie the insecurities and self-doubts which have produced
his remarkable spirit of the "monkey" and the "tiger."

This poem, written late in Mao's life when he must have
been contemplating all the varied roles he had played as Public
Man, provides confirmation for the psychological interpretation which has run through this entire book.

NOTES

CHAPTER 1 / *The Problem*

1. For an analysis of the linkage between Chinese cultural patterns for controling aggression and the Chinese propensity for theatrical behavior see Lucian W. Pye, *The Spirit of Chinese Politics* (Cambridge: M.I.T. Press, 1968), especially Chap. 9.

2. Lowell Dittmer with great insight has recognized that Mao's personality conforms to Harold Lasswell's definition of the "dramatizing" character, and that Liu Shao-ch'i was a model of Lasswell's "compulsive" character. See Lowell Dittmer, "Power and Personality in China," *Studies in Comparative Communism*, Vol. VII, Nos. 1 and 2 (1974), pp. 21–49; and Lowell Dittmer, *Liu Shao-ch'i and the Chinese Cultural Revolution* (Berkeley: University of California Press, 1974), Chapter 6.

For our purposes it may be helpful to follow briefly Dittmer's lead and pin down more clearly Mao's "dramatizing" character by contrasting his style with that of Liu Shao-ch'i who as a "compulsive" personality was a "natural" opponent for Mao in the Cultural Revolution. Lasswell's descriptions of his two generalized types of political men seem to fit perfectly the differences between Mao and Liu. "The dramatizing character may resort to traces of exhibitionism, flirtatiousness, provocativeness, indignation; but in any case all devices are pivoted around the task of 'getting a rise out of' the other person. . . . The compulsive inclines toward carefully defined limits and the well-worked-out ordering of parts; the dramatizer excels in scope and abundance of loosely classified detail. The hallmark of the former is the imposition of uniformity, while the latter tolerates diversity and excels in nuance. The compulsive desubjectivizes a situation, while the dramatizer remains sensitized to psychological dimensions; the one denies novelty, while the other welcomes it; one squeezes and compresses the dimensions of the human situation which the other complies with and allows to spread. The compulsive monotonizes the presentation of the self to the other, while the latter multiplies the faces and facades which can be presented to other persons." Harold D. Lasswell, *Power and Personality* (New York: W. W. Norton, 1948), p. 62.

3. It is interesting that in the history of the study of modern China there is considerable legitimacy for intellectual history but not for the role of personality. The ideas of intellectuals, and the ways Chinese responded to Western ideas, have been treated as self-evident forces in shaping modern China. The power of such ideas is almost always treated in isolation from the personalities and the emotional responses of the Chinese. See such studies as Benjamin Schwartz, *Chinese Communism and the Rise*

Notes

of Mao Tse-tung (Cambridge: Harvard University Press, 1951); and Joseph R. Levenson, *Confucian China and Its Modern Fate:* Vol. I, *The Problem of Intellectual Continuity,* 1959; Vol. II, *The Problem of Monarchial Decay,* 1964; Vol. III, *The Problem of Historical Significance* (Berkeley: University of California Press).

4. Harold D. Lasswell, *Psychopathology and Politics* (Chicago: University of Chicago Press, 1930), p. 50.

5. The theory of narcissism, in grossly oversimplified form, holds that in earliest infancy when separation of ego and non-ego has not taken place, the ego is extremely weak, and anything pleasant is considered ego. The baby, if his environment is appropriately supportive, senses no differentiation between himself and the world, and thus he and his world are one, his every wish becomes a command, and his sense of his own goodness is the center of his magical universe. When he cannot relieve every pain by crying and hence commanding his world, he experiences deep frustrations, anxieties over his own goodness, and possibly the beginnings of guilt. Thus omnipotence and self-esteem are intimately linked to a longing for the "oceanic feeling of primary narcissism." Later after the child has developed a sense of his separate ego and differentiation between ego and non-ego has taken place, it is possible to revive the fantasy of being incorporated as one in the world, of recapturing the sense of omnipotence and inherent goodness that went with primary narcissism. It is this form of "secondary narcissism" which is the basis of the narcissistic personality, who is constantly in search of self-esteem (as in Lasswell's theory of the political man) that is the basis of our theory of the charismatic leader. Narcissism makes possible the focusing of tremendous psychic energies on the ego. For technical details about narcissism see: Sigmund Freud, "On Narcissism: An Introduction" in *Collected Papers,* ed. Ernest Jones, trans. Joan Riviere (New York: Basic Books, 1959), Vol. IV, pp. 30–59; and Otto Fenichel, *The Psychoanalytical Theory of Neurosis* (New York: W. W. Norton, 1945).

6. I am indebted to discussion with Dr. Steve Pieczenik, M.D., for help in arriving at this concept of the *mutual exploitation of vulnerabilities* as the basis of the charismatic relationship between leader and followers.

7. "Examples of Dialectics," *Miscellany of Mao Tse-tung Thought,* Part I (Arlington, Va.: Joint Publications Research Service 61269–1, February 20, 1974), p. 214.

CHAPTER 2 / *Impressions of the Private Man*

1. Chen Ch'ang-feng, *Ken-sui Mao Chu-hsi Ch'ang-cheng (With Chairman Mao on the Long March)* (Peking Tso-chia Ch'u pan she, 1959).

2. Siao Yu, *Mao Tse-tung and I Were Beggars* (London: Hutchinson & Co., 1961), p. 31.

3. Li Jui, *Mao Tse-tung t'ung-chih ti ch'u-ch'i ke-ming huo-tung (Comrade Mao's Early Revolutionary Activities)* (Peking: Chung-kuo Ch'ing-mien Ch'u-pan she, 1957).

4. Jerome Ch'en, *Mao and the Chinese Revolution* (London: Oxford University Press, 1965), p. 210.

5. Li Jui, *Comrade Mao's Activities,* p. 45.

Notes

6. Chou Shih-chao, "Ti-i-shih-fan Shih-tai ti Mao-chu-hsi" ("Chairman Mao at the First Teachers' Training School"), *Hsin Kuan Ch'a*, Vol. II, No. 2 (1965), p. 11.

7. Ch'en, *Mao*, p. 211.

8. Edgar Snow, *Red Star Over China*, rev. ed. (New York: Grove Press, 1968), p. 96.

9. Li Ang, *Hung-se Wu-t'ai (The Red Stage)* (Chungking: Sheng-li Ch'u-pan-she, 1942), p. 76.

10. Chang, Kuo-t'ao, *Wo ti Hui Yi (Memoirs)*, Vol. I (Hong Kong: Ming Pao Publishing Co., 1971), p. 137.

10A. Sheng Shan (pseudonym) "Mao Tse-tung As I Know Him," Chung-hua Yüeh-pao *(China Monthly)* No. 718, July 1, 1975, p. 45.

11. *Hung-ch'i p'iao-p'iao*, No. 12 (May 1959), pp. 148–156.

12. *Ibid.*

13. Li Jui, *Comrade Mao's Activities*, p. 164.

14. The newsletter was published in *Red Flag Daily*, No. 14, August 28, 1930, as cited in Hsiao Tso-liang, *Power Relations Within the Chinese Communist Movement, 1930–1934: A Study of Documents* (Seattle: University of Washington Press, 1961), p. 36.

15. Snow, *Red Star Over China*, p. 90.

16. Chao Ch'ao-kuo, *Yenan i-yueh (A Month in Yenan)* (Shanghai: Hsin-min pao-she, 1946), p. 60.

17. Robert Payne, *Journey to Red China* (London: William Heinemann Ltd., 1947), pp. 84–85.

18. Snow, *Red Star Over China*, p. 95.

19. Gunther Stein, *The Challenge of Red China* (London, 1943), p. 83.

20. Chai Tso-chün, *Tsai Mao-chu-hsi shen-pien (With Chairman Mao)* (Wuhan, 1959), pp. 10–17, cited in Ch'en, *Mao*, p. 209.

21. Stuart Schram, *Mao Tse-tung* (Harmondsworth: Penguin, 1966), p. 237.

22. Nikita Khrushchev, *Khrushchev Remembers*, trans. Strobe Talbott (Boston: Little, Brown and Co., 1970), p. 462.

23. Nikita Khrushchev, *Khrushchev Remembers: The Last Testament*, trans. Strobe Talbott (Boston: Little, Brown and Co., 1974), p. 252.

24. Howard L. Boorman, "Mao Tse-tung: the Lacquered Image," *The China Quarterly*, No. 16 (Oct.–Dec. 1963), pp. 1–55.

25. A. L. Sulzberger, *An Age of Mediocrity: Memories and Diaries, 1963–1972* (New York: Macmillan, 1973), pp. 7–8.

26. *Hung-ch'i p'iao-p'iao*, No. 12 (May 1959), p. 151.

27. Nym Wales, *Inside Red China* (New York: Doubleday, Doran & Co., 1939), p. 276.

28. Violet Cressy-Marcks, *Journey Into China* (New York: E. P. Dutton & Co., 1942), p. 163.

29. Edgar Snow, "Random Notes on Red China (1936–1945)," *Chinese Economic Political Studies* (Cambridge, Mass.: Harvard East Asia Center, 1957), pp. 71–72.

30. Chen Hsueh-Chao, *Yenan Fang Wen Chi (A Visit to Yenan)*, Pei-chi Shu-tien, 1940, pp. 133–134.

31. Cressy-Marcks, *Journey*, p. 188.

Notes

32. *Mao Chu-hsi Tsai Hupei (Chairman Mao in Hupei)*, Wuhan, Hupei Jen-min Ch'u-p'an-she, 1958, p. 54.

33. *Hung-ch'i p'iao-piao*, No. 10 (January 1959), p. 21.

34. Kung Chu, "Ts'an-chia Chung-kung Wu-chuang T'ou-cheng Chi-shih" ("Recollection of Participation in the Armed Struggle of the Chinese Communists"), *Ming Pao*, Vol. VI, No. 11 (November, 1971), pp. 98–99.

35. Chao Ch'ao-kuo, *Month in Yenan*, p. 63.

36. Payne, *Journey to Red China*, p. 49.

37. Snow, *Red Star Over China*, p. 94.

38. Robert Payne, *Mao Tse-tung: Ruler of Red China* (New York: Henry Schuman, 1950), p. 225.

39. Agnes Smedley, *Battle Hymn of China* (New York: Alfred Knopf, 1943), pp. 268–9.

40. Agnes Smedley, *The Great Road: The Life and Times of Chu Teh* (New York: Monthly Review Press, 1956), p. 226.

41. André Malraux, *Anti-Memoirs* (New York: Holt, Reinhart and Winston, 1968), p. 372.

42. Private communication with a diplomat stationed in Peking during the 1950s.

43. Robert Loh, *Escape from Red China* (New York: Coward-McCann, 1962), p. 179.

44. Siao, Yu, *Mao Tse-tung and I*, p. 31.

45. Payne, *Journey to Red China*, p. 122.

46. Wales, *Inside Red China*, p. 276.

47. Payne, *Mao Tse-tung*, p. 37.

48. *Ibid.*

49. Smedley, *Great Road*, p. 170.

50. Payne, *Mao Tse-tung*, p. 217.

51. Snow, *Red Star Over China*, p. 150.

52. *Chung-kung Yen-chiu (Studies on Chinese Communism)*, June, 1970, p. 114.

53. "Mao's Talk at Hangchow," (December 21, 1965), *Issues and Studies* Vol. V, No. 10 (July 1969), p. 91.

54. Versions of this letter which was circulated among cadres at the beginning of the anti-Lin-Piao campaign in 1972 have been published in *Issues and Studies* Vol. IX, No. 4 (January 1973), p. 95, and the *Tsing-tao Jih-pao*, Hong Kong, November 4, 1972.

55. Margaret Mead and Martha Wolfenstein, eds., *Childhood in Contemporary Cultures* (Chicago: University of Chicago Press, 1955), p. 246.

56. *Issues and Studies* Vol. IX, No. 4 (January 1973), p. 95.

CHAPTER 3 / *Impressions of the Public Man*

1. Edgar Snow, *The Long Revolution* (New York: Random House, 1972), p. 170.

2. *Ibid.*, p. 205.

3. Stanley Karnow, *Mao and China* (New York: Viking Press, 1972), p. 7.

Notes

4. Robert S. Elegant, *Mao's Great Revoluton* (New York and Cleveland: World Publishing Co., 1971), p. 62.

5. Robert Jay Lifton, *Revolutionary Immortality: Mao Tse-tung and the Chinese Cultural Revolution* (New York: Vintage Books, 1968), p. 19.

6. A. Doak Barnett, *Uncertain Passage: China's Transition to the Post-Mao Era* (Washington, D.C.: Brookings Institution, 1974), pp. 8–9.

7. Michel C. Oksenberg, "Policy Making Under Mao, 1948–68: An Overview," in John M. H. Lindbeck, ed., *China: Management of a Revolutionary Society* (Seattle: University of Washington Press, 1971), p. 83.

8. Possibly the most rigorous attempt to distinguish Mao's views from those of Liu Shao-ch'i is to be found in Harry Harding, Jr., "Maoist Theories of Policy-Making and Organization" in Thomas W. Robinson, *The Cultural Revolution in China* (Berkeley: University of California Press, 1971), pp. 113–164.

9. Elegant, *Mao's Great Revolution*, p. 447.

10. *Selected Works of Mao Tse-tung*, Vol. III (Peking: Foreign Languages Press, 1964), p. 183, cited in Jerome Ch'en, "The Development and Logic of Mao Tse-tung's Thought, 1928–49," in Chalmers Johnson, ed., *Ideology and Politics in Contemporary China* (Seattle: University of Washington Press, 1973), p. 106.

11. Boyd Compton, *Mao's China: Party Reform Documents, 1942–1944* (Seattle: University of Washington Press, 1952), Chapter I.

12. Khrushchev, *The Last Testament*, p. 240.

13. Benjamin Schwartz, *Ideology in Flux* (Cambridge: Harvard University Press, 1968), pp. 102–113; Stuart Schram, ed., *Authority, Participation and Cultural Change in China* (New York: Cambridge University Press, 1973), pp. 40–50.

14. "Talk at the Hangchow Conference of the Shanghai Bureau," (April 1957) *Miscellany of Mao Tse-tung Thought* (Arlington, Va.: JPRS, 61269-1, February, 1974), Part I, p. 65.

15. "Talks with Directors of Various Cooperative Areas," (November, December 1958) *Miscellany of Mao Tse-tung Thought*, Part I, p. 133.

16. "Talk at the Hangchow Conference of the Shanghai Bureau," (April 1957), *Miscellany of Mao Tse-tung Thought*, Part I, p. 80.

17. "Examples of Dialectics (Abstractive Compilation)," (1959?), *Miscellany of Mao Tse-tung Thought*, Part I, p. 203.

18. *Ibid.*, p. 204.

19. "Speech at the Second Session of the Eighth Party Congress" (May 17, 1958), *Miscellany of Mao Tse-tung Thought*, Part I, p. 112.

20. "Examples of Dialectics (Abstracted Compilation)," p. 204.

21. "Speech at the Second Session of the Eighth Party Congress," p. 92.

22. "Talk on Methods of Solidarity," (August 1964), *Miscellany of Mao Tse-tung Thought*, Part II, p. 405.

23. "Interjections at Conference of Provincial and Municipal Committee Secretaries (Collected)," (January 1957), *Miscellany of Mao Tse-tung Thought*, Part I, p. 47.

24. See James Chieh Hsiung, *Ideology and Practice: The Evolution of Chinese Communism* (New York: Praeger, 1970).

25. Michel Oksenberg, *op. cit.*, p. 105-6.

Notes

26. Edward E. Rice, *Mao's Way* (Berkeley: University of California Press, 1972), p. 62.

27. "Speech at the Lushan Conference," *Chinese Law and Government*, Vol. I, No. 4 (Winter 1968–1969), pp. 27–43.

28. Roderick MacFarquhar, *The Origins of the Cultural Revolution: Contradictions among the People* (New York: Columbia University Press, 1974).

29. Oksenberg, in Lindbeck, *China*, p. 88.

30. Quoted in *ibid.*, p. 90.

31. Jerome Ch'en, *Mao* (Englewood Cliffs, N.J.: Prentice-Hall Spectrum Paperbacks, 1969), p. 94.

32. Quoted in MacFarquhar, *Origins of Cultural Revolution*, p. 204.

33. Oksenberg, *China*, p. 89.

34. Richard H. Solomon, *Mao's Revolution and the Chinese Political Culture* (Berkeley: University of California Press, 1971).

35. *Selected Readings from the Works of Mao Tse-tung* (Peking: Foreign Languages Press, 1967), pp. 130–132.

36. One version of this event is reported in Solomon, *Mao's Revolution*, p. 205.

37. *Selected Works of Mao Tse-tung* (New York: International Publishers, 1954), p. 13.

38. See Nathan Leites, *The Study of Bolshevism* (Glencoe, Ill.: The Free Press, 1953).

39. "Speech at the Lushan Conference," p. 28.

40. "Speeches at the Second Session of the Eighth Party Congress," *Miscellany of Mao Tse-tung Thought*, Part I, p. 98.

41. "Kwangsi Campaign" written in the fall of 1929, published in *Mao Chu-hsi Shih Tz'u*, trans. Dorothy Grouse Fontana (Peking: Jen Min Wen Hsueh Ch'u Pan She, 1968), p. 6. The Ting River is in Fukien, where Mao was advancing, while Chiang Kai-shek was fighting with warlords in Kwangsi.

42. "Ninth Day of the Ninth Moon," written in October 1929, *ibid.*, p. 7.

43. "New Years Day," written in 1929, published in *Mao Tse-tung Nineteen Poems*, ed. Chou Chen-fu and foreword by Tsang Keh-chia. (Peking: Foreign Language Press, 1958), p. 13.

44. "On the Road to Kuang Ch'ang," written in February 1930, *Mao Chu Hsi Shih Tz'u*, p. 9. Fontana translation.

45. "Withstanding the First Encirclement," written in spring 1931, *ibid.*, p. 11.

46. "Withstanding the Second Encirclement," written in summer 1931, *ibid.*, p. 14.

47. "Tapoti," written in February 1933 after the Fourth Encirclement; *Mao Tse-tung Nineteen Poems*, p. 15.

48. "The Long March," written in September 1935, *ibid.*, p. 18.

49. "Liupan," written in October 1935, *ibid.*, p. 19.

50. "The Peoples' Liberation Army Occupation of Nanking," written in April 1949, *Mao Chu Hsi Tz'u*, p. 30. Fontana translation.

Notes

CHAPTER 4 / *The Home and Mother*

1. Richard Solomon has suggested that swimming represents for Mao a way of breaking free from all controls, particularly those of his father and the traditions of being constrained by the obligations of filial piety. See Richard H. Solomon, *A Revolution Is Not a Dinner Party: A Feast of Images of the Maoist Transformation of China* (New York: Doubleday, 1975).

2. In *The Morning Deluge* (Boston: Little, Brown and Co., 1972), p. 18, Han Suyin reports that Tse-hung was adopted. Other biographies make no mention of this fact, but since Tse-hung was about the same age as Mao Tse-t'an it seems likely that she was adopted. She must, however, have been treated very much as a natural daughter since her adopted status was not well known.

3. Robert Payne, *Mao Tse-tung: Ruler of Red China* (New York: Henry Schuman, 1950), p. 25.

4. Edward E. Rice, *Mao's Way* (Berkeley: University of California Press, 1972), p. 3.

5. Edgar Snow, *Red Star Over China*, rev. ed. (New York: Grove Press, 1968), p. 132.

6. *Ibid.*, p. 134.

7. *Ibid.*, p. 132.

8. Hsiao San (Emi Hsiao), *Mao Tse-tung ti Ch'ing-nien Shih-tai* (*Mao Tse-tung's Youth*) (Hong Kong: Hsin-min-chu Ch'u-p'an-she, 1949), p. 19. Interestingly in a revised edition published in Peking in August, 1949, this episode about the food was deleted.

9. Francis L. K. Hsu, *Under the Ancestor's Shadow* (New York: Columbia University Press, 1948).

10. Snow, *Red Star Over China*, pp. 124–125.

11. Han Suyin, *Morning Deluge*, pp. 16–17.

12. Payne, *Mao Tse-tung: Ruler of Red China*, p. 25.

13. Snow, *Red Star Over China*, p. 131.

14. Li Jui, *Mao Tse-tung t'ung-chih ti ch'u-ch'i ko-ming huo-tung* (Peking: Chung-kuo Ch'ing-nien ch'u-pan She, 1957), p. 8.

15. Snow, *Red Star Over China*, p. 150.

16. Li Jui, *Mao Tse-tung*, p. 8.

CHAPTER 5 / *Brothers and Sister*

1. Edgar Snow, *Red Star Over China*, rev. ed. (New York: Grove Press, 1968), p. 151.

2. "Speech at a Report Meeting" (October 24, 1966), in *Long Live Mao Tse-tung Thought*, translated in *Current Background* (Hong Kong: American Consulate General, No. 891, Oct. 8, 1969), p. 71.

3. Snow, *Red Star Over China*, p. 131.

4. Literally, the title is "Water Margin Tales" but Pearl Buck, in translating this

Notes

romantic tale of a bandit gang, captured its basic spirit by calling it, *All Men Are Brothers* (New York: John Day, 1933).

5. Siao-yu, *Mao Tse-tung and I Were Beggars* (Syracuse, N.Y.: Syracuse University Press, 1959), p. 11.

6. Edgar Snow, *The Long Revolution* (New York: Random House, 1971, 1972), pp. 220–221.

7. Martha Wolfenstein, *Disaster, A Psychological Essay* (Glencoe, Ill.: The Free Press, 1957).

CHAPTER 6 / *The Father*

1. Howard L. Boorman, ed., *Biographical Dictionary of Republican China*, Vol. III (New York: Columbia University Press, 1970), p. 2.

2. Edgar Snow, *Red Star Over China*, rev. ed. (New York: Grove Press, 1968) p. 132.

3. *Ibid.*

4. Robert Payne, *Mao Tse-tung: Ruler of Red China* (New York: Henry Schuman, 1950) chapter 2.

5. Hsiao San, *Mao Tse-tung T'ung-chih ti Chung-shao-nien shih-tai (Mao Tse-tung's Youth)* (Hong Kong: Hsin-min-chu Ch'u-pan-she, 1949), p. 9.

6. Li Jui, *Mao Tse-tung t'ung-chih ti ch'u-ch'i ko-ming huo-tung* (Peking: Chung-kuo Ch'ing-nien Ch'u-pan she, 1957), p. 6.

7. Snow, *Red Star Over China*, p. 132.

8. *Ibid.*, p. 131.

9. Report by Dr. C. P. Li in *New York Times*, September 11, 1973, p. 32.

10. Snow, *Red Star Over China*, p. 133.

11. *Tokyo Shimbun*, September 27, 1972. Richard H. Solomon brought this published conversation to my attention.

12. Snow, *Red Star Over China*, pp. 132–133.

13. *Ibid.*, p. 133.

14. *Ibid.*

15. Quoted in "Chairman Mao's Youth and Boyhood," published in booklet form with the title, *Material for Study*, by Red Guards, Peking, no date but probably 1966. Translated in *Current Background* (Hong Kong: American Consulate General, No. 900, Jan. 30, 1970), p. 13.

16. *Ibid.*, p. 14.

17. Snow, *Red Star Over China*, p. 132.

18. *Ibid.*, p. 133.

19. See Lucian W. Pye, *The Spirit of Chinese Politics* (Cambridge: M.I.T. Press, 1968); Richard H. Solomon, *Mao's Revolution and Chinese Political Culture* (Berkeley: University of California Press, 1971).

20. *Tokyo Shimbun*, September 27, 1972.

21. Snow, *Red Star Over China*, p. 132.

22. *Ibid.*

23. *Ibid.*, p. 133.

24. *Ibid.*, p. 142.

25. *Ibid.*

26. Quoted in *Chairman Mao's Activities in Revolutionary Practice*, no publication date given, but appeared in 1966 in Peking during the Cultural Revolution and translated in *Current Background* (Hong Kong: American Consulate General, No. 900, Jan. 30, 1970), p. 13. The editor of this pamphlet elaborates on Mao's theme of the dangers of laziness and observes, "Once a nation is lazy, revisionism will appear, and the Soviet Union is a good example." Then in an interesting but peculiarly Chinese twist, he links laziness with gluttony, the supreme temptation of self-indulgence in an oral culture. "When the Soviet Army Song and Dance Ensemble came to Changsha last year, its members were lazy and gluttonous, and they constantly looked around for good things to satisfy their gluttony. When they came to visit the seedless orange orchard planted by the Provincial Committee itself, they became so gluttonous that they asked us whether they could have some. When we answered in the affirmative, they ate as many as they could. Then they asked us whether they could take some away, and we told them that they could take as many as they wished. They also asked us how many days these oranges could be kept because they wanted to take some home for their wives and children. We asked them, 'Haven't you seedless oranges in Moscow?' They said: 'Not even oranges with seeds, let alone seedless oranges.'

"On another occasion, more than thirty people came to visit Shaoshan, and twelve of them were Soviet revisionists. Our hostel served them with chicken, and they ate with their fingers. They filled their pockets with fruits, and they were so gluttonous that they knew not there was such a thing as shame.

"When Chairman Mao wrote his article more than 50 years ago in 1914, he was only 20 years old. Now some people have degenerated because starting from laziness they have glided down the black line of laziness, gluttony and avarice. This question was pointed out by Chairman Mao fifty years ago."

27. Talk at the Hangchow Conference, December 21, 1965, published in Chinese in *Long Live Mao Tse-tung Thought* (no date or place of publication given), translated in *Current Background* (Hong Kong: American Consulate General, No. 891, Oct. 8, 1969), p. 52. It is strange for Mao in 1965 to speak of "traders" as models for children—it is almost as if he had forgotten that the Chinese economy was socialized and was thinking about the world his father had known.

28. Dr. Nelson Fu of the Baptist Mission Hospital in Changting treated Mao and said he needed extensive rest. Edward E. Rice, *Mao's Way* (Berkeley: University of California Press, 1972), p. 62.

29. James P. Harrison, *The Long March to Power* (New York: Praeger, 1972), p. 468.

30. *Ibid.*, p. 497.

31. For a most insightful appreciation of the psychology of justice in French culture see Nathan Leites, *The Rulers of the Game in Paris* (Chicago: University of Chicago Press, 1966).

32. Snow, *Red Star Over China*, pp. 132, 133.

33. *Ibid.*, p. 133.

34. Mao's experience in seeking to find a higher and abstract authority to control immediate and concrete authorities is remarkably similar to what the early Lutherans

Notes

and Calvinists did in evoking the concept of a "Heavenly Father" to counter the authority of temporal fathers. Robert Bellah has argued that this approach of early Protestants made it possible for them to maintain the notion of rigid submission to authority while in fact innovating concepts of justice. This was possible because the concept of a Heavenly Father was appropriately grand to evoke the notion of supreme authority but adequately vague to allow individual definition (see Robert Bellah, *Beyond Belief* (New York: Harper & Row, 1970). Mao with the classics and then with Marxism similarly combined abstract authority with his own personal innovations.

35. Snow, *Red Star Over China*, p. 175.

CHAPTER 7 / Students and Teachers

1. Edgar Snow, *Red Star Over China*, rev. ed. (New York: Grove Press, 1968) p. 134.

2. *Ibid.*, p. 136.

3. Stuart Schram, *Mao Tse-tung* (London: Penguin, 1966) pp. 20–23.

4. Snow, *Red Star Over China*, p. 135.

5. Schram, *Mao Tse-tung*, p. 22.

6. Snow, *Red Star Over China*, p. 135.

7. *Ibid.*

8. *Ibid.*

9. *Ibid.*, p. 136.

10. *Ibid.*, p. 134.

11. Siao-yu, *Mao Tse-tung and I Were Beggars* (Syracuse, N.Y.: Syracuse University Press, 1959), pp. 18–23.

12. *Ibid.*, p. 20.

13. *Ibid.*, pp. 19–20.

14. Snow, *Red Star Over China*, p. 137.

15. *Ibid.*

16. *Ibid.*

17. *Ibid.*

18. *Ibid.*, p. 151.

19. Siao-yu, *Mao Tse-tung and I*, pp. 24–25.

20. *Ibid.*, p. 150.

21. *Ibid.*, p. 30.

22. Snow, *Red Star Over China*, p. 138.

23. Siao-yu, *Mao Tse-tung and I*, p. 26.

24. Snow, *Red Star Over China*, p. 139.

25. *Ibid.*, p. 140.

26. *Ibid.*

27. Schram, *Mao Tse-tung*, p. 33.

28. Snow, *Red Star Over China*, p. 142.

29. *Ibid.*

30. *Ibid.*

31. *Ibid.*

32. Schram, *Mao Tse-tung*, p. 34.

33. Lucian W. Pye, "Personal Identity and Political Ideology," in Bruce Mazlish, ed., *Psychoanalysis and History* (Englewood Cliffs, N.J.: Prentice-Hall, 1963), pp. 165–166.

34. Robert Payne, *Mao Tse-tung: Ruler of Red China* (New York: Henry Schuman, 1950), pp. 44–45.

35. *Ibid.*, p. 45.

36. Snow, *Red Star Over China*, p. 143.

37. Payne, *Mao Tse-tung: Ruler of Red China*, p. 45.

38. *Ibid.*, p. 45.

39. Snow, *Red Star Over China*, p. 143.

40. *Ibid.*

41. *Ibid.*

42. *Ibid.*

43. *Ibid.*

44. *Ibid.*

45. *Ibid.*, p. 144.

46. *Ibid.*, pp. 144–145.

47. Payne, *Mao Tse-tung: Ruler of Red China*, pp. 49–50.

48. Snow, *Red Star Over China*, p. 145.

49. *Ibid.*

50. *Ibid.*

51. "Instructions Given at the Spring Festival Concerning Educational Work." (February 13, 1964) in *Long Live Mao Tse-tung Thought*, translated in *Current Background* (Hong Kong: American Consulate General, No. 891, October 8, 1969), pp. 42–43.

52. Snow, *Red Star Over China*, p. 145.

53. *Ibid.*, p. 146.

CHAPTER 8 / *Wives and Children*

1. Edgar Snow, *Red Star Over China*, rev. ed. (New York: Grove Press, 1968), p. 147.

2. Lucian W. Pye, *China: An Introduction* (Boston: Little, Brown and Co., 1972), p. 223.

3. Siao-yu, *Mao Tse-tung and I Were Beggars* (Syracuse, N.Y.: Syracuse University Press, 1959), p. 52.

4. Snow, *Red Star Over China*, p. 146.

5. Mao not only mentioned the figure of his salary to Edgar Snow, but in 1964 when he was seventy years old he observed in a speech that ". . . In 1918 I was at the Peking University library receiving eight silver dollars a month and utterly disregarding the amenities of life. . . ." "Minutes of Spring Festival Talk" (13 February 1964), *Miscellany of Mao Tse-tung Thought*, Part II, p. 328.

6. Snow, *Red Star Over China*, p. 152. Mao must have been confused as to the T'ang poet's reference since the Pei Hai in Peking dates only from the Ming period.

Notes

7. *Ibid.*

8. Han Suyin, *The Morning Deluge* (Boston: Little, Brown and Co., 1972), p. 64.

9. Stuart Schram, *Mao Tse-tung* (London: Penguin, 1966), p. 51.

10. *Ibid.*, p. 56.

11. *Ibid.*, p. 55.

12. Snow, *Red Star Over China*, p. 155.

13. Edward C. Rice, *Mao's Way* (Berkeley: University of California Press, 1972), p. 23.

14. *Ibid.*, p. 23.

15. Schram, *Mao Tse-tung*, p. 57.

16. Snow, *Red Star Over China*, p. 155.

17. Edgar Snow, *Red Star Over China* (New York: Grove Press, 1968), p. 486.

18. Schram, *Mao Tse-tung*, p. 57.

19. Donald W. Klein and Anne Clark, *Biographical Dictionary of Chinese Communism, 1921–1971*, Vol. II (Cambridge: Harvard University Press, 1971), p. 677.

20. Howard L. Boorman, ed., *Biographical Dictionary of Republican China*, Vol. III (New York: Columbia University Press, 1970), p. 5.

21. Suyin, *Morning Deluge*, p. 86.

22. Robert Payne, *Mao Tse-tung* (New York: Weybright and Talley, 1950), p. 61.

23. Snow, *Red Star Over China* (New York: Random House, 1938), p. 156n.

24. Jerome Ch'en, *Mao and the Chinese Revolution* (New York: Oxford University Press, 1967), p. 378.

24A. Sheng Shan, (pseudonym) "Mao Tse-tung As I Know Him," *Chung-kua Yüeh-pao (China Monthly)*, No. 718, July 1, 1975, p. 46.

25. Tung Lin, *Mao Chu-hsi Ke-ming te I-chia (The Revolutionary Family of Chairman Mao)* (no date or publisher, but a Red Guard publication, probably from Peking in 1966 or 1967), pp. 9–10.

26. Rice, *Mao's Way*, p. 30.

27. *Ibid.*, p. 66.

28. *Ibid.*, p. 66.

29. Kung Ch'u, *Wo Yu Hung Chun (The Red Army and I)* (South Wind Publishing Company, 1954), p. 144.

30. *Ibid.*, p. 396.

31. Rice, *Mao's Way*, p. 66.

32. Robert Payne, *Mao Tse-tung: Ruler of Red China* (New York: Henry Schuman, 1950), p. 143.

33. Rice, *Mao's Way*, p. 102.

34. *Ibid.*, p. 102.

35. Chen Ch'ang-feng, *Ken-sui Mao Chu-hsi Ch'ang-cheng (With Chairman Mao On The Long March)* (Peking: Tso-chia Ch'u-pan She, 1959), p. 8.

36. Yang Tzu-lieh, *Chang Kuo-t'ao Fu-jen Hui-i-lu (Madame Chang Kuo-t'ao's Recollection)* (Hong Kong: Tzu Lien Ch'u-p'an She, 1970) pp. 333–334.

37. Helen Foster Snow (Nym Wales), *The Chinese Communists: Sketches and Autobiographies of the Old Guard* (Westport, Conn.: Greenwood Publishing Co., 1972), p. 250.

38. *Ibid.*, p. 251.

Notes

39. Chow Ching-wen, *Ten Years of Storm: The True Story of the Communist Regime in China* (New York: Holt, Rinehart and Winston, 1960), p. 184.

40. Rice, *Mao's Way*, p. 103.

41. *Ibid.*, p. 104.

42. Li Ang, *Hung-se Wu-t'ai* (The Red Stage) (Chungking: Sun-li Kung-shih Ch'u-pan se, 1942), p. 75.

43. *Survey of China Mainland Press* (Hong Kong: American Consul General, No. 4181, May 20, 1968, p. 10.) Cited in Edward E. Rice, *Mao's Way*, p. 108.

44. *Chung-kung Yen-chiu (Studies on Chinese Communism)*, June 1970, p. 114.

45. "Chairman Mao's Revolutionary Family" (first draft) *Shuang-ch'en-yueh*, No. 1, Jan. 10, 1968 (A Red Guard Publication), translated in *Current Background* (Hong Kong: American Consulate General, No. 616), p. 8.

46. *Chairman Mao's Activities in Revolutionary Practice* (Red Guard booklet, no date or place of publication but apparently produced in 1966 on "Material for Study"), translated in *Current Background*, (Hong Kong: American Consulate General, No. 900), p. 5.

47. *Ibid.*

48. Tung Lin, *Revolutionary Family*, p. 17.

49. Schram, *Mao Tse-tung*, p. 265.

50. Mao Tse-tung, "Speech at the Lushan Conference" (July 23, 1959), translated in *Chinese Law and Government*, Vol. I, No. 4 (Winter 1968–1969), p. 39.

51. Snow, *Red Star over China*, p. 486.

52. Han Suyin, *Morning Deluge*, p. 86.

53. "Chairman Mao's Revolutionary Family," p. 8.

54. Tung Lin, *Revolutionary Family* pp. 21–22.

55. Klein and Clark, *op. cit.*

56. Edgar Snow, *The Long Revolution* (New York: Random House, 1972), p. 222.

57. *Chung-kung Yen-chiu (Studies on Chinese Communism)* (June 1970), pp. 114–130.

58. "Chairman Mao's Conversations With His Nephew, Mao Hsuan-hsin" in "Talks and Writings of Chairman Mao" *Translations on Communist China*, No. 128, JPRS 52029 December 21, 1970), p. 42.

59. Mao Tse-tung, "Speech at the Hankow Conference" (April 6, 1958) *Miscellany of Mao Tse-tung Thought*, Part I, p. 89.

CHAPTER 9 / *Political Creativity: The Skills*

1. Leo C. Rosten, *The Washington Correspondent* (New York: Harcourt, Brace, 1937), pp. 243–244, quoted in A. F. Davies, *Politics As Work* (Melbourne Politics Monograph, Department of Political Science, University of Melbourne, 1973), p. 30.

2. This task has been masterfully performed in such works as Joseph Levenson, *Confucian China and Its Modern Fate* (Berkeley: University of California Press, 1958); and Mary C. Wright, *The Last Stand of Chinese Conservatism* (New York: Atheneum, 1966).

3. See Karl A. Willfogel, "The Legend of Marxism," *China Quarterly* No. 1 (1960), pp. 72–86; and Benjamin Schwartz, "The Legend of the 'Legend of Maoism,' " *China Quarterly*, No. 2 (1960), pp. 35–42.

Notes

4. John Rue, "Is Mao Tse-tung's *Dialectical Materialism* a Forgery?" *Journal of Asian Studies*, Vol. 26, No. 3 (1967), pp. 464–468.

5. Stuart R. Schram, "Mao Tse-tung and the Theory of Permanent Revolution," *China Quarterly*, No. 46 (April 1971), p. 223.

6. Harold D. Lasswell, *Psychopathology and Politics* (New York: Viking, 1930).

7. Davies, *Politics As Work*, p. 66.

8. *Ibid.*, p. 158.

9. Snow, *Red Star Over China*, rev. ed. (New York: Grove Press, 1968), p. 133.

10. *Ibid.*, p. 132.

11. Siao-yu, *Mao Tse-tung and I were Beggars* (Syracuse, N.Y.: Syracuse University Press), p. 24.

12. Snow, *Red Star Over China*, p. 140.

13. *Ibid.*, p. 133.

14. Stuart R. Schram, *The Political Thought of Mao Tse-tung* (New York: Praeger, 1963), pp. 12–14.

15. Snow, *Red Star Over China*, p. 142.

16. *Ibid.*, p. 150.

17. *Ibid.*, p. 140.

18. "Talk at the Hatan Forum on Four Clean-ups Work," (March 28, 1964), *Miscellany of Mao Tse-tung Thought* (Arlington, Va.: JPRS 6129-1, February 1974), Part II, p. 338.

19. "Some Interjections at a Briefing of the State Planning Commission's Leading Group," (May 11, 1964), *Miscellany of Mao Tse-tung Thought*, Part II, p. 349.

20. "Remarks at a Briefing in March, 1964," *Miscellany of Mao Tse-tung Thought*, Part II, p. 345.

21. "Criticizing P'eng Chen," (April 28, 1966), *Miscellany of Mao Tse-tung Thought*, Part II, p. 383.

22. "Speech at the Ninth Plenum of the Eighth CCP Central Committee," (January 18, 1961), *Miscellany of Mao Tse-tung Thought*, Part II, p. 242.

23. "Talk on Sakata's Article" (August 24, 1964), *Miscellany of Mao Tse-tung Thought*, Part II, p. 401.

24. "Minutes of Spring Festival Talk" (February 13, 1964), *Miscellany of Mao Tse-tung Thought*, Part II, p. 336.

25. *Ibid.*

26. "Talk 28, at the Hantan Forum on Four Clean-ups Work," (March 28, 1964), *Miscellany of Mao Tse-tung Thought*, Part II, p. 338.

27. For an analysis of the bond between leader and followers which uses the insights of depth psychology see: Irvine Schiffer, *Charisma: A Psychoanalytic Look at Mass Society* (Toronto: University of Toronto Press, 1973).

28. "Speech at the Hangchow Conference" (May 1963), *Miscellany of Mao Tse-tung Thought*, Part II, p. 319.

29. George Urban, ed., *The Miracles of Chairman Mao* (London: Torn Stacey, 1971).

30. Snow, *Red Star Over China*, p. 146.

31. These excerpts are from Stuart R. Schram, *The Political Thought of Mao Tse-tung* (New York: Praeger, 1963), pp. 152–60.

Notes

32. "Directives After Hearing Reports of Ku Mu and Yu Ch'iu-li on Planning Work," (January 1965), *Miscellany of Mao Tse-tung Thought*, Part II, p. 445.

33. *Ibid.*, Part I, p. 98.

34. "Speech at the Hangchow Conference," (May 1963), *Miscellany of Mao Tse-tung Thought*, Part II, p. 322.

35. "Speech at the Ninth Plenum of the Eighth Congress of the CCP," (January 18, 1961), *Miscellany of Mao Tse-tung Thought*, Part II, p. 241.

36. "Speech at the Second Session of the Eighth Party Congress," (May 1958), *Miscellany of Mao-Tse-tung Thought*, Part I, p. 99.

CHAPTER 10 / *Political Abandonment: The Fears*

1. See for example: Roderick MacFarquhar, *The Origins of the Cultural Revolution: Contradiction Among the People* (New York: Columbia University Press, 1974); Stanley Karnow, *Mao and China: From Revolution to Revolution* (New York: Viking Press, 1972); A. Doak Barnett, *Uncertain Passage: China's Transition to the Post-Mao Era* (Washington, D.C.: Brookings, 1974).

2. A useful study of the relationship of directors and board chairmen to presidents and executive officers is: Myles L. Mace, *Directors: Myth and Reality* (Boston: Harvard Business School, 1971).

3. The relationship of emperor to ministers has been described in: Michael Loewe, *Imperial China: The Historical Background to the Modern Age* (New York: Praeger, 1966); E. A. Kracke, Jr., *Civil Service in Early Sung China, 960–1067* (Cambridge: Harvard University Press, 1959); John F. Fairbank, ed., *Chinese Thought and Institutions* (Chicago: University of Chicago Press, 1957).

4. Sebastian de Grazia, ed., *Masters of Chinese Political Thought* (New York: Viking Press, 1973), p. 357, quoted from W. K. Liao, tr., *The Complete Works of Han Fei Tzu*, 2 vols. (London: Probsthain, 1950).

5. "Selections from Chairman Mao," *Selections from Chairman Mao*, No. 90, JPRS 49826, February 12, 1970, p. 26.

6. Edgar Snow, *Red Star Over China*, rev. ed. (New York: Grove Press, 1968) p. 154.

7. "Speech at the Expanded Meeting of the CCP Political Bureau," (April 1956), *Miscellany of Mao Tse-tung Thought* (Arlington, Va.: JPRS 6129-1, February 1974), Part I, p. 31.

8. Snow, *Red Star Over China*, p. 146.

9. Quoted in Red Guard Publications entitled, *Chairman Mao's Activities in Revolutionary Practice*, translated in *Current Background* (Hong Kong: American Consulate General, No. 900, January 30, 1970), p. 17.

10. "Speech at the Sixth Plenum of the Eighth Central Committee," Dec. 19, 1958, *Miscellany of Mao Tse-tung Thought*, Part I, p. 146.

11. *Ibid.*, p. 30.

12. The first volume of Roderick MacFarquhar's projected three volume study of the origins of the Cultural Revolution establishes very clearly an inexorable trail of conflicts and issues which goes back to the Hundred Flowers phase of 1956–1957 in

which the one constant theme seems to be Mao's basic problem of managing conflicts. For the vacillations between complete suppression and uncontrolled clashes, see: *The Origins of the Cultural Revolution: Contradiction Among the People, 1956–1957, op. cit.*

13. *Mao Tse-tung Ssu-hsiang Wan-sui (Long Live the Thoughts of Mao Tse-tung)*, Vol. II, (N.P., 1967), p. 262.

14. "Interjection at Conference for Pronounced and Municipal Committee Secretaries," (January 1957), *Miscellany of Mao Tse-tung Thought*, Part I, p. 48; Chinese Text, *Wan-Sui*, Vol. I, pp. 75–76.

15. *Ibid.*

16. "Speech at Expanded Meeting of the CCP Political Bureau," (April 1956), *Miscellany of Mao Tse-tung Thought*, Part I, p. 34.

17. "Notes from Chairman Mao's Talks with Leading Comrades on an Inspection Trip," (Aug.–Sept. 1972), *Studies on Chinese Communism* Vol. 6, No. 9 (Sept. 1972), p. 21.

18. *Chairman Mao's Activities in Revolutionary Practice*, p. 21.

19. For an analysis of the basic problem of suppressing aggression and the role of hostility in Chinese political culture see: Lucian W. Pye, *The Spirit of Chinese Politics* (Cambridge: M.I.T. Press, 1968).

20. "Speech at Politburo Meeting," (October 24, 1966), *Selections from Chairman Mao*, No. 90, JPRS 49826 (February 12, 1970), p. 11.

21. See Jerome Ch'en, *Mao and the Chinese Revolution* (London: Oxford University Press, 1965), p. 94; and MacFarquhar, *Origins of Cultural Revolution*, p. 204.

22. *Mao Tse-tung Ssu-hsiang Wan-sui*, Vol. II, p. 542.

23. Klein and Clark, *Biographical Dictionary of Chinese Communism*, p. 432.

24. Nikita Khrushchev, *Khrushchev Remembers: The Last Testament*, trans. Strobe Talbott (Boston: Little Brown and Co., 1974), pp. 243–244.

25. "Speech at the Lushan Conference," *Chinese Law and Government* Vol. 1, No. 4 (Winter 1968–1969), pp. 27–43.

26. *The Case of Peng Teh-huai* (Hong Kong: Union Research Institute, 1968), p. 36.

27. *Ibid.*, p. 4.

28. "P'eng Teh-huai's Letter," *Miscellany of Mao Tse-tung Thought*, Vol. I, p. 188.

29. "Comment on P'eng Teh-huai's Letter," *ibid.*, p. 187.

30. Jerome Ch'en, *Mao and the Chinese Revolution*, p. 85.

31. MacFarquhar, *Origins of Cultural Revolution*, pp. 312–317.

32. Stanley Karnow, *Mao and China From Revolution to Revolution* (New York: Viking Press, 1972), p. 137.

33. "A Summary of Chairman Mao's Talks to Responsible Local Comrades During His Tour of Inspection," *Chinese Law and Government*, Vol. 5, Nos. 3–4 (Winter 1972–1973), p. 35.

34. *Ibid.*, pp. 37–38.

35. "Mao Tse-tung's Private Letter to Chiang Ch'ing," (July 8, 1966), *Chinese Law and Government*, Vol. 6, No. 2 (Summer 1973), pp. 96–97.

36. Copies of the purported document drafted by the "571" plotters appeared in Hong Kong in later 1971. Translations appear in *Issues and Studies* (May 1972), pp. 78–83.

Notes

37. "Summary of Conference of Provisional and Municipal Committee Secretaries," *Miscellany of Mao Tse-tung Thought*, Part I, p. 57.

38. *Ibid.*, p. 58.

39. "Second Speech at the Eighth Party Congress," (May 17, 1958), *Miscellany of Mao Tse-tung Thought*, Part I, p. 101.

40. "Critique of Stalin's *Economic Problems of Socialism in the Soviet Union*," *Miscellany of Mao Tse-tung Thought*, Part I, p. 191.

41. *Ibid.*, p. 192.

42. "Talk with Director of Cooperative Areas," (December 1958), *Miscellany of Mao Tse-tung Thought*, Part I, pp. 133–134.

43. C. L. Sulzberger, *The Age of Mediocrity: Memories and Diaries, 1963–1972* (New York: Macmillan, 1973), p. 8.

44. Marvin Kalb and Bernard Kalb, *Kissinger* (Boston: Little Brown and Co., 1974), Chapter 10.

45. "Dialogues with Responsible Persons of the Capitol Red Guards Congress," July 28, 1968, *Miscellany of Mao Tse-tung Thought*, Part II, pp. 484, 492, and 494.

INDEX

Index

Political creativity, 229-60; secret of, 229

Political justifications: supremacy of, 160

Popular style, elite vs., 60-61

Populism, 43, 60-61

Power: importance of gradations of, 153; of Mao in Chinese Communist Party, 272-73; of slogans, in Chinese culture, 253; words as source of, 242-43, 254-55 (*see also* Words); *see also* Leadership; Willpower

Pragmatic policies: consolidation of, 43

Primogeniture, 93, 94; *see also* Firstborn son

Privacy: effects of absence of, 71

Professional revolutionary, *see* Revolutionary career

Purges, 134, 271, 273, 281-95

Reason, 10; in operational code, 49-54; suspicion of, 95

Rebel: Mao's appeal as, 11

Rebellion: developing feeling for, 98-99; lesson in, 121; source of, 126-27; source for learning spirit and tactics of, 116, 307-8; *see also* Revolution

Red Guards, *see* Cultural Revolution

Red Star Over China (Snow), 209n

Religion, 75, 77, 78

Repression, 258

Responsibilities: of firstborn, 16, 94, 97, 98; of parenthood, avoided, 141-42, 223-24, 306-7

"Return Students," 279-81

Revolution: continuing problems of, 313-14; developing feeling for, 98-99; glorification of, 43; *see also* Chinese Revolution; Rebellion

Revolution of 1911, 159, 160, 162

Revolutionary career: and Autumn Harvest Uprisings, 206-7; critical period in moving toward, 193-98, 200-1; explanation of sensitivity to commit-

ment to revolution, 86; revolutionary spirit, 307

Rice, Edward, 197, 204, 209-10

Risk-taking: in operational code, 49-54

Ritualization of emotions, 6-7

Romanticism: Maoism and, 40

Roosevelt, Franklin D., 13-14, 230

Rosten, Leo, 231

Rousseau, Jean-Jacques, 168, 242

Rural life: glorification of, 60-61

Russian Affairs Study Group, 198

Russian leadership: ambivalence toward, 42; *see also* Stalin, Joseph

San Kuo Chih Yen Yi (Romance of the Three Kingdoms), 154, 190, 241

Schram, Stuart, 230; on Mao, 144-45; on Mao as theoretician, 235; on Mao's description of Changsha military activity, 160; on Mao's first marriage, 199

Schwartz, Benjamin, 230

Selected Readings from Mao Tse-tung, 248-49

Selected Works of Mao Tse-tung (Mao), 63, 240, 248

Self-confidence: acquiring, 75-88

Self-Education College, 104-5

Sexual behavior: after first marriage, 204-5; Yang Ch'ang-chi and, 196

Shame, 279

Shaw, George Bernard, 163

Sheng Shih-ts'ai, 104

Sheng-shih Wei-yen (Words of Warning; Chung Kuang-ying), 147

Shui Hu Chuan, 98, 100, 156

Shun, 156

Siao Yu: on Mao, 19, 101, 149; on Mao's arguments in school, 154; on Mao's leaving school, 157; on Mao's love for Tao Szu-hung, 186; on Mao's manner of walking, 34; on Mao's schoolmates, 151

Sibling relationships: birth of siblings

343

Index

345